To Dad
Happy Father's Day
With Love From
　　　　　　Aileen and Billy
　　　　　　　x x x

1993

ALISTAIR MacLEAN

A Life

Jack Webster, a journalist since the 1940s, is currently Features Writer of the *Glasgow Herald*, working mainly on profiles of personalities. He is the author of six previous books, including *The Dons* and *A Grain of Truth*, and of three award-nominated television films.

ALISTAIR MacLEAN

A Life

Jack Webster

CHAPMANS

Chapmans Publishers Ltd
141-143 Drury Lane
London WC2B 5TB

First published by Chapmans 1991
This paperback edition first published by Chapmans 1992

ISBN 1 85592 576 1

Printed and bound in Great Britain by
Clays Ltd, St Ives plc

CONTENTS

Complete works of
ALISTAIR MacLEAN

ALISTAIR MACLEAN WRITING UNDER THE PSEUDONYM IAN STUART
1961   The Dark Crusader   1962   The Satan Bug

WRITTEN FROM ALISTAIR MACLEAN OUTLINES
1980   Hostage Tower   John Denis
1981   Air Force One is Down   John Denis
1989   Death Train   Alastair MacNeill
1989   Night Watch   Alastair MacNeill
1990   Red Alert   Alastair MacNeill
1991   Time of the Assassin   Alastair MacNeill

WRITTEN FROM A FULL-LENGTH SCREENPLAY BY ALISTAIR MACLEAN
1992   Golden Girl   Simon Gandolfi

Illustrations

INTRODUCTION

The mantle of fame is no doubt a mixed blessing which many would gladly cast aside. It has burdens as well as benefits, responsibilities alongside rewards and in the end, like it or not, you become a part of public property. To that extent, it is very likely that someone will write your biography.

It is reasonable that Alistair MacLean's legion of readers around the world, charmed by his story-telling for more than thirty years, should want to know more about the man himself. In the years of following his fiction, they came to know very little of their favourite author, for the simple reason that he was an intensely private person, shunning a limelight which would have revealed him as an enigmatic figure to rival the most complex of his own fictional characters.

He was at once highly intelligent, creative, amusing, reserved, stubborn, even violent. In getting to the bottom of this Jekyll-and-Hyde of a man, I would have benefited from his own investigative skills. Instead, I had to rely on a painstaking pursuit of his relatives and friends, all the way from his childhood home in the Highlands of Scotland, through Glasgow, London, Geneva, Venice, Dubrovnik and on to California and wherever the well-concealed dramas of his extraordinary life were to unfold.

Unravelling the mysteries of Alistair MacLean became a fascinating story in itself, an adventure which threatened to raise as many questions as it solved. Many close witnesses delved deeply in furrowed concentration, anxious to do him the justice of a fair historical assessment, balancing admiration and affection with an acknowledgement of his faults and weaknesses.

His first wife and three sons, the beneficiaries of his will but hardly a united family, took different stances over the prospect of a biography. For reasons best known to himself, MacLean's eldest son Lachlan, who lives near London, made it plain he would give me no cooperation at all. The youngest son, Alistair, assured me no direct member of the family would consent to reveal the private side of his father's life. Equally, he assured me of no personal animosity, wished me well with the biography and was even kind enough to point me in the direction of certain valuable witnesses to the story. The middle son, Michael, assured me of a welcome to California and could not have been more helpful when I visited his home at Topanga Canyon, near Los Angeles.

Their mother, Gisela, who figured in the first of MacLean's two divorces, was evidently opposed to a biography but agreed to answer my questions when I knocked on the door of her splendid villa overlooking Lake Geneva. She talked freely and frankly about her former husband, produced photographs and accompanied me to his grave in the Swiss village of Celigny. Her courtesy was extended to a second visit and was matched by the cooperation of MacLean's two brothers and other members of the family. From the witness of so many people, I have absorbed the flavour of this distinguished Scotsman and tried to reproduce it as faithfully as possible.

While defending his own privacy, Alistair MacLean was worldly enough to know that he would inescapably become the subject of biographical study one day. He was too famous and too popular for it to be otherwise. Though it was perhaps not one of his better ventures, he chose to write the biography of the great Captain Cook and had plans to produce others. In tackling the life of Cook, he made this frank admission: 'A true biography is a fully-rounded portrait but there are colours missing from my palette. I do not know enough about the man.'

While certain colours have been denied the palette of his own biography, I can only hope the surviving picture still manages to tell the story as vividly as it revealed itself to me.

Alistair MacLean junior thought his father's private life had been mundane and boring and that I faced an uphill task. If the task was uphill then it was for very different reasons. For the real-life story of Alistair MacLean turned out to be far more captivating than I could ever have imagined it to be.

Jack Webster

1

The story of Alistair MacLean had come full circle that bright and windy day of 4 May 1987, when a modest gathering of friends and relatives assembled in the trim little kirk of Daviot, just south of Inverness, in that broad and dramatic sweep of the Scottish Highlands.

They had come with their private thoughts to pay last respects to the quiet lad who had gone forth from this parish, through a life which was tortuous and controversial, to battle his way through the Second World War and to rise from the modest role of a Scottish schoolmaster to the heights of bestselling novelist, earning and spending countless millions in a career which ranged from undiluted triumph to something nearer self-inflicted tragedy.

The organ set an atmosphere of hushed reverence as they filed into the hard wooden pews which characterize the kirk in Scotland. A tasteful arrangement of flowers did nothing to intrude on the plain rural dignity of this house, from which his father, another Alistair MacLean, had conducted a ministry which enriched the life of this parish and brought him fame as a preacher far beyond its boundaries.

Sunday after Sunday the young MacLean would listen with growing attention to the skills of a master wordsmith, pouring forth from that formidable pulpit, little knowing that the genes of a great preacher were already stirring within a new generation.

Now that he was gone, his father's old pulpit became the focal point of a memorial service in which the mixed emotions went beyond a quiet sense of thanksgiving. There was anger and annoyance over the arrangements.

Unaware of the situation, MacLean's first wife, Gisela, took her place beside her former sister-in-law, Margaret, and whispered, 'There are not many people; but then it is a long time since Alistair left here.'

There was more to it than that. Having played its own insidious part in the life of Alistair MacLean, the demon drink had dogged his footsteps all the way to that farewell service. It began when a local newspaper, in its obituary notice, chose to label a famous son 'the Daviot Drunk', raising fears in the parish minister, the Reverend Lilian Bruce, that an invasion of disrespectful media people might bring vulgarity to an occasion which she wanted to be 'sincere, dignified and untrammelled'.

If the media had been so inclined they could have invaded the privacy of the service and there was little Miss Bruce or anyone else could have done about it; though she did manage to turn away a harmless little lady from the local radio station in Inverness who appeared at the door with a microphone.

Beyond that, there were no more than two or three genteel reporters, turning up very properly for a service which should have been a glorious celebration of Scotland's most widely read modern author.

What angered the family was that the minister's attitude had excluded so many local people who should have been there. Left to make the arrangements, MacLean's brother Gillespie, who lived locally, had agreed to a compromise announcement in the newspapers, fearing that his insistence on a full public service might deprive them of his father's old church.

That announcement said that seating for the memorial service was 'by arrangement only'; given the nature of the Scots people, it was not surprising that it was taken as a hint of privacy and that very few turned up.

Disappointment was softened by the sincerity of the occasion, in which MacLean's elder brother, Ian, and his old schoolfriend, Tom Fraser, read lessons from the Old Testament and the congregation joined in the singing of the 23rd Psalm to the tune of Crimond – 'The Lord's My Shepherd' – and in the appropriate verses of 'There's a wideness of God's mercy like the wideness of the sea'.

The eulogy, which deserved a wider audience, came from Alistair MacLean's long-time friend and publisher, Ian Chapman; and there was a particularly poignant moment when Alison Rapson from Muir of Ord, herself a Mod gold medallist, sang the same Gaelic song, 'I Love the Shepherd', which was sung by MacLean's mother when she carried off the gold medal at the Mod in Dundee in 1913.

Among the few outsiders who did appear that day was one of Alistair's shipmates from the wartime adventures, Charlie Dunbar from the town of Keith in Banffshire, who hadn't seen his old friend since those victorious days of Japanese surrender in the Far East.

So much had happened since then. But now they stood in quiet remembrance of a famous son whose childhood had been spent right here in the heart of the Highlands. Much more than the Guns of Navarone had now been silenced as the call of benediction brought the service to a close and folk shuffled out to the late-spring sun, which lent to that idyllic corner of Scotland a sense of everlasting peace.

From the kirk of Daviot, encircled by gravestones so old that many an inscription had long since worn to the weather, you could cast around this melancholy landscape and feel that little had changed since the days of Alistair MacLean's childhood in the twenties and thirties. It was not too hard to fit his early days to this rural canvas; only the roar of an articulated lorry on the carriageway now separating kirk from manse could disturb the notion that time may well have stood still in the cradle of the author's life.

His first wife was accompanied by two of their sons, Lachlan and Alistair, as well as MacLean's two surviving brothers, Ian and Gillespie, and their wives Bunty and Margaret, his lawyer, David Bishop from London, his loyal secretary, Sabrina Carver, and Ian Chapman, chairman of Collins the publishers, with his wife Marjory.

Before adjourning to the Kingsmills Hotel, outside Inverness, for lunch, they lingered by the two grey granite stones of the MacLean family, taking pride of place by the kirk door.

One stone was devoted to his father alone, a much-loved minister of Daviot and Dunlichity, whose parishioners remembered 'a brilliant scholar, an eloquent preacher, a distinguished author, a faithful pastor and a loyal friend'.

The second stone was for his beloved mother, Mary Lamont

MacLean, and his brother Lachlan, about whom it was said 'To know him was to love him'. Now there was an addition.

Though the earthly remains lay in a plain little cemetery far away in Switzerland, another name was now restored to the place where it began, black-printed words which gave intimation of the death of Alistair Stuart MacLean, MA, D.Litt., author, born Shettleston, Glasgow, 21 April 1922, died Munich, Germany, 2 February 1987.

And then, beneath it, the words which he had borrowed from Tennyson's poem 'Ulysses', for his own bestselling novel of the sea:

> Come, my friends,
> 'Tis not too late to seek a newer world.

2

To find the roots of his family, Alistair MacLean looked no further than the Western Isles of Coll and Tiree, great strongholds of the clan, which lie to the north-west of Mull, just off Ardnamurchan Point, in that cluster of Scottish islands which can roll mellifluently from the tongue or pull you up in such rich staccato as Rhum, Eigg and Muck.

His more immediate antecedents, however, were to be found on the mainland of Scotland, at the district of Strachur, lying southward across Loch Fyne from the Campbell stronghold of Inveraray. In more recent times, the lands of Strachur have been owned by another famous MacLean, Sir Fitzroy, whose wartime exploits with the Partisans of Yugoslavia would indirectly bring him into the author's life at a later stage.

It was at Strachur in 1885 that Alistair's father was born, in the home of his maternal grandfather, old Donald MacVean, the shoemaker, whose daughter Mary had married Lachlan MacLean, later to be Captain MacLean of the Duff Steamship Company of Glasgow.

Lachlan and Mary set up their own home at the village of Kilmelford, sixteen miles south of Oban, in one of the most picturesque settings which Scotland can offer. The wooded slopes among lochs and tumbling streams made it more of a fishermen's paradise than the likely location for the manufacture of gunpowder, yet that is what took place within that sylvan setting until 1867, when a major explosion brought a return to the less hazardous pursuit of farming.

Their son Alexander became known as Alistair, the name under which he wrote his books, little knowing that he would yet produce a son who would bring it international fame.

Forsaking the sea-going tradition, the first Alistair MacLean embarked instead on a Bachelor of Divinity degree at Glasgow University, which he gained in 1909. His first full parish ministry was at Tarbert, back in the calf country of Loch Fyne, a small fishing town built on a bay which gave shelter to a multitude of brown sailing boats.

There were evenings in Tarbert, he said, when the sun was set and windows were lit and the tide grumbled round the piers, that it became a fairy town in which you could imagine you saw the ghosts of ancient mariners stealing round the coast. In the beauty of its parish church he had preached in Gaelic every Sabbath and, many years later, had only to close his eyes to see again those fine grey heads bending over their psalters and to hear again those old, quavering voices softly singing to the Lord who dwelt in Zion.

The pulpit power of the Reverend Alistair MacLean became known across the land, and city churches were never slow to lure such talent. In 1913, after three years in Tarbert, he answered the call of Shettleston Parish Church in the east end of Glasgow, with a population of 46,000.

He would later reflect on his Glasgow experience:

Someone has said that a minister sees you at your best, a lawyer at your worst and a doctor as you really are. But I can assure you that, after ten hectic years in that great east end parish, I had a doctor's and a lawyer's close-up view of human nature. I saw it as it was, in its raw, in all its complexities and simplicities, its greatnesses and meannesses, and came away firmly believing in the presence of God in life and in the greatness, goodness and ultimate beauty of character in men and women.

At the Shettleston manse in the district of Mount Vernon, the bachelor minister was looked after by Janet MacNeill, an island girl from Gigha, commonly known as God's island. By now, however, he had also met the vivacious Mary Lamont from the Possilpark district of Glasgow, whose golden voice had brought that gold medal home from the 1913 Mod, the annual festival of An Comunn Gaidhealach, the central body of all things Gaelic in Scotland.

Mary's father, Archie Lamont, had left Tiree to go to sea (providing another seafaring element in the background of the future novelist) but was working at a bonded warehouse in Glasgow when his attractive daughter walked down the aisle of St Columba Church, in the Anderston district of the city, on 7 November 1916. The First World War was at its height and the young couple were no sooner settled into the Shettleston manse at Buchanan Gardens, Mount Vernon, than the Reverend Alistair MacLean was off to the gory fields of France as a chaplain to the Scottish soldiers.

In her husband's absence at the war front, Mary gave birth to their first child, Lachlan, still supported on the domestic front by the faithful Janet, whose indispensable place in the MacLean household was typical of a tradition among Highland womenfolk. It was something to be maid at the manse.

Back home in the victory of 1918, in time to father his second son, Ian, the Reverend Alistair MacLean maintained a long-standing connection with the Highland districts of Daviot (pronounced Dave-iot) and Dunlichity, where his step-uncle, the Reverend Alexander Stewart, had conducted a memorable ministry. On the death of Mr Stewart, the folk of Daviot were in no doubt about who they wanted as his successor. If their bid seemed wildly ambitious, it worked to their advantage that Alistair MacLean had been gassed in the battlefields of France, while serving with the Black Watch, and was advised by doctors that the fresh air of the countryside should be considered before the pollution of Glasgow.

He promptly accepted the invitation and in 1922, with Mary having just given birth to their third son, Alistair, the MacLean family bade farewell to the hanging smoke of Glasgow and faced the open spaces of the Highlands, north to Daviot and Dunlichity, with their home at the manse of Daviot, six miles south of Inverness.

At least they were no strangers in their new abode, the parish folk remembering with affection the appearance of Mr MacLean, resplendent in military uniform, when he came to preach for his uncle while on leave during the war. Mr Stewart had been a fine Christian gentleman, if not much of a preacher, a bachelor looked after by his three quaint sisters, Miss Marion, Miss Jessie and Miss Mary, but he dropped dead one day in the fields of the glebe, that stretch of farmland apportioned to rural ministers by which they could augment their meagre stipends.

Mr MacLean's arrival not only brought a new standard of preaching but raised excitement in the parish that a proper family would inhabit the manse. Single families could so affect the balance of a rural community that the MacLeans, with three boys, could raise the local school roll by 10 per cent. They would also bring unaccustomed quality to the hymn-singing with the voices of both Mr and Mrs MacLean; sometimes it would sound like a duet, with a muted backing from the more inhibited body of the kirk.

Thus the MacLeans settled into the manse at Daviot, a sturdy three-storey house of red sandstone, hewn from the old Daviot Quarry and set within wooded grounds from which they could walk across the field or follow the driveway through the trees to the old road and round to the church, just a few hundred yards away.

In the mapping out of a childhood setting for Alistair MacLean, the good Lord could not have scooped a more picturesque hollow of the Highlands, an idyllic corner which must in time have stirred the smouldering imagination of the introverted boy. The valley of Strathnairn rose in summer from lush greenery to hills that were mauve and snow-flecked; and you could just as easily picture it in winter, with the wind howling in the trees and the ghosts of Highland superstition flitting through the glen.

The towering rock above the quarry bears down on the Auld Kirk of Daviot, with its gleaming white walls and big red door and a spire which rises in prayerful pose to the heavens, topped off somewhat ludicrously with the strut of a weather-cock.

The glebe, with its manse and steading, sloped down to the River Nairn, while higher to the right stood the big house known as The Doune, home to the Mackintoshes who farmed the adjoining lands of Balvonie and would be the nearest neighbours of the MacLean family. Four of the Mackintosh ladies still live in the district (there were nine children altogether), two of them at The Doune, lending a bygone charm and that sense of rural continuity which endures all change.

The centre of Alistair MacLean's childhood home was the kitchen of the manse, with its big open fire and family table, Mrs MacLean expecting suitable standards from her boys and knowing that she could rely on Janet to demand even more, to the point that she was regarded by the young MacLeans as a bit of a martinet.

Janet MacNeill had accompanied them north from Shettleston to

engage a tramp by the roadside, listen to his hard-luck story and give him half-a-crown. Before leaving Inverness, he would see the same tramp disappear into the nearest pub; but he had done his Christian best for the man.

While eschewing political postures, the Reverend Alistair MacLean was nevertheless active in local county council affairs and amassed a wide range of friends and acquaintances. While a man of such impeccable standards sought no favours, the sons soon found that a respect for their father brought benefits which they had no intention of scorning.

The man who owned the cinema in Inverness so regarded the minister that the boys were never charged for admission to the pictures. Though the legal age was seventeen, Ian remembers driving around in his father's old red Clyno car while still only fifteen and never once being stopped by the local constabulary. The mystery cleared when he discovered they were mostly West Highland Bobbies who owed their jobs to the sympathetic interest of the county councillor – the Reverend Alistair MacLean.

3

By the mid-twenties, the lives of the MacLeans at the manse and the neighbouring Mackintoshes had become closely intertwined. They were all in church on a Sunday and if, for some reason, Mr Mackintosh of The Doune happened to be absent, Mr MacLean went straight from his pulpit, and before lunch, to see what was wrong. The affinity was such that Mrs Mackintosh was present at the birth of the fourth MacLean boy, Gillespie, in 1926.

By the following year, Alistair was ready to join his two elder brothers, Lachlan and Ian, at Daviot Public School, the standard Scottish unit of local education for all which, unlike the English system, uses 'public' in its literal sense. At Daviot they came under the influence of Miss Joan Mackintosh, headmistress of the two-teacher school, where the traditional three Rs of Reading, Writing and 'Rithmetic were drummed into generations of children. Once you were taught by ladies like Miss Mackintosh, you stayed taught. She was also the organist at Daviot Parish Church (rehearsing her mistakes with customary diligence, as the boys recalled) and was a familiar visitor to the MacLean kitchen.

The arrival of Alistair MacLean as an infant pupil at Daviot School coincided with the return to her native parish of another Miss Mackintosh, taking up her post as second teacher to Miss Joan Mackintosh, to whom she was not related. Miss Barbara Mackintosh was, however, another of the nine children from The Doune, a clear-minded witness who lives alone in Inverness, taking a quiet pride in the fact that she was the very first teacher of the man who would bring such distinction to Daviot.

A charming lady of sterling quality and twinkling good humour, Miss Barbara (she became Mrs Fraser) paints a clear picture of the parish school of the twenties. Because of the family friendship, she retains a vivid memory of Alistair MacLean's first day at school.

'He arrived wearing the MacLean tartan kilt and a green polo-neck jersey and I remember thinking that he was so like his father,' is her recollection. 'He was a quiet little boy who gave me no trouble at all.'

With a total school roll of around forty, the small sandstone building, which stands recognizable to this day, was partitioned in two, Miss Joan taking the senior half of the school and Miss Barbara the lower half. With such small numbers, there were only seven pupils in Alistair's class, of which he ranked about third. The outstanding talent of his year was little Mary McCallum, the gamekeeper's daughter.

The school day started at nine o'clock with The Lord's Prayer and was followed in winter by arm-flapping exercises at the side of their desks, intended to stimulate circulation, keep them warm and put them in condition for the day's work. A big coal fire burned brightly in the classroom, and when it was particularly cold the children pulled their forms closer to the hearth. Alistair MacLean took his instruction from an old-fashioned blackboard and used slate-pencil on a wooden-framed slate for most of his class work. Once again, they were drilled in the basics, with much emphasis on grammar, punctuation and spelling. Once a week they filled up the inkwells and settled down to copybook writing, laboriously gaining the knack of the light upward stroke and the heavy downward, a discipline which produced generations of good calligraphy.

Like his elder brothers, Alistair arrived at school with the disadvantage of not being allowed to speak English at home, a curious restriction for a boy whose father both wrote and delivered the language with a fine eloquence and must have known that his children would require it in whatever direction their lives would lead.

Whatever his deficiencies, he was soon adding to his knowledge of English in the school playground where, even in the twenties, very few Highland children were speaking Gaelic. That was in direct contrast to places like South Uist, where Miss Barbara had recently been teaching and where the children knew no English at all, a problem compounded by the fact that she knew no Gaelic.

As a late starter to the language he would later use to entertain countless millions, Alistair was fortunate in his teachers, who left no unexplained mysteries about how to analyse, parse and punctuate. Perhaps with the same curiosity as foreign-born writers, like Joseph Conrad or Tom Stoppard, the young MacLean was coming to English from the base of another culture and applying himself to it with all the more determination. He would respond with interest to Miss Mackintosh when she gave him essays on subjects like: Write the autobiography of an old boot. Found in a ditch, where had it been? What was its history?

At lunchtime, the MacLean boys were near enough to go home to the manse, while most country children carried their 'piece' and would be supplied with cocoa on colder days. Sometimes the piece would be eaten on the morning trek to school and you would find them scouring a farmer's field for a lunchtime turnip.

Once a week they crossed the narrow village road to the green, with its magnificent view of the valley of Strathnairn, to engage in what was known as 'drill', before it took on the clumsier title of physical education.

Prize-giving day could be a mixed blessing but the highlight of the year was the visit to the neighbouring school of Moy for an afternoon of sporting rivalry. Boarding the train for the short trip, which was still a major adventure, the Daviot children were met by the piper of the Clan Chief Mackintosh of Mackintosh and marched to the sports field at Moy. After hours of competition, they were royally fed before being piped back to the train for the short journey home.

From April to November the MacLean boys went barefoot to school, as a saving on shoe-leather, and from the age of seven or eight you would find them out grouse-beating over the moors by Meallmore, walking thirty miles a day to make some money.

As the eldest of the four, Lachlan, who was also like his father in appearance, was growing into a delightful boy, gentle, kind and thoughtful, an accomplished pianist and already with thoughts of being a doctor. The second son, Ian, who more resembled his mother, was of an out-going nature, while still sublimating much of his energy in manual work. With the responsibility of the glebe, there was always a measure of farm work to be done and young Alistair's particular chore was to bring in the old cross-Ayrshire cow, called Blackie, in time for milking. There were pigs and poultry to feed and wood to cut, and when that was over Ian was soon by the side of Alf Mackintosh at the farm, helping with the horses and counting it a wasted day if he had not already gone striding over Daviot with the gun and brought home a rabbit for the pot. Such were the ways of rural youngsters.

It is an advantage of country life that the mixture of occupations in a small community brings together youngsters who would not have the same chance to meet in the social divisions of a city. Since the children knew no barriers, it was not unnatural that Alistair MacLean from the manse should find a soul-mate in Tom Fraser, son of a railway surfaceman who died at thirty-two, leaving his wife to bring up four children in a fair measure of poverty. It was one of those bonds of loyalty and friendship which was to endure for a lifetime, taking no account of different intellectual levels. Whenever they met up again, it was as if they had never been apart.

The friendship could just as easily have been with one of the boarded-out bairns from Glasgow, who found their way to every rural parish in Scotland, though Daviot was late in receiving them, due to some resistance from the Mackintosh of Mackintosh.

Alistair and Tom Fraser became inseparable, at school and beyond, a pair of young adventurers who had nothing to learn about boyhood pranks. On a Sabbath morning they would wait till the gardener at Daviot House went off to Mr MacLean's church before raiding his fruit trees. Alistair won a multi-colour torch in a *Wizard* competition and he and Tom had much fun on the public highway, flashing the torch at passing vehicles and inducing them to stop, before vanishing over the nearest dyke.

The pair of them extended their capers to Daviot Church, where you would find them mounting the steps of Mr MacLean's pulpit and addressing their imaginary congregations with a fine flow of irreverence, a memory which came back to Tom Fraser that May day of 1987 when he rose to read the lesson at Alistair's thanksgiving service. Boys were forever boys.

Having benefited from the protection of his two elder brothers, Alistair extended the favour to his younger brother, Gillespie, when he arrived at Daviot School in 1931. At home, however, he thought the kid was spoiled and would hiss threats of 'I'm going to bash you!'

In the summer they would visit the three Miss Stewarts at Kilmelford, the step-grand-aunts, holy ladies who set the boys out on the
rocks by the loch to read their Bibles on the Sabbath. Alistair was
suddenly clipped on the ear by one of the aunts one day, having
been caught folding a copy of the *Wizard* inside the pages of the
Bible.

Through it all, at school or in the manse kitchen, they would find
themselves under the scrutiny of Miss Mackintosh, the headmistress. Wherever she sniffed the hint of academic promise, she
launched herself into additional tuition with a view to securing her
pupils a bursary for Inverness Royal Academy. One by one, the
MacLean boys came under that special attention and found their
way to the Highland capital. Sometimes it meant leaving behind the
less gifted, who could finish their school careers in the supplemen-
tary class at Daviot and leave at the age of fourteen.

Though the distance to school in Inverness was a modest six
miles, communications in rural Scotland were then so scant that you
either walked, cycled or took up residence nearer at hand. A Latin
master at the Academy, a Mr Robson, supervised a boarding house
for long-distance pupils, most of the forty residents coming from
the Western Isles. Lachlan was the first of the MacLeans to arrive
at Hedgefield and was soon an established member and keen sports-
man for the house.

Two years later, Ian collected his bursary and took up residence,
but with a vastly different reaction. He detested the place, appreciated neither food nor discipline and was soon walking out and refusing to go back. The minister of Daviot was at least better equipped
than most to solve the crisis. Further along the road at Moy, the
Reverend Hector Cameron had four boys and a girl; surely there
must be a case for a school bus, they said. That was how the matter
was resolved, not only quelling Ian's rebellion but making it possible
for Alistair to savour the greater intellectual opportunity of Inverness
Royal Academy while living at home with his parents.

When home on leave during the war, Alistair MacLean visited
the school, resplendent in naval uniform. It was a common practice
among former pupils during the war. For one thing, the girls
admired them!

His old headmaster of those far-off days, Dr Donald John Macdonald, born on St Columba's Day, 1900, has clear recollections of

his famous pupil. Straight from his days as a Gordon Highlander in the First World War, Dr Macdonald graduated at Aberdeen University and spent the rest of his career at the Royal Academy. A small, neat man with an impish sense of humour, he lives in the Abbeyfield residential home for the elderly.

He has a clear recollection of teaching English to Alistair MacLean, describing him as a good scholar without hitting the high spots – one of those in-between pupils.

'When he left the Academy, of course, I had no idea he would be famous one day, otherwise I would have kept every scrap he ever wrote. I wish I had some of his essays. But you often discover that the people who become famous in life were not at all famous at school. One of the lessons you learn in a lifetime of teaching is to keep an open mind about young people.'

It didn't surprise Dr Macdonald that Alistair MacLean turned out to be a writer, considering his father's gift for words, but he wouldn't have anticipated the success he attained.

In contrast to Barbara Mackintosh at Daviot, who read *HMS Ulysses* but didn't feel inclined to read any more, Dr Macdonald has read MacLean avidly and found him extremely readable, though his type of book would not normally have been his choice.

Claiming his old pupil with pride, Dr Macdonald was intrigued not only by his gift for disentangling a situation but by the way he developed a kind of mathematical mind for punctuation.

Naturally, much as he remembers the boy, he has a much clearer recollection of the father, so renowned as a preacher and sometimes appearing at the West Church of Inverness on a Sunday evening, when people would queue up to hear him.

Mr Mackintosh of The Doune, a Tory by nature, was not too keen on the socialist politics of his minister, acknowledging however that he had been in a working-class district of Glasgow and that his socialism was more of a Christian nature than a party one. He thought better of the fact that the Reverend Alistair MacLean could happily roll up his sleeves at harvest time and work in the fields.

Mrs MacLean had emerged as a woman of great presence, tall and dominant with a pleasant speaking voice as well as a glorious singing one. She was strong in character, popular in the parish but made no bones about joining her husband in bitter opposition to the Roman Catholic Church. They claimed to have seen life in the raw during their days in Glasgow and were highly critical of the priests in their treatment of the poor.

As for Dr. Macdonald, he took to lay preaching in his retirement and found his way on several occasions to the old pulpit at Daviot. Recalling the power of the Reverend Alistair MacLean, he says, 'I swear I was always aware of his presence, just sitting there beside me.'

4

Alistair MacLean was gaining his early impressions of life through that frenetic decade of the Roaring Twenties, towards the thirties, when the flappers were determined to flap and the jazz trumpets rasped in a world which tried hard to restore a sense of normality.

Quietly, though, a generation of young women realized that the carnage of a foreign field had left them to spinsterhood, with memories only of that last embrace before the train steamed out of sight for ever. Outby, the General Strike had raged, but rural youngsters like Alistair MacLean still lived a sheltered existence in the peace and beauty of the Scottish Highlands.

His father had his own memories of that most appalling war in all history, stark and chilling but now receding as a lingering nightmare. Within his study, where he so regularly shut himself away that he ate with the rest of the family on Sundays only, he would turn his thoughts to the book reviews he wrote for the *Glasgow Herald*, under the pen-name of Bookworm, little knowing the significance that family connection with the newspaper would have in years to come.

He was contented with his family and professional life, centred on his beloved Daviot Church, which was known to the old cattle drovers as 'the kirk of the golden cockerel', standing there since 1826 and just the latest in a succession of buildings which had occupied that site of worship for centuries, between the Priest's Hillock and the ruined stone fort of Dun Daviot Hill.

Inside the kirk itself, neat and trim, well scrubbed and wholesome, you still found the essence of the Scottish Presbyterian ethos. In the Auld Kirk of Scotland there had long been a no-nonsense symmetry of design, seats which made no pretence at comfort and would not only give you corns where corns were never meant to be but were intended to keep you awake through droning sermons. Those sermons could search the soul of the innocent and send you out to reassess sins you didn't know you had.

The Reverend Alistair MacLean was usually a more understanding and compassionate man than that. Perhaps he needed to be. When praising Mr MacLean's talents as a preacher, Alistair's first teacher, Miss Barbara, could recall individual sermons of sixty years' distance. She remembered him picking one of the whisky names and preaching on the theme 'Take Mr Haig and throw him down the stair!' The demon drink was the target of his violent and, on this occasion, intolerant thought; all the more revealing since Mrs MacLean had confided in close friends that her husband enjoyed a dram or two himself. The man's imbibing was well under control but such was Mrs MacLean's detestation of alcohol in any shape or form that she seemed to regard it as a problem. In crossing swords with Mr Haig and wishing him a speedy descent on the staircase, the minister at least knew what he was talking about.

Meanwhile, the boys were developing personalities of their own. Ian could appreciate his elder brother, Lachlan, but paid little heed to young Alistair. Junior siblings are seldom of much consequence at that stage. So it was that Ian MacLean, now a retired seafaring man in Herefordshire, detected nothing of the future novelist. 'He didn't strike me as a bright boy, just a dour wee customer who was quietly introspective and rather liked his own way. If he was reading at all, it was likely to be the *Wizard* or the *Hotspur*, just like any other Highland boy.'

Many a man of the cloth has been embarrassed by family rebellion over religious observance but the Reverend Alistair MacLean was spared the ordeal, a reward for his own liberal outlook. He was such an open-minded man that there was no question of his sons being dragooned into church attendance. As a result, they more or less fell in with the party line and were to be found in church every Sunday, all togged out in their MacLean tartan kilts.

On every second Sabbath, when his father preached at the neighbouring Culloden, Lachlan went along as his organist. Having acquired one of the first cat's-whisker wireless sets in the district, he regularly tuned into Radio Luxembourg to find what was happening in the music world beyond. He would then play a voluntary in church, after which his father would come home saying, 'I seem to have heard that tune before, Lachlan.' It would turn out to be a slowed-down version of 'Home on the Range' or some other rhythmic melody not quite acceptable in the Auld Kirk of Scotland, at least not without a suitable camouflage.

Before eight o'clock, at Daviot every Sunday morning, Lachlan and Ian were charged with activating the primitive heating system in their father's church. That amounted to two twin-burning paraffin heaters which, even when coaxed into something resembling life, made little impression on a damp Highland morning. On one particular Sabbath Lachlan was ill and Ian was left to prime the stove on his own. Instead of nursing the beastly thing into action, he rushed the process to the point that, when Miss Mackintosh arrived to practise her mistakes on the organ, she was met by palls of smoke and soot. Daviot Church was on fire. When the blaze was finally quelled, the pews were found to be a charred mess and the walls bulged outwards.

Whatever reaction the boy expected from an irate father, the imperturbable cleric stood by with kindly understanding, accepting it as an act of God which didn't exactly conflict with his own private desire to renovate the place anyway. The Lord worked in mysterious ways. The outer walls had to be buttressed against collapse and the opportunity was taken to lower the ceiling and do away with the gallery, so often superfluous when the downstair pews were more than enough to house the flock. (Ironically, the renovations of 1991 were designed to restore all that Mr MacLean had sought to remove.)

The capacity of the kirk was fully stretched, however, one day in 1934 when the folk of Daviot and Dunlichity turned out in force to celebrate the silver jubilee of Mr MacLean's ministry. It was the kind of occasion when he would hear in his own lifetime the tributes more commonly reserved for obituaries. With Mrs MacLean and the boys in the congregation, he took stock of his own career and told his listeners, 'More than twelve years ago I came home – home to the parish I had loved since my boyhood days; and it has always been a great source of pride to me that you called me to succeed my uncle, the Reverend Alexander Stewart. He was a fine spirit,

God's man, and he left behind him one of those memories that "shineth more and more unto the perfect day".

'I can only add that I have been very happy in this parish of my youth and of my work. So far, I have had a very fortunate life. I have been fortunate and happy in my beloved wife, in our four boys, who are no better and I hope no worse than other boys, and in our housekeeper and friend, Miss Janet MacNeill. I am happy in knowing that the bond of friendship between you and me is a bond that is deep and secure.'

He quoted Queen Elizabeth when she addressed a deputation from the House of Commons who went to visit in her old age. With trembling hands, the Queen rose up and said, 'Though you have had and though you will have many princes mightier and wiser than I who sit upon this seat, let me tell you that you have never had and you never will have one who loved you better.'

Taking up the theme, Mr MacLean said, 'In all humility and sincerity, I think I can make the same claim for myself here tonight. You will have, no doubt at all, many a better man, many a better minister, but you will have none who has for you an affection more real than mine.'

Flowery by modern standards, but a self-effacement at odds with public opinion. One after another, ministers rose to laud his qualities. To the Reverend D. Macgillivray, late of Petty, who had known him since he was sixteen, there was simply no minister in Scotland or out of it who could compare to Mr MacLean for simplicity or clearness of thought in his sermons, for beautiful diction and a stately style of elocution. His published sermons were popular throughout Britain.

The Reverend Neil Maclennan from Inverness had first set eyes on him in the quadrangle of Glasgow University, where someone had prophesied, 'See that youth? That is one you are going to hear of by and by.' How true it had become. He loved the Gaelic people and their language and was happy at Daviot, in the silence of the hills and the peace of the glens. He was spoken of as a poet and a mystic but, far from being a dreamer, he was a man with his feet on solid earth.

Without seeking the limelight, Mrs MacLean was the power behind the throne and now they had come to an important milestone in their life's journey. They could look to the future with every reason to thank God and to take courage.

The neighbouring Hector Cameron of Moy, Moderator of the Presbytery of Inverness, echoed the wish of all that the MacLeans would be long spared to the people of Daviot and Dunlichity. It was not his privilege to see into the future.

5

The eulogies of that silver jubilee night of 1934, when the Reverend Alistair MacLean was only forty-nine, were well ordered, in the light of subsequent events. Any notions that this outstanding man of the kirk might be set for another twenty-five years in the pulpit were shattered just two years later, when he was struck down by a cerebral haemorrhage and died in the prime of his life.

Those same country folk who had so recently honoured him in his lifetime were back at Daviot Church to pay their last respects at a memorial service in which his friend, the Reverend Hector Cameron, preached from the text of Revelation: 'And I heard a voice from heaven saying unto me, Write, Blessed are the dead which die in the Lord from henceforth: Yea, saith the Spirit, that they may rest from their labours; and their works do follow them.'

The beautiful church at Daviot was crowded that Sunday morning and later they gathered round the memorial outside. Mary MacLean stood in the breeze, casting her eyes across the parish where they had raised their children and sought to fulfil their lives together. By her side stood three of her four sons: Gillespie, just ten: Alistair, fourteen; and Lachlan who, at nineteen, had just started his medical studies at Glasgow University, his father's alma mater. Nearby stood the ever-faithful Janet, while the organ was played, imperfectly as ever, by Miss Mackintosh. The only missing face was that of Ian, who had gone off to sea the previous year, joining the British India Navigation Company in London as a cadet. He was already sailing the high seas between Britain, the United States, Australia and New Zealand, away for ten months at a time and therefore unable to be

at his father's funeral. As he stood by the memorial stone, Lachlan
was already wincing from a pain which he had so far managed to
conceal from his mother, not wishing to add to her burdens.

Daviot and Dunlichity were in a state of shock with the tragic end
to Mr MacLean's ministry. Of immediate concern to Mary
MacLean was the fact that she would now have to vacate the manse
of Daviot and find herself a new home, with the additional hazard
of trying to keep three boys on the meagre income of a Church of
Scotland pension. Thank goodness Ian at least was off her hands
and earning his own living at sea.

Having grown up in Glasgow, and with Lachlan now studying
medicine there, it seemed the sensible decision to head back south
to the city where she had started out as the young minister's wife.
As well as providing a home base for Lachlan at university, it would
take Alistair and Gillespie closer to senior schools and city amenities
which, for all the lack of rural fresh air and freedom, would have
certain advantages.

How little we know of the effect of childhood experience on the
hearts and minds of the young; the revelations usually come later.
Alistair MacLean was just turning fifteen when the family headed
south in the spring of 1937, but he had already distilled enough of
his Highland background to write thoughtfully of it at a future date.

He pondered on the irreversible and inescapable factor of the
transmission of hereditary characteristics through the genes and the
weight of environmental influence which would inevitably leave its
mark. He wrote:

I think of the wonder of sailing on a summer's dusk in the Western
Isles, bathed in that magical quality of light, diffuse and limpid
and wholly indescribable, which I have found nowhere else in the
world except the Aegean in autumn: of driving grouse across the
bleak and windswept Grampian moors for the benefit of short-
sighted American millionaires: of going to three different
churches on a Sunday, each in its own way as bleak and windswept
– inside, not out – as the above-mentioned moors: of cleaning
out the byre by the light of a storm lantern in the darkness of a
January morning with two feet of snow on the ground: of reading
the *Wizard* under the blankets with the aid of a torch in the attic
of a venerable Georgian manse deep in a remote Highland glen

because not only did the single candle, which was the sole means of illumination, afford little more light than an anaemic glow-worm but the cold in that unheated attic was often so intense that to expose hands, wrists and face was to invite a condition only one degree removed from frost-bite: of the golden harvests of late summer where, because of some unaccountable richness of the soil, the corn was a foot higher than the head of the tallest man: of the illicit removal of salmon from the fishing rights of an absentee Sassenach landlord, who was universally – if the limits of the universe be regarded as the bounds of our glen – and powerfully detested for no reason that I could ever discover other than that he *was* a Sassenach: of what seemed to be half the men in the parish crowding into the manse study to hear the broadcast report of the Scotland-England soccer international at Hampden on my father's radio, the only one in the glen: of fishing for cod with the long lines, or inshore off the island of Gigha – using the wicker-work creels – for lobster and monstrous crabs for whose intransi-gent belligerence I formed a life-long respect: of sleeping under the stars on a pile of sweet-smelling, new-mown hay, a practice much frowned upon: of the wonders of Hallowe'en, which we took to be All Saints night, blissfully unaware that in Celtic myth-ology the last night of October was reserved for the activities of witches of the less desirable kind: of endless reading – I had read all Scott by the time I was ten . . .

Thus we gain a glimpse of what was forming within the heart and mind of the young Alistair MacLean before he raised anchor from his Highland home to move southward on the next stage of his life's voyage.

Having been raised in the remoteness of the north, where a social day out to Inverness was a highlight of the year, the MacLean boys took their farewell not only with sadness in their hearts but with apprehension about the big city, having no idea what Glasgow would be like. It was the spring of 1937, just after the abdication of Edward VIII, when they waved goodbye to friends at Daviot Station and went south to their new home, which was to be a tenement flat, two stairs up, at 26 Carrington Street, just off Great Western Road. Though Mrs MacLean had her own connections in Glasgow, it was Mr Cameron, the minister from Moy, who helped her find a place.

Since you couldn't live handsomely on a kirk pension, Mrs MacLean let out two rooms to students, who had a bedroom and drawing-room to themselves. It helped to eke out the living. In a reasonably spacious flat, the other bedroom was occupied by Lachlan, Alistair and Gillespie while Mrs MacLean slept in a box-bed in the kitchen. They had a sitting-room-cum-dining-room to themselves.

In these days of social security, it is hard to imagine the frugal living of the vast majority of people; that they managed at all in those distant days was generally a miracle wrought by a prudent and careworn mother. In that bare living of the thirties, the MacLean boys were fed and clothed but, in all truth, there wasn't much left for anything else.

They were lucky to get threepence every few weeks to go to the Gem Cinema at the foot of Carrington Street. Alistair wasn't particularly keen on the pictures and he had taken to reading a lot in those days, in contrast to his later life when he felt he had had a surfeit of it.

Still a quiet and lonesome boy, he gained a bursary to Hillhead High School while young Gillespie was sent to Woodside Secondary. Gradually they adjusted to their new environment, becoming familiar with nearby locations like West Princes Street, already well known as the murder scene of Miss Gilchrist, for which the German-Jewish gentleman called Oscar Slater served nearly twenty years in Peterhead Prison for a crime he didn't commit.

Lachlan was glad to have the family so close to him, not only for the convenience of his medical studies but for comfort in the illness which continued to trouble him. He had already had an operation at Inverness Royal Infirmary but matters took a turn for the worse and he was rushed back, this time to the Western Infirmary in Glasgow. He underwent another operation, when it was confirmed that he was suffering from cancer of the stomach. This time there would be no recovery and the delightful Lachlan, of such talent and admirable nature, died just a few weeks before his twenty-first birthday.

Mrs MacLean needed all the resources of her strong character to cope with the devastation, having lost her husband and now her eldest son, all within two years. At the delicate age of sixteen, Alistair MacLean grieved quietly in his room, constantly reminded of the

tragedy by the empty bed in the corner. It was a spectre which was
to haunt him for the rest of his life, even to his last weeks when he
would still raise the name of Lachlan.

Mrs MacLean drew closer to her two teenage boys, while Ian had
to cope with his emotions in distant waters. It seemed only yesterday
that they were such a big, happy family at Daviot, the fire roaring
in the kitchen, Janet keeping them all in order and Mr MacLean
withdrawing to his study to write.

The devastation was no less when it reached Daviot, especially in
the Mackintosh household where the beautiful young Catherine had
her own good reason for breaking her heart. Even today, she sits at
The Doune, gazing towards kirk and manse with very private
thoughts and recollections.

She told me how she and Lachlan had fallen in love, a discovery
which developed and blossomed right to his deathbed in the Glasgow infirmary. Through her seventies, she had remained faithful to
his memory and was carrying a torch for Lachlan into the eventide
of her days, there at Daviot where they had found each other nearly
sixty years earlier.

Rural folk not given to tears filled Daviot kirk to capacity that day
when they brought his body home to the scene of his childhood for
a highly emotional funeral service. Thereafter he was laid to rest in
the layer by his father's kirk door, with a new granite stone and that
inscription which said that 'To know him was to love him'.

Mrs MacLean and the boys returned to Glasgow, a city in the
grip of the famous Empire Exhibition at Bellahouston Park, the
biggest event ever staged in Scotland. Alistair and Gillespie went
across town to visit that remarkable spectacle, which had drawn
more than thirteen million people from all over the world; but not
even that could divert them from the thought of what had happened
to their beloved eldest brother.

Mrs MacLean gathered the remnants of their family life and did
her best to console the boys. A semblance of normality was retained
for a time when Janet stayed on, but now she had to find a living
for herself and landed in service with a Mrs Bell in Bearsden, on the
northern perimeter of Glasgow. She was never far away, however,
returning to the MacLean household on three or four evenings a
week and always on Sunday.

Another link with Daviot was the appearance of Alastair and

Hector Cameron, two sons of the Reverend Hector Cameron from
the manse at Moy. Those sons of the local ministers had all been
pupils at Inverness Royal Academy together and used to go on joint
holidays to a cottage at Nairn, supervised as ever by the indispensable Janet.

Alastair Cameron, who had moved to Glasgow to study accountancy in 1937, remembered Alistair MacLean as a difficult boy to
know, reserved in manner and looking for protection from Lachlan
in those earlier days, when brother Ian would sometimes bully him.
Alastair Cameron became a regular visitor at Carrington Street,
where he and Alistair MacLean would discuss football and generate
an enthusiasm for Glasgow Rangers, of which they both became
keen supporters. Mrs MacLean's brother, Archie Lamont, a div-
orcee who moved in with them until his second marriage, worked
at the Post Office and could usually arrange tickets for matches at
Ibrox Park.

Meanwhile, Alistair MacLean had started his Glasgow schooling
at Hillhead High after the summer break of 1937, joining the fourth
year of the Scottish secondary system, which enabled pupils to sit
their leaving certificate examinations in the fifth year, generally at
the age of seventeen.

He was not over-impressed with his new school, however, later
describing it as 'a snooty establishment in the West End, which had
the misfortune to model itself on an English public school, either
ignorant of or ignoring the fact that English public schools, like
numerous Italian red wines, do not travel very well'.

By the summer of 1939, just before the start of the Second World
War, he had gained his Higher Leaving Certificate with passes in
English, History, Latin, Mathematics and Science. He won the
special science prize in the fourth year and came first again in his
certificate year, confirming that interest in the subject's literature
which persisted throughout his life and became the basis of a vast
knowledge which served him well in the fabric of his novels. In that
final year, which showed he was no academic slouch, he was listed
as having come third in English.

Among his fellow pupils at Hillhead High was a boy called Gordon Jackson, who went on to become the famous Scots actor, best
remembered for his television role in *Upstairs, Downstairs*, though a
distinguished performer in films long before that.

With the boys settled in their schooling, Mrs MacLean busied herself in the urban environment of Glasgow, by now deeply caught up in all things to do with the Gaelic community and its culture, as well as church affairs in the strongly Protestant tradition. She had brought as many as possible of their belongings from Daviot, including her husband's popular book *High Country*, which she would sit down and re-read in her quiet moments. She found comfort in his flowery gift for language. It wasn't *HMS Ulysses* or *The Guns of Navarone*, but it was a clear sign that the facility for words which would catapult his son to fame in the next generation existed just as surely in the father, who chose to fashion it instead for God's purpose.

When his elder brother, Ian, went off to sea in 1935, Alistair MacLean began to entertain ambitions of following his example. Despite the seafaring tradition which came from both grandfathers, his love of the sea and messing about in boats did not manifest itself strongly in those pre-war years. There had been boats to sail when they visited the relatives at Kilmelford and, when Janet took the boys to her own home in Gigha, there was excitement to find that her family were all fishing folk.

The romance of the sea, however, was filtering strongly into the house at Carrington Street, Glasgow, in letters from Ian, who was riding distant oceans and stirring in young Alistair those dreams of adventure.

Dreams had to be set aside when Alistair completed his Higher Leaving Certificate at Hillhead. There was a mother to help and, with the headmaster expecting him back for the sixth-year studies, he was to be found instead taking up a post at the shipping office of F. C. Strick, who ran a service from Glasgow to the Persian Gulf.

But war clouds were gathering towards the end of that decade, with its mellow saxophones playing counterpoint to the royal rumpus over the Prince of Wales and the sound of jackboots on the streets of Germany arousing fears that Hitler's war was now inevitable.

Plodding up and down to his job in the shipping office, Alistair MacLean had never taken to Glasgow and said he had only to catch the fragrance of a primrose and he was back again on the banks of the River Nairn in Inverness-shire. Glasgow left him with only one burning ambition, and that was to take the first available opportunity to leave it, which he was to do on two significant occasions in his life. The first would not be long delayed.

Ian had been home only three times between 1935 and 1940, now coming ashore to sit his second mate's examinations in Glasgow, a city quite strange to him despite the fact that he had been born there and it was where his mother was now living once more. Having completed his exams, he was no sooner back to duty than his ship, the *Domala*, was attacked by German bombers and sunk in the English Channel, off Southampton. More than a hundred of his mates were lost in the tragedy and he counted his blessings to be among the lucky ones.

It was not all glamour at sea, as Alistair would acknowledge, but it was still his choice of service in the future which would inevitably face him, now that conscription was being introduced.

If he didn't volunteer for the navy, he would soon have no say in where he went. So he bade goodbye to the shipping office of F. C. Strick, reluctantly took farewell of his mother and young Gillespie and reported to his first base, which was *HMS Victory* at Portsmouth. After training, he was sent to join the converted pleasure steamer, the *Bournemouth Queen*, which had been brought into service on the east coast corvette patrol.

With the Phoney War now over, the war of Alistair MacLean was under way.

6

Having joined the navy and spent his early days on the *Bournemouth Queen*, Alistair MacLean now headed north to Glasgow, *en route* to Scott's of Greenock, the famous Clydeside shipyard, where he was to be among those on stand-by duty for the building of *HMS Royalist*, a Dido class cruiser destined for service on what was to become known as the Russian Convoys, heroic adventures in which supplies were being carried to Murmansk to enable the Soviet Union to fight off the Nazi menace.

Hitler had been obsessed with the idea that the Allies intended to invade northern Norway and had thus declared that 'Norway is the zone of destiny in this war'. It was indeed, as Churchill confirmed, and for that reason Hitler sent the *Tirpitz*, acknowledged as the most powerful battleship in the world, into the fjords of that Scandinavian coast. The route to Russia was northwards into the frozen wastes of the Arctic, round the top of Scandinavia to the Barents Sea and into the port of Murmansk.

With the supplies being brought by the merchantmen from North America, the Royal Navy's job was to escort them on that last, dangerous stretch to the Soviet Union, meeting up at places like Scapa Flow, just off the northern tip of Scotland, a strategic point, the importance of which was repeatedly emphasized by Winston Churchill. Indeed, he made it his business to visit Scapa and took time to record in his diaries the memory of a previous visit during the First World War. This time, he was staying with Sir Charles Forbes, Commander-in-Chief of his flagship, *Nelson*. The rest of the fleet was hiding round the corner in Loch Ewe and the Admiral took Churchill to visit them.

He was later to write:

On every side rose the purple hills of Scotland in all their splendour. My thoughts went back a quarter of a century, when I had last visited Sir John Jellicoe and his captains in this very bay and had found them with their long lines of battleships and cruisers drawn out at anchor, a prey to the same uncertainties as now afflicted us.

Another day, another generation. Among the ships now heading up past Loch Ewe, where Churchill had paid that secret visit, was *HMS Royalist*, with the young Alistair MacLean on board, not long past his twenty-first birthday and remembering his own childhood among those 'purple hills of Scotland' so near to him now. He was part of a ship attached to the Home Fleet at Scapa Flow which would escort those supply vessels to their Soviet destination.

They would go through frozen hell and back again in the most nightmarish experience any of those young men would ever know; but MacLean was among those who would say very little about it in the years to come. He merely distilled his own experience, with the help of some other legends from that war, and let it all spill out a dozen years later in *HMS Ulysses*. The fiction had enough reality for 600 sailors to recognize their own ship and for many more to identify with the nightmare when his book reached the bestseller list.

Alistair MacLean's growing love of the sea was put to its most severe test as the reality of those Russian adventures began to dawn. At first, there was little fear, more a sense of excitement in the protected anchorage of Scapa Flow where a dozen ships of the Royal Navy would meet up with those merchantmen in readiness for the run to Murmansk.

The night closed in but in the loom of the star-lit sky dark outlines of moored ships could be picked out. The pervading silence was broken by the hawking cry of wind-carried seabirds. All sorts of possibilities were discussed among those young sailors as ships of all sizes and tonnage crept into the anchorage. When would the convoy set sail? What of the smaller craft with their assorted deck cargoes of tanks and equipment – could they be expected to survive the Arctic storms? To what extent would they slow down the convoy, making it an easy target for skulking German submarines? Those hell-runs to Murmansk meant steaming six days each way and escorting thirty or forty ships at a time, with MacLean taking up his position as a leading torpedo operator on the *Royalist*, which sailed as an escort carrier on the far outside of the formation.

Battered by hurricane and mountainous seas – and apart altogether from torpedo attacks – the smaller ships, which were down to their marks with tanks on deck, seemed to have little chance of ever reaching harbour. Many didn't. Back in Scapa and preparing for the second run, MacLean and his mates now knew too much to be without fear. They could only try to close their minds to impending tragedy – a torpedo strike, a dull detonation, smoke and flames. The scenario had become all too familiar.

There was the unspoken terror that a German U-boat attack or an air strike could mean abandoning ship, an option which offered nothing but instant death. The extreme cold and damp were bad enough on board but a man in the water would last only seconds. Apart from enemy action, ships could capsize through the speedy formation of ice on the superstructure. It was all grist to the mill of *HMS Ulysses*.

As the ferocity of the war at sea increased, so too did their chances of survival decrease. Life took on a new poignancy, not least in the letters which MacLean and his friends were trying to write before the start of another run to Murmansk. All kinds of thoughts were passing through their young heads. Was this the last their loved ones would ever hear from them? 'Lost at sea' – was that to be their epitaph? Yet they were not without their optimism.

Tom Brown, an engineer from Drymen, near Glasgow, who sailed on *Royalist* for its entire wartime service, confirms the mixed emotions of those young men. On the one hand they were waiting for the worst to happen while, on the other, believing that it wouldn't actually happen to them.

That faith in survival, as they moved out to those Arctic wastes, was fully justified in the case of Alistair MacLean and his shipmates. Indeed, just as *HMS Ulysses* was claimed as a lucky ship, so too was *HMS Royalist*, her crew marvelling from time to time about the fact that she ran through those hell-trips to Murmansk with nothing worse than a hole in a funnel. Their faith extended to thoughts about what they would do after the war.

On board the *Royalist*, they counted themselves lucky to be the first ship equipped with 'proximity shells', a deadly weapon which detonated when it was near an aeroplane and therefore did not require to hit its target to cause havoc. The Germans feared it.

Though he did not remember MacLean from their days on board *Royalist*, Tom Brown was among those who readily unravelled the fiction of *HMS Ulysses*. It was only when I talked to him about this book, however, that he learned for certain that the author was indeed a leading torpedo operator on his own vessel.

'You were there to be shot at all the time,' said Tom. 'It was a hell-run right enough, in which you were just living from day to day.'

While MacLean's ship took part in only two full runs to the outskirts of Murmansk, it was heavily engaged in bombing German oil installations on the Norwegian coast.

Then, in the spring of 1944, it left Scapa Flow with others to face up to the dreaded *Tirpitz* in Kaa Fjord. The Germans were caught napping and suffered heavy damage, their famous battleship last seen burning furiously as the navy proceeded to put it out of action for three months. The *Tirpitz* had to endure another devastating attack from the air later that year (her attackers included planes from the Dambusters squadron) before she finally capsized, taking more than half her 1,900 crew with her.

Throughout their ordeal, the crew of the *Royalist* had to sling their hammocks in sleeping quarters which were cramped and claustrophobic. Not even the forced proximity and mutual danger of the circumstances succeeded in unwinding the reticence which followed Alistair MacLean for all his days. He spoke very little about his background and only those closest to him knew that he was a son of the manse and that his mother was a Mod gold medallist. He let slip that he was upset by not having had a better education but made it plain that he would do something about that after the war.

Only with the destruction of the *Tirpitz* did Churchill declare that all British heavy ships were free to move towards the Far East. The nightmare of the Arctic behind them, MacLean and his crewmates could at least look forward to warmer weather as they headed first for the Mediterranean. But their war was far from over.

HMS Royalist served on convoy duty into Malta, then, in August 1944, as flagship for Task Force 88 in Operation Dragoon, the Allied landing in southern France. From there she moved to the Aegean where, on the night of 14–15 September, along with the destroyer *Teazer*, she intercepted two armed blockade runners to the north of Suda Bay in Crete. Both were sunk after a spirited resistance.

The *Royalist* then bombarded shore targets on other Greek islands, an incident which must have lodged well in the mind of Alistair MacLean for the time when he would come to write *The Guns of Navarone*. By coincidence, it was on one of those islands – at the picturesque town of Lindos on Rhodes – that a Scots film director would later find his location for much of the epic of Navarone.

Before the *Royalist* headed for the Far East in the penultimate stage of the Second World War, Alistair was home on leave for an uncommonly long period. Mrs MacLean was delighted to see her son but wondered about the length of his stay. By chance, she caught sight of a wound in his back, which he was reluctant to explain and which gave rise to one of those strange little mysteries which came to surround him from time to time.

The long leave, it turned out, was for the purpose of attending hospital in Glasgow. A clue to the explanation of the wound may be given in *HMS Ulysses*, where MacLean described a shell exploding in its barrel, hurling two men against a bulkhead where the backs of their heads were smashed to an eggshell pulp. Another man was unbelievably lucky, having been flung, as if by the driving piston of the Coronation Scot, through an open door behind him.

A similar incident took place on board *HMS Royalist* during target practice, when a shell exploded too near the ship and backfired to cause death and injury. There is reason within the family to believe that MacLean himself was the man who was thrown to safety through the open door.

When the ship returned to Portsmouth from the Aegean, Charlie Dunbar from Banffshire joined the crew for his first taste of life aboard a real fighting vessel, a little apprehensive at the prospect. As he struggled below with his kitbag and hammock, low in spirits and wishing he was back home in Scotland, he found himself just in time for tea. Casting an eye round the mess, he sat in awe of his

new mates, mostly battle-hardened sailors from the Russian convoys. But he was aware that one sailor in particular had cocked an
ear at the sound of his accent.

'He came over and asked where I was from,' he said. 'I told him
I was Charlie Dunbar, cinema projectionist at the Playhouse in
Keith, and he explained that he was Alistair MacLean from the
same north and north-east part of Scotland. It was a relief to find I
was no longer on my own and thereafter he kept asking how I was
settling in.'

Still only twenty-two himself, MacLean took a paternal interest
in the new arrival, not unhappy to find a kindred spirit from a Moray
Firth coast so close to the scene of his own childhood.

With Mountbatten emphasizing the importance of films for the
morale of his men, Charlie was soon in demand to continue his
work as a projectionist on board the *Royalist*. He stored his cinema
equipment under Y gun-turret and there he rigged up an electric
element on which he could brew up tea. Alistair used to wander in
for what the north-east Scots call a 'fly-cup' and a chat with Charlie.

He was not an easy conversationalist, speaking quickly and without modulation, but he showed a keen interest in the film equipment.
He had not seen many films in his lifetime and was not at all familiar
with the names of the stars. At the end of the show, however,
he would help Charlie dismantle the apparatus and put it back in
storage.

The ship sailed from Portsmouth to Alexandria, where it spent
three months undergoing a refit, including better ventilation for its
onward voyage to the Far East. Through the Suez Canal and across
the Indian Ocean, they were heading for Trincomalee, which
became an important British naval base after the fall of Singapore.
Conditions on board were still cramped and hot and there was
always the danger of attack from the air, on surface or under water.

On shore visits the crew would play football, but despite his interest in the game Alistair didn't take part. He did participate in Ludo
games, known to the sailors as Uckers, though not with much
enthusiasm. They also played cribbage and, with hobbies an essential, they used to knit, make rugs and even try crochet-work, without
any sense of that being effeminate.

Shipmates remember Alistair, when not on watch, pacing back
and fore on the after-deck, alone with his thoughts. During action-

stations, when everyone had special duties, his squad stood by for
'damage control'. Part of his work was maintaining telephone contact
throughout the ship and repairing electrical damage if it suffered
attack. He was known to have a good knowledge of the ship's circuits
and was a handy man for getting repairs carried out.

He was not given to sustaining grudges. He and Charlie fell out
one day, to the point of strained silence. But it was not long before
he picked up a dish-towel and started drying dishes for Charlie.
Nothing was said. He just smiled and they were friends again.

In south-west India they went on shore duty together, rounding
up crew members who had been drinking jungle juice and had run
amok. Alistair was frog-marching one lad back to the jetty when he
broke loose, looked up indignantly and said, 'The Lord will guide
my footsteps.' A few steps later he fell headfirst into the water and
it took more than the Lord to get him out. Back on board there was
much vomiting and Charlie Dunbar can still recall Alistair's concern
through the night for lads who might be swallowing their tongues.
He had a reputation for compassion among his fellow men.

Sailing in shark-infested waters and having seen the handiwork
of these killers, there was a debate in the mess one night about what
they would do if the ship were sunk. Most of them favoured going
down but Alistair said he would take his chance with the sharks, in
the hope of being picked up in time.

'Despite the temptations of Far Eastern ports,' Charlie remembers, 'Alistair was a clean-living man. He didn't drink to excess –
what I read about him later didn't seem like the same man – and
had no time for idle chatter, to the point of being abrupt with those
who did. He was a good chap to have around in a tight situation.'

The occasional fight would break out but was never allowed to
get out of hand. If two crew members persisted, they could request
permission for a grudge fight, usually held when in port. It was
announced when the fight would take place and the crew formed a
spectators' circle. The participants wore boxing gloves and an officer
acted as referee. There were no set rounds, just a continuous fight
until one either gave in or was knocked out. The two then had to
shake hands and admit the grudge was now over. However one
views such matters, it was evidently an effective way of settling
disputes.

In May 1945, the month of Victory in Europe, *HMS Royalist* took part in Operation Dracula, the invasion of Rangoon, and later that month, led by the battleship *Queen Elizabeth*, took part in attacking the Japanese heavy destroyer *Haguro*, which was sunk off Penang by torpedoes from *HMS Venus*. The invasion of Malaya followed quickly and the fleet was heading for Port Dickson when it received word of the bomb at Hiroshima – and the Japanese surrender.

Alistair MacLean and his mates returned to Singapore for Lord Mountbatten's ceremony of official surrender and were in time to see Japanese soldiers being set to cleaning the parade ground, to the point of picking grass from between cobblestones. Indian soldiers, incensed by what had happened to Allied forces in the prison camps, stood over them with bayonets, prodding them or simply kicking backsides as an outlet for their rage.

Then they all watched proudly as a first-lieutenant from the *Royalist* stood as the right-hand guard of the Japanese officers involved in the surrender. The Second World War was finally over that August day of 1945, known officially as VJ-Day, though it would take until December before the *Royalist* crew set sail for home.

Before leaving the Far East, they ferried men who had been prisoners of the Japs at the notorious Changi Jail in Singapore to India and Ceylon. They also took the Governor-General back to Malaya, where they were given a civic reception in Kuala Lumpur. By the end of the war there was already communist activity in Malaya and Charlie Dunbar remembers how the *Royalist* was sent to Penang to show the flag, with detachments of Royal Marines on board. When given shore leave, the NCOs were issued with revolvers to protect themselves in the event of a communist attack. Dunbar verified that Alistair MacLean never did use that revolver, nor was there any suggestion that he killed anyone when ashore. The point gains relevance later in his story when he would tell tales which allegedly troubled his conscience. Perhaps the imagination of the writer was at work. Certainly they used to gather round at the end of the war and indulge in what sailors knew as 'swinging the lamp'. These were exaggerations being manufactured when they asked each other what tales they would tell the grandchildren about their adventures in the Second World War.

In the light of subsequent events, I thought it might be interesting to ask the Naval Records Department of the Ministry of Defence to furnish whatever information they might have on Leading Torpedo

Operator Alistair MacLean of *HMS Royalist*, the man who would later write a bestseller about his experiences on those Russian Convoys. The information could be supplied only to the next of kin, so I asked his brother Ian to lodge the request. Back came a standard, pre-printed letter saying it was regretted that 'it has not been possible to identify your late brother, Alistair MacLean'. If he could provide further detail, they would make a further search. As far as the Royal Navy was concerned, did the man who wrote *HMS Ulysses* never exist? Perhaps that was wishful thinking on the part of some senior ranks, who did not look kindly on the book. Given further proof that he did exist, however, the Ministry responded that they had found an ex-LTO Alistair Stuart MacLean, service no. JX 282131, who had entered the navy at *HMS Victory* and served until 26 March 1946, when he was released in Class A. He held the rates of Ordinary Seaman, Able Seaman and Leading Torpedo Operator and was listed as having served at *HMS Spartiate* and on *HMS Royalist*.

At least his existence was now officially recognized.

7

With the war behind him, Alistair MacLean headed home from the Far East to prepare for demobilization, already turning his thoughts to what he would do in Civvy Street. His ship arrived in Portsmouth and the immediate excitement was the prospect of a reunion in London with brother Ian, whom he had not seen at all in the last five years and only three times in the last ten.

As a merchant seaman, Ian had had a vastly different, if no less dangerous, war. Apart from carrying supplies to the various theatres, he was engaged in ferrying many of the 250,000 mules which were landed in Karachi, ready to play their part with Wingate's Chindits and the 14th Army in Burma.

Though there were strict limitations on what Alistair could write to his mother at home and to his brother at sea, there was enough in his letters to Ian to prompt a reply: 'I think your future lies in writing, Alistair. With the descriptions and the way you compose your letters, you should really end up writing books.' At the end of the war, Ian had been standing by a ship under construction in Sunderland, where he met his future wife, Bunty; but now he was due in London, and for him, too, the big moment was the get-together he had arranged on one of the British India ships at the King George V Dock. Some top brass were expected on board when Ian arrived and the crew were all lined up for the occasion. But as he took up his own position by the gangway, he was less interested in the ceremonial than in catching a first glimpse of his young brother.

Suddenly, there he was, coming towards the ship and up the

gangway. Yes, this was him all right, last seen as a boy in his school-days, now grown to a man, still only twenty-three but a veteran of those Russian Convoys which would write themselves large into the pages of British naval history. The kid had been there, no longer a kid. Even though he was to say very little about the experience, it was plain that he had been through tough times. Within the smallish, spare figure, the good-looking face was gaunt, mature too far beyond its years. But to hell with serious reflection! This was celebration time. They repaired to Ian's cabin, joined by another Scots sailor from Oban, and the drink began to flow in the spirit of party time.

Even the top brass visiting the ship looked in to check on the occasion and, in the spirit of victory, joined in the celebration. Alistair was thoroughly enjoying himself. With the war now won, they were alive and well and in a mood of gratitude that the good Lord had seen them safely home. Whatever scars may have been imprinted on mind and soul, they had to think of the future, and fell to discussing what they might do.

Alistair thought he would go to university and take a degree, without too many plans about the route thereafter. It would give him time to sort out thoughts and feelings. They were basically a High-land family but the focus of attention now had to be Glasgow, where their mother lived. In the days of Daviot, their lives were contentedly self-contained; if they looked towards an urban area at all it was Inverness. Glasgow meant nothing to Ian. It didn't mean much more to Alistair, except that it was where he had spent those final years before the war and where he could now expect to pursue his univer-sity studies – at his father's alma mater, which at least gave him a warm remembrance of that gentle human being who had presided over his childhood. He was gone all too soon, when Alistair was not yet capable of appreciating the full flavour of the man but only of sensing a rich fellowship ahead. It was not to be.

So it was back home to the embrace of his mother in Glasgow, catching up with all that had been happening in his absence. Young Gillespie, for example, had remained at Woodside School until 1941, when the Luftwaffe carried out its devastating raids on Clyde-bank, the famous shipbuilding town near Glasgow, a destruction of a single community which ranked with that of Coventry. Gillespie had been at the Scouts in St Columba Church when the raids started and spent the first night in the church vaults. Thereafter, he was

promptly dispatched to the rural safety of Daviot, back to stay with
the Mackintosh family at The Doune, from which he cycled every
day to school at Inverness Royal Academy. It felt good to be back
at Daviot, scene of happier times, blighted only by the sadness of
his father and Lachlan. At call-up age, however, he was off to his
training at the Bridge of Don Barracks in Aberdeen, and was already
a sergeant in the Intelligence Corps when, at the end of the war, he
was badly injured in an explosion in Germany. He was taken back
to a hospital in Surrey, where he lay unconscious for six months.

Mrs MacLean had not had her worries to seek, between losing
her husband and eldest son before the war, having two more at sea
through the worst dangers and now with her youngest boy lying in
hospital, unaware of what was happening. Alistair went down to see
Gillespie once a fortnight.

A more pleasant surprise was the reappearance of Alastair
Cameron, the minister's son from Moy, with whom he had enjoyed
a friendship before the war in Glasgow. Appropriately, Alastair had
joined the Cameron Highlanders in 1939. He arrived home on leave
at Tomatin Station in May 1940 to hear casually from the local
postman that his father, the Reverend Hector Cameron, had just
died. Staying for the funeral meant that he missed being back in
time for the tragedy of Dunkirk. Like Mrs MacLean three years
earlier, it was now Mrs Cameron's turn to vacate her northern
manse and she, too, headed south to Glasgow, where her father
bought her a house in Drumchapel. Alastair Cameron's sister, Edith,
who was already in Glasgow, had stayed with the MacLeans at one
time and came to regard Alistair as a strange young man. She would
see him walking towards her in the street then suddenly spotting
her and crossing to the other side. He seemed averse to close contact
with people, particularly women.

Home from the war in 1946, Alastair Cameron was finding his
way back to the MacLeans in Carrington Street and continuing the
friendship as if it had never been broken. Alistair and Alastair,
separated only by a different spelling, became close associates once
more, resuming their routine of going to Ibrox Park every second
Saturday afternoon to watch their beloved Rangers. Players who
had just surfaced before the war, like Willie Waddell, were now
established stars, having had their careers severely dented by six
years of war. There was Dougie Gray and Jock Shaw, big George

Young and Scot Symon and a forward line of Waddell, Gillick, Thornton, Duncanson and Caskie. The sheer relief that the war was now behind them brought a great camaraderie among people rediscovering each other, and nowhere more so than in Glasgow, always given to excesses of welcome (or aggression, according to the mood!).

After the match they would go for a beer and spend Saturday night at the pictures, often at the Grosvenor in Byres Road. It was still Glasgow of the slums and the smoke of heavy industry, of tram-cars and trolley-buses, Glasgow of the Locarno or Green's Playhouse Ballroom, dancing to Joe Loss or Felix Mendelsohn and his Hawaiian Serenaders.

In a previous generation, the connection between the Camerons and the MacLeans had not always been so cordial. Alastair's uncle, Hugh Cameron, had once been engaged to Mrs MacLean, who was warmly welcomed in the family. Then along had come the Reverend Alistair MacLean and 'stolen' her from Hugh, giving rise to resentment in the Cameron household.

Peace was restored in time, however, when the MacLeans formed their friendship with Hugh's brother Hector at Moy. Family differences had long since been forgotten and the two young men were set for university, Alistair with his eye on an honours degree in arts while Alastair Cameron was changing course from his pre-war accountancy to do medicine instead, facing a daunting six years of further study.

For those who had made a start to their university careers before war service there was the concession of a reduced course, but Alistair MacLean's pursuit of an honours degree in English language and literature would take him the full four years, as for any other beginner. It coincided with the start of a vintage period in university life in this country. It had happened after the First World War, when battle-hardened veterans of the Somme and Passchendaele came home in a spirit of celebrating survival and lent a vigour and maturity to student life which was quite unprecedented.

The same thing happened after the Second World War, and MacLean was part of that generation of young men which enlivened the academic and social activity in memorable fashion. In a spirit of abandon, some were hell-bent on enjoying themselves while others, perhaps already married with responsibilities, simply wanted to buckle down to work and gain a degree as quickly as possible. As a group, they constituted between a third and a half of the student intake in 1946, dominating the scene with their worldly ways and overshadowing the youngsters who had come straight from school at seventeen or eighteen.

There were men like Donald MacMillan, one of the first people into Belsen concentration camp in Germany at the end of the war; and Norman Buchan, a veteran of the North African campaign, who would go on to hold office in the Labour Government under Harold Wilson.

But if some of the younger men and women stood in awe of the ex-servicemen, they must have been learning a lesson just the same. For MacLean's younger contemporaries included some distinguished names of the future. William Kerr Fraser would return one day as Principal of Glasgow University; George McNicol, remembered by some for a rectorial stunt in which he was caged in the city's George Square, ended up as Principal of Aberdeen University. An up-and-coming lady learning law became known as Winnie Ewing, sensational victor for the Scottish National Party at the Hamilton by-election of 1967; and a Campbeltown lad heading for a first-class honours degree in engineering was to revolutionize the supermarkets of Britain. He was, of course, James Gulliver, whose Argyll Foods company owned Presto and Safeway.

In this golden age of student activity, high-class debate and socializing, which was often wild, it has to be said that Alistair MacLean took virtually no part at all. Such was his quiet routine of attending classes and the occasional tutorial with John Farrish, his lecturer, returning to private study at Carrington Street as soon as possible, that there are many from his own honours year who cannot even remember him. Even his student friend, Alastair Cameron over in the medical faculty, cannot recall having seen him within the precincts of the university. There were no coffees at the Students' Union or rendezvous around the campus or enthusiasm for debating or other combative skills. There were only those weekend meetings when they put their studies behind them and headed for the football or the cinema.

Yet if MacLean had only known it, his final year at Glasgow University marked the hatching of a plot which was taking shape under his very nose and would have made wonderful material for

the budding fiction writer. His fellow students included ex-servicemen like Ian Hamilton and Billy Craig, deeply conscious of their
Scottish history and heritage and secretly discussing a plan to put
right a long-standing grievance of the Scottish people and return
the Stone of Scone to what they regarded as its rightful place.

The famous stone, upon which Scots kings had been crowned in
days of independence, had lain in Westminster Abbey for 650 years,
ever since Edward I removed it from Scone and broke his promise
to return it.

In a clandestine operation which entranced the nation, Ian Hamilton, later destined to be a sheriff and Advocate Depute, led
the team, which eluded all security and, on Christmas night
of 1950, removed the Stone from under the Coronation Chair
behind the High Altar of the Abbey. The newspaper headlines
tracked the mystery day by day until the Stone finally turned
up on the steps of Arbroath Abbey, itself a symbol of Scottish
independence.

As an indication of the reigning mood of nationalism at Glasgow
University, the students in Alistair MacLean's final year elected
John MacCormick, a leading home-rule politician of his day who
had organized the Scottish Covenant of 1949, to be their Rector.

Viewing these events from a safe distance, Alistair MacLean
remained basically apolitical and thought it more important to be a
good European and a good Scot than to be just a good Scot. So he
was not a Nationalist, though he did sympathize with many of the
nationalistic aspirations, to the extent that Scotland should have
greater autonomy, if only because it had a much clearer perception
of its own problems and how to solve them than Westminster would
ever have. The extremists who advocated home rule, he wrote later,
would never be listened to, for the simple reason that the vast majority of people, in Scotland as well as Britain, were not by nature
revolutionary.

So instead of politics and a lively student life, Alistair MacLean
devoted himself to his work and hoped that he would land one of
the coveted first-class degrees. In the lead-up to his final examinations, he appeared with a heavily bandaged right hand and the story
that he had been struck by a brewer's lorry. A specialist took a
serious view of the injury and said the hand might never recover.
Determined as ever, Alistair found his own remedy for restoring the

condition, using a tennis ball for gripping exercises and bringing the hand back to order. That was not achieved before the exams, however, and he claimed that, because of the bandaged limb, the examiners couldn't read his writing. He missed the first-class degree but landed a very good second-class one.

His diligence at university was fuelled largely by his determination that he wouldn't be a burden on anyone during his student days. There was still his widowed mother to think about so he went to earn some money in his spare time by sweeping streets and working at the Post Office.

Avoiding the excitements of the university, he confined his adventures to vacation time. Gillespie had recovered from his serious injuries sustained at the end of the war and emerged from a Surrey hospital with instructions to find work in the fresh air. That led him into forestry work on the Campbell estate at Furnace in Argyll, where he was joined during the summer holidays by Alistair and two of the Cameron boys, Alastair and Ewan who had hewn coal as a Bevin Boy in the war and was now a dental student in Glasgow.

In the two months of summer they cleared undergrowth to give young trees a chance to develop and remained for hay-time and the making of silage. It was hard work in that summer of 1947, Scotland's most glorious of the century, but they played hard as well and would set off in the evenings to the nearby town of Inveraray. Friday night was dancing night when they might land at Lochgilphead or Ardrishaig.

Alastair Cameron had brought his motor-bike and you would find them setting out on their nocturnal adventures with Alistair MacLean on the pillion-seat, holding a rope by which he pulled brother Gillespie along on his push-bike. On one occasion when they changed places, a thoughtless rabbit crossed the road at a bad time, went straight into the spokes of the bicycle and sent Alistair heelster-gowdie into the ditch. The rabbit didn't do himself much good either. At Glasgow Fair time, they went dancing every night of the week, returning in poor shape for the morning, when the forester came looking for his city helpers.

Forestry work at Furnace became a pattern of the summer holidays, but in Alistair MacLean's final year of his honours degree they decided to do something different. Alastair Cameron answered an advertisement seeking porters for the King George V Sanatorium at Godalming in Surrey, and for two months of that year they found themselves doing nothing more glamorous than cleaning out toilets and sweeping floors. But they enjoyed themselves, not least MacLean, who was in no hurry to return to Glasgow and showed an enthusiasm for staying on when the others had gone.

But there was more to it than that. He had met a German girl, who was working in his ward at the sanatorium, though it was not until he was inveigled into going back for the hospital dance at Christmas that Alastair Cameron fully appreciated the situation.

It became clear that Alistair had fallen deeply in love with Gisela Heinrichsen from Schleswig-Holstein, who had come to this country to learn English in 1949, taking whatever kind of limited position was permitted to those so recently regarded as the enemy.

His general reticence included a shyness towards women, to the extent that he had never displayed an eye for the opposite sex. He did have a girlfriend during the forestry days at Furness, but this was different. He was totally bowled over by the German girl and Alastair Cameron could understand why.

Gisela was a tallish, good-looking girl and they were obviously hitting it off together. With Alistair graduating and deciding to take the teaching qualification at Jordanhill College, the romance reached a stage where Gisela applied for a job at Mearnskirk Hospital, on the southern outskirts of Glasgow. In the early fifties it was not yet the fashion to set up house together in advance of marriage – not that they would have approved of the arrangement anyway – so Gisela settled into accommodation at the hospital while Alistair continued to live with his mother in Carrington Street, at the other end of town.

For all her lady-like qualities, Mrs MacLean, who commanded respect and deference from the sons to her dying day, was hardly more keen on Germans than she was on Roman Catholics, a prejudice dating back to the First World War, when her brother John was killed at the Somme. She could express herself quite forcibly on such matters, though without much success, since Alistair was to marry a German and Gillespie a Catholic.

From a different standpoint, brother Ian was no less opposed to the intended marriage, having met the bride-to-be, considered the couple to be incompatible and told Alistair bluntly that they wouldn't see eye to eye over the years and that he would be a fool to marry her. Ian was given to seeing things in black-and-white terms.

Of course, such overtures have a history of falling on deaf ears and Alistair MacLean went ahead and married his attractive German bride on 2 July 1953, at the same St Columba Church in Glasgow where his parents had been married thirty-seven years earlier. It was a small family affair, at which Mrs MacLean and Gillespie were joined by people like her brother, Archie Lamont, and Ian's wife Bunty. Ian was spared the embarrassment of his remarks by the fact that he was still at sea. He simply wished his brother well and kept the rest of his reservations to himself.

8

By the time of the wedding, Alistair MacLean was established as a teacher at Gallowflat School, in the ancient burgh of Rutherglen, which directly adjoined the city of Glasgow's southern boundary. Gallowflat was an old-fashioned red sandstone building in the traditional mould of west of Scotland schools (it is now an annexe of Stonelaw High). Though he soon developed a distaste for the profession, he had gone to teach English, history and geography, sharing a wartime Nissen hut in Reid Street with the ebullient George Bradford, an Ayrshire man who had been teaching English there since 1948.

MacLean was introduced to the staff-room by the head of his department, Willie Murray, better known by his initials of WAM, and George Bradford gained an early impression that he was a bit standoffish, with a quizzical, Highland look about him. The staff surveying the newcomer were themselves a rich mixture of distinctive characters, many of them back from the war with a breadth of experience which made them a unique generation of schoolmasters. They sat in little groups, playing cards or reading the papers. MacLean took to sitting alone by the big open fire, smoking quietly from heavily nicotined fingers and making his own private judgements, still only in his twenties and yet himself a veteran of the Russian Convoys and the Japanese surrender in the Far East.

Gallowflat was the school for those who had not made the grade for Rutherglen Academy, an early separation which was far from infallible. That sense of inferiority may itself have spurred fresh effort because the list of former pupils is peppered with successful businessmen, police chiefs, famous athletes – and schoolteachers.

While George Bradford next door had the A and B classes, MacLean found himself with a category sometimes referred to as the no-hopers, a total misnomer as events would prove. He listened to colleagues' advice but went ahead and faced up to these less academic classes in his own particular style. The problem for some was discipline but not for Alistair MacLean.

He reinforced his square-shouldered, padded jacket by sticking an old-fashioned Scottish tawse, the leather belt of punishment, inside the chest of it, a visible and effective presence which meant he seldom had to use it. The children liked him. Strict on discipline but scrupulously fair and mixing it all with a wry humour, he soon came to be known as Dandy MacLean, after a fictitious character of the day.

From an austere façade, he would break into playful pokes with an enormous classroom pointer, which could turn quickly from a blackboard illustration to the reawakening of an idle dreamer. In an age when some so-called forward thinkers of education have managed to replace discipline with sloppiness, Willie McIntosh speaks for his generation in loud praise of MacLean and his colleagues at Gallowflat for the way they dealt with rumbustious youth.

Willie, who now runs his own taxi business in Rutherglen, is full of gratitude for the methods and the care with which that generation of teacher brought out the best in pupils who were classed as low achievers. He proudly turns out a class photograph to illustrate the type of youngster in question. There, at the end of the row, stands Mr MacLean, complete with tweed suit and tartan tie, still sporting the middle parting in his full head of dark hair, more reminiscent of pre-war Glasgow than of a period which had already heard the first echoes of Elvis Presley and Bill Haley.

He worked his own simple system of incentive, which he called 'correct tick'. Whatever he had been teaching was the subject of a test on the following week and, if the correct ticks didn't reach eight out of ten, the pupil wrote 100 lines for every point below the eight. Five out of ten meant 300 lines of his punitive phrase, 'I must remember not to forget to learn my history.' Modern educationists would raise their hands in horror at such wasteful effort but Willie McIntosh is not a modern educationist. He has to run a business from a modest background of schooling and reckons the system made up in effectiveness what it lacked in sophistication.

'I was becoming so sick of writing lines that it dawned on me I had better brush up my performance or I would be doing this for the rest of my schooldays,' he said. 'So for the first time in my life, I actually began to study and to enjoy it.'

MacLean fired Willie's imagination and is remembered as an excellent teacher of those who wanted to learn. It surprised his pupils to discover later that he didn't enjoy his work. None of that was conveyed to the children.

Some felt there was a sadistic streak in his nature, an interesting observation in view of subsequent events. Of course, boys were forever boys and MacLean became the teacher to sort out the lavatory smokers. Those under suspicion were confined during playtime to a quadrangle outside his window, where he could keep an eye on them. Willie McIntosh was wrongly suspected and a visit from his father brought an acknowledgement of the injustice. MacLean was fair as ever, resorting only rarely to that leather-thonged belt which, in Scotland, was variously known as the tawse, the strap, the tag or the scud. He created just enough fear to gain attention and encourage diligence.

Teaching next door, George Bradford had already gathered that MacLean's heart was not in the job. He gave it his full application, to the point of writing his own interpretation passages while others would copy them from books or newspapers. But having done his job he was strictly a nine-to-four man, out through the school door the moment the bell rang and heading as quickly as possible for the bus-stop at Boots shop, on the corner of Main Street and Stonelaw Road.

In the staff-room at Gallowflat, it had not taken MacLean long to find his soul-mate. Within that array of war-hardened ex-servicemen was a certain Dougie Seggie from Cambuslang, the neighbouring town, who had started teaching technical subjects at Gallowflat before the war but was soon off to the RAF. Now more wise and worldly, he would sit there taking a measured, askance view of mankind before drawling some wry, nasal pronouncement. When Alistair MacLean and Willie Murray were engrossed in more academic discussion, the artisan in Dougie would pass comment about 'these parsers and analysers'.

Nevertheless, he knew a kindred spirit when he saw one and was soon engaging the newcomer in conversation – not that he had much to say for himself at first, and what he did say was delivered in a lilting mumble which was hard to pick up. But the daily talk came round to sailing, and the discovery of a mutual interest in messing about in boats gave them common ground. As the ideas began to gel and they felt they knew each other well enough, Dougie and Alistair struck on the idea of jointly looking for a suitable craft at a price they could afford. Dougie had had a rowing boat but this would be something different.

By the time the search began, Dougie and Violet Seggie were married and living in furnished accommodation at 33 Drumsargard Road, Burnside, Rutherglen, a semi-detached villa of pre-war vintage. Though Alistair had not struck his colleagues as the type to go wenching, he did arrive in the staff-room one day with his arm in a sling and a story that he had 'walked into a bus' while visiting London and was taken to a hospital, where he met this nurse.

It was his convoluted, tongue-in-cheek way of introducing the name of Gisela, by then working at Mearnskirk Hospital, Glasgow. Before they were married in 1953, Dougie Seggie mentioned that he and Violet were moving out to Larkhall and that the furnished rooms in Drumsargard Road would be available. MacLean jumped at the chance of a house within walking distance of Gallowflat and negotiated with Mr and Mrs Menzies, who had moved down the Ayrshire coast to live but had left their son in the Burnside house. There would be a downstairs sitting-room, an upstairs bedroom, with a boxroom and shared kitchen.

That was where Alistair and Gisela began their married life, after their July honeymoon in that year of the Coronation and in time for the new school session of 1953–54.

Though money was in short supply, MacLean and Seggie had not forgotten their ambition to own a boat. Alistair was reading the *Oban Times* when he spotted the advertisement of a Loch Fyne skiff for sale. It had been built at Ardrishaig (about the time of the Ark, according to Dougie's later judgement) and its stern had been cut square to accommodate a Bergius engine.

Managing to scrape together the £200 required, the two teachers became joint owners of the *Silver Craig*, bought from two old fishermen up the west coast of Scotland at Loch Gairloch, north-east of the Isle of Skye. When they needed extra hands to bring the vessel south, who should turn up but Dr Alastair Cameron, back from practising in Canada and ready to bring a further pair of hands in Dr Harvey Miles from West Kilbride, son of an ICI scientist at Ardeer, Ayrshire. Off the merry crew drove in Dougie Seggie's old car for the far north of Scotland, proudly taking charge of the *Silver Craig* and preparing for its southward voyage to the Clyde.

Straight away they ran into trouble with the folk of the Highlands for daring to sail on the Sabbath. The noise of the engine could be heard for miles, leaving nobody in any doubt that they were committing a sin. The wrath of God would surely be upon them. Well, they weren't far wrong. In no time at all they ran into a severe storm and got themselves into a fankle.

Despite his wartime experience, Alistair's skill had been in the torpedo-room and, in general terms, he was no more than a dedicated amateur as far as sailing was concerned. Dougie had discovered that the engine had no reverse so there was really no means of stopping the boat. When other vessels in radio contact – the *Silver Craig* had no radio – suddenly scarpered from the vicinity, the lads from Glasgow found they had an ocean to themselves. The storm of the Atlantic came roaring in and it was their great good fortune that a lady on shore, who had lost her husband at sea, was vigilant enough to raise the alarm.

Alastair Cameron, now retired from his medical practice at Cumbernauld, still remembers it as the most terrifying experience of his life. Alistair MacLean was no less frightened and went quietly away to record the voyage in a prose style which was beginning to form within him. There had been times when he would tease Willie Murray about a regular column he wrote in a Glasgow evening newspaper, called 'The Chronicles of Hackers' Park', a weekly account of the on-goings at a local football ground. 'Is that the best you can do, Willie?' he would ask.

Any challenging retort was silenced when Willie opened a 1954 copy of the famous old *Blackwood's Magazine* to read a story entitled 'The Cruise of the *Golden Girl* – by Alistair S. MacLean'. There was now no doubt that his younger colleague had a definite talent for the written word. But if readers of *Blackwood's* thought MacLean's short story was a piece of fiction, they could not have been more wrong. It was none other than a lightly camouflaged account of the cruise of the *Silver Craig*, as endured by Dougie Seggie, Alastair Cameron, Harvey Miles and himself. He didn't even attempt to change their names. What Dougie Seggie had described to me in colourful, layman's language, MacLean had shaped into the kind of prose which would one day make him famous. As a sample of his magazine story:

Four hours after leaving Kyle, Dougie and I, blissfully asleep in the fore cabin, were startled into wakefulness by a violent jolt, a loud crash, and water rushing into the cabin above our heads. We knew at once that we were doomed. This was it. Sinking fast and helplessly trapped below decks. Take to the boats! Only we had no boat.

The scene on deck ten seconds later – the delay in arriving there being due to a cabin door never designed to allow two people to get through at once – did little to reassure us . . .

The rocks drew perilously near. Beyond the outer harbour mouth now, we were exposed to the full force of the sea, and we knew that the *Golden Girl* could not last long if once she struck . . .

They ran into one horrendous emergency after another and all but lost their lives on that adventure. (For the full text of 'The Cruise of the *Golden Girl*', see the Appendix at the end of this book.)

The factual sequel to the story was that they managed to bring the *Silver Craig* to the safety of Kilcreggan on the Clyde, where they pulled it up and began to caulk it (sealing between the timbers), going down at weekends in an attempt to get it ship-shape.

MacLean and Seggie were now the proud owners of a Loch Fyne skiff, glad to be alive and looking forward to their sails in the river. As a third pair of hands, Dougie invited another friend of his, big Willie Campbell from Hamilton, to join the crew. Willie, a foreman joiner and later clerk of works with the Scottish Special Housing Association, was a square-cut hulk of a man, strong, fearless but gentle, the kind of man to whom MacLean took an instant liking.

Willie had seen life in the raw. As an engineer in the Commandos, he had been on the beaches of Dunkirk, fought in North Africa and landed on the Normandy shores half an hour ahead of the official hour of D-Day. As well as the creative work of his carpentry, he could handle explosives, blow up bridges and comport himself with such courage that he was awarded the Military Medal for his efforts on D-Day. Three days later he was wounded. Several years later, when they saw the film of *The Guns of Navarone*, Seggie and his friends were in no doubt upon whom Alistair had modelled his character of Andrea, played by Anthony Quinn. Willie Campbell was staring them in the face.

Having been through the hell of the Russian Convoys, Alistair detected in big Willie another kindred spirit, a humorous jack-of-all-trades, who would be a decided asset to their maritime adventures. It wouldn't be long before he was put to the test.

Alistair and Dougie had built a little wooden dinghy which would take them to the *Silver Craig* at anchor and could be towed thereafter. The home-made craft was called into unexpected service one evening when they were without the engineering skills of Dougie. Not to put too fine a point on it, Alistair had entered the commercial market of carrying fare-paying passengers on the Clyde estuary, as a means of easing the drain on the classroom salary. It was therefore essential to ensure public safety and see that the boat would keep sailing.

Charging Willie with the engineering responsibilities of the evening, Dougie explained that the *Silver Craig*'s magneto was in an exposed position and that the boat would bob along nicely only as long as he didn't allow the water to come up and touch the flywheel. One of the first things Willie did was to let the water touch the flywheel!

Now they had no means of going anywhere and, with the emergency of stranded passengers, Alistair took to the wooden dinghy, clipped in the oars and tried to tow the *Silver Craig* by rowing. When the wind defeated him, there was no option but to call out Troon lifeboat.

The story having reached the ears of Glasgow newspapers, a reporter called at MacLean's home to ask Gisela if she had heard about 'the accident'. No, she hadn't. Her alarm was calmed by news that the *Silver Craig* had been taken in tow and was on its way to port. The law was not overjoyed with MacLean and his adventures.

Alistair was now thoroughly enjoying the camaraderie of the Clyde and particularly his warm friendship with Dougie and Willie. They would spend much time working on their thirty-four-foot boat at

Shandon or Kilcreggan, caulking, painting, repairing, before sailing off in a spirit of abandon, full of life and laughter and playing out their Para Handy fantasies, standing on deck and spouting doggerel about their escapades which could reduce them to convulsions.

Every now and then would come an incident which silenced the laughter and called for their combined skills. Dougie was back on board when they were sailing by the narrows near the Gare Loch one day and found themselves in the path of a battleship heading for a breaker's yard at Faslane. It was not the most opportune moment for a breakdown but that is what happened with the *Silver Craig*, as Dougie strove frantically to revive her engine and bring it putt-putting to safety in the nick of time. (He still pulls a serious expression and contemplates how close that battleship came to being run down!)

Whatever else happened at sea, they held to a golden rule that there would be no drinking until the boat was tied up. Sailing down by the Mull of Galloway one day, where they fabricated Mulberry Harbours during the war, they ran across an Irish boat cutting up naval scrap. The bhoys from the Emerald Isle had no such inhibitions about drinking. Cases of Guinness were everywhere and most of it was disappearing down the throats of the carefree crew. Alistair handed them over a pot of soup to stabilize events and off they set for Belfast. Somewhere along the way, they missed their route and the *Silver Craig*, now heading for Portpatrick, met the Irishmen coming back. A storm was blowing up and soon they were in the local bar and doing more than justice to the black stout of their native land. Alistair sought reassurance that they would not be setting out till morning but no such assurance could be given.

After a couple of hours of lubrication, they set sail into the teeth of a wild and stormy night, ignoring all warnings and pleas. Providence looks after such people and, in the absence of any tragic report, they could finally assume that they had reached Belfast.

MacLean and his crew huddled over the wee coal fire and waited for more hospitable conditions. A master of improvisation, Willie Campbell came to the rescue one night when the *Silver Craig* lost its anchor. Having shaped up a substitute, it was a little difficult to explain to two policemen why he was heaving one and a half hundredweight of steel in a sack at two o'clock in the morning.

Forever the enthusiast, Willie would provide tar-coating for the deck. It was not until two visitors arrived on board that its non-drying properties were discovered. One, the commodore of local yachting, slipped and fell to a sticky fate. The other, a religious zealot for whom Willie was told to mind his language, ended up so tar-encrusted that Willie had never heard such expletives.

The staff at Gallowflat School, always curious about this famous boat which MacLean and Seggie were telling them of, were finally rewarded with a memorable staff outing, in which they were taken on a cruise from Shandon to Garelochhead. They tied up at a rotting old pier and, while it may have been difficult to climb out of the boat, an evening's lubrication on shore made the return a more feasible and hilariously acrobatic feat.

In their quieter moments, Alistair was confiding in Dougie that he was trying his hand at writing short stories. Having just seen an example of his work in the 'Golden Girl' story, Dougie understood the potential. Another had appeared in Argosy. Now there was a hint that he had entered a short-story competition in the Glasgow Herald newspaper, but little more was said.

Gisela remembers when Alistair received the letter indicating he had won something, but he didn't think it would be the first prize. 'He was called into the Herald office and we agreed that, if it was a runner-up prize, he would come home to tell me. Only if by some chance he had won it was he going to phone. I remember waiting at home – and the phone rang. He had won the first prize of a hundred pounds. We were so delighted because we needed some extra money.

'The house in Drumsargard Road, where we had the rooms, was now on the market and we were asked if we wanted to buy it; but we couldn't afford it and had already received notice to quit. We had only a few pieces of furniture and were planning to move to another furnished place, this time at 343 King's Park Avenue, not far away.'

The joy of Gisela and Alistair MacLean, whose take-home pay at that time was about £24 a month, was shared with the general public next morning, 6 March 1954, when the Glasgow Herald announced the prize-winners in their short-story competition. The results were:

First prize (£100) – 'The *Dileas*', by Alistair S. MacLean, 33 Drumsargard Road, Burnside, Glasgow

Second prize (£50) – 'Now Such Light', by Iris I. J. M. Gibson, Wellmeadow House, Paisley

Third prize (£25) – 'The Epicurean', by D. R. Miller, 110 Eldon Street, Greenock

Fourth prize (£25) – 'Timothy's Earthquake', by Henry R. Saunders, Rowantree Cottage, Gartocharn, Alexandria, Dumbartonshire

The report went on:

Mr Alistair S. MacLean, the winner of the first prize, is a Rutherglen schoolteacher. He is 32 and was brought up in Inverness-shire, where his father was minister at Daviot. He is Gaelic-speaking and owns and sails a Loch Fyner, built at Ardrishaig. These facts, in conjunction with war service in the navy, may be taken to supply the background of his winning short story. He was educated at Inverness Royal Academy, Hillhead High School and, after his naval service, at Glasgow University, where he took his degree in 1950.

There were 942 entries, some from as far away as India, Canada and the United States, from grandmothers and grandfathers and schoolchildren and all ages in between. Having listed the difficulties which faced the adjudicators in reducing 942 stories to a short leet, the *Herald* writer said:

In the end, the choice fell on a story of exciting action in which the Highland dialect is used sparingly to suggest the setting, in which the simple emotions of courage and affection are treated with undemonstrative conviction.

What was not revealed was that the judges, six highly literate journalists on the staff of the *Herald*, found themselves in heated division over who should win first prize. Alastair Phillips, who started his own column in 1937 and still writes it in the nineties, backed the MacLean story, supported by Colin Murray, the literary editor, and Innis Macbeath, a leader-writer. The supporters of Iris Gibson, who became a doctor at the Southern General Hospital, Glasgow, were deputy editor Richard Biles (father of actress Anne Kristen), feature-writer Anne Donaldson and senior leader-writer Alex Sturrock. There was some horse-trading even before they could agree on the top two and it was finally left to the casting vote of the editor, Sir William Robieson, to split the deadlock; his choice of 'The *Dileas*' (pronounced Jee-lus) was surely vindicated by subsequent events.

The title in Gaelic means 'The *Faithful*', which was the name of a boat involved in a shipwreck up the west coast of Scotland, a subject and location in which Alistair MacLean was very well versed! But with such a mass of reading to undertake, how easy it would have been for the judges to overlook this story altogether. If that had happened, it is very likely we would never have heard the name of Alistair MacLean in the context of international bestselling novelist. A short story here or there was liable to have been the extent of his literary adventures.

Ironically, he very nearly disqualified himself by submitting an earlier short story for consideration by the *Glasgow Herald*. The rules said no one who had previously written for the paper could enter. Luckily, that earlier attempt was sent back with a rejection slip.

At Gallowflat School there was a rush to congratulate their prize-winning colleague on his success. Naturally, among those delighted with the result was the headmaster, James Butler, who had on occasion welcomed MacLean to his home in Larkhall. There he met Butler's son, David, home from St Andrews University, where he was studying English. That meeting with David Butler would form the basis of an amazing coincidence in years to come. Meanwhile, in the staff-room at Gallowflat, there were a few winks and hints that Alistair's short-story success was one in the eye for Rutherglen Academy, where the higher intellectual level of the pupils was seen by some to be reflected in the calibre of staff as well. It rankled. What would they now be thinking of a teacher from the inferior Gallowflat managing to show such literary prowess?

Local rivalry was one thing; but a chance happening of much greater significance would arise almost immediately – a meeting which would change the whole course of Alistair MacLean's life.

9

Much as he disliked teaching, the last thing on Alistair MacLean's mind that Saturday morning in March 1954 was that his prize-winning short story might open the escape hatch and lead him to a lucrative career as an international bestselling novelist.

The short story, often with the tang of the sea about it, had become a hobby, a balancing mental exercise for the more practical adventures on the *Silver Craig*. His medium had been magazines like *Blackwood's* and *Argosy* and the only difference that Saturday morning was that he had triumphed in a competition of nearly a thousand entries and was now receiving the high-powered publicity which only a newspaper can offer.

He looked again and again at the prominent display in the week-end section of the *Glasgow Herald*, but was just as enthusiastic about the cheque for £100, which would make all the difference to Gisela and himself, especially with a baby on the way.

What Alistair MacLean didn't know was that among those who took time to read his story that wet afternoon was Marjory Chapman, who had worked for Collins the publishers in Glasgow, along with her husband, Ian, who was in the Bible department.

At their furnished rooms in Ancaster Drive, near Anniesland Cross, Ian Chapman was writing letters when he noticed his wife had tears on her cheeks. What on earth was wrong?

Quite simply, she had just been so moved by 'The *Dileas*' that she was handing over her *Glasgow Herald* to see what he thought of the winning story. Soon they were enthusing together over this unknown schoolteacher's ability to write. It was a first-class story, they kept telling each other. What else could he do? The publisher's instinct was unlikely to let it rest there.

Unable to find a telephone number at MacLean's furnished rooms, Ian Chapman continued his letter-writing with a new urgency, dropping a note to the address given in the *Glasgow Herald*, asking the competition winner to phone him as soon as possible.

Alistair MacLean pondered over the letter till curiosity got the better of him. He went to a telephone and called Mr Chapman at Collins in Cathedral Street. Though both were northern Scots, the latter had difficulty in following MacLean's indistinct speech but managed to communicate sufficiently to invite him out to dinner and to bring his wife with him, so that they could make up a foursome.

Ian and Marjory Chapman arrived at the old Royal Restaurant in the centre of Glasgow to be met by Alistair alone. In the days before the Swinging Sixties, heavily pregnant women were less inclined to be seen in public dining places and Gisela had decided to stay at home.

Over a pleasant dinner, Alistair was encouraged to talk about his background, which included his war service on the famous Russian Convoys, and in the course of the evening they were to discover that he was actually in the same honours class at Glasgow University as Marjory Chapman, which explained why they both felt that they had met before.

In the conviviality of the evening, the Chapmans had managed to unwind the natural reticence of the Rutherglen schoolteacher and to put the point which had engaged their minds from the start. They suggested he should write a novel for Collins. MacLean showed little enthusiasm for the idea, confirming that the short story was really his main interest. But the Chapmans were not giving up.

They met him on a number of occasions through the spring and summer of 1954, enough to show that he was not ruling out their proposition altogether. MacLean could be awkward with new faces but he had taken a liking to the Chapmans and was intrigued to find the common ground that he and Ian were both sons of the manse. Ian Chapman had been born at St Fergus, near Peterhead, where his father, the Reverend Peter Chapman, was minister before they moved along the Moray coast to Auldearn, not far from MacLean's own childhood scene of Daviot.

Just as the MacLeans headed for Glasgow in the thirties, so did

the Chapmans, when Ian's father became a minister in the Gorbals
and they settled into Queen Mary Avenue, on the south side, where
their neighbours included Sir Hugh Roberton, illustrious founder
of the Glasgow Orpheus Choir.

Ian went to Shawlands Academy before joining the RAF in 1943.
An eye problem put an end to his flying ambitions and he ended up
with three years as a coalminer at Plean Colliery, near Stirling. An
outstanding musician, he had put aside an earlier ambition to be a
concert violinist as he faced up to the realities of post-war Britain
and applied for a job with William Collins in Glasgow. In 1947 he
was engaged as a trainee at a wage of £2 a week and four years later
was selling Bibles across America before returning to the Glasgow
office. There he had met Marjory.

Like the MacLeans, they were married in 1953, and now they
were exchanging backgrounds and views with the man they had
targeted as a potential writer for Collins. Quietly, MacLean had
conceded, at least to himself, that it was worth a try.

There were other, more pressing, matters on his mind as Gisela
was taken to Stobhill Hospital, Glasgow, in September, when she
gave birth to their first son, Lachlan. With the news that mother
and baby were both well, he conveyed to Ian Chapman some other
news which was music to the publisher's ears. Using his wartime
experience, he had decided to make an attempt at that novel they
were talking about.

Less than ten weeks later, he stimulated further joy by phoning
to tell Ian he could come out and collect 'that thing'. What thing?
The book? Yes, the manuscript was ready, for better or worse.

With the Chapmans by now living in Rutherglen, Ian jumped into
his little Ford Popular and drove across to 343 King's Park Avenue,
the little semi-detached bungalow which was the MacLeans' new
address, now that they had been asked to move from Drumsargard
Road, Burnside. Alistair appeared in his carpet slippers but felt the
domestic scene of a new baby and an array of nappies was too
complicated for inviting his visitor to come into. Though it was
pouring rain, he left Ian Chapman on the doorstep while he disappeared inside, returning with a brown paper parcel, tied up in
old-fashioned string. It was hardly an auspicious start.

In an on-rush of self-doubt, Chapman drove home, wondering
what he had let himself in for. After all, he was a lesser employee

of Collins with no authority to commission anything. With his encouragement, this man had written a manuscript in less than three months, so it couldn't be any good anyway, and . . .

Back home he untied the string, unwrapped the pathetic package on the kitchen table and there, in front of him, was a title-page which said: '*HMS Ulysses*, by Alistair S. MacLean'. He and Marjory began to read the opening words of the very first novel from the man who would change the face of modern story-telling:

> Slowly, deliberately, Starr crushed out the butt of his cigarette. The gesture, Captain Vallery thought, held a curious air of decision and finality. He knew what was coming next and, just for a moment, the sharp bitterness of defeat cut through that dull ache that never left his forehead nowadays. But it was only for a moment – he was too tired really, far too tired to care . . .

Page after page they read, more and more enthralled as they went by this drama of the Russian Convoys during the Second World War. No one surely had written like this about the sheer horror of what those courageous men went through in the attempt to take supplies to the Soviet Union. Under attack and cast into a burning sea of oil, screaming, dying in a barbarous combination of drowning and cremation, their plight was recaptured by MacLean in frightening relief:

> For ten, fifteen seconds the *Ulysses* held her course, arrowing through the burning sea to the spot where gregariously atavistic instinct for self-preservation held two hundred men knotted in a writhing, seething mass, gasping out their lives in hideous agony. For a second, a great gout of flame leapt up in the centre of the group like a giant, incandescent magnesium flare, a flame that burnt the picture into the hearts and minds of the men on the bridge with a permanence and searing clarity that no photographic plate could ever have reproduced: men on fire, human torches beating insanely at the flames that licked, scorched and then incinerated clothes, hair and skin: men flinging themselves out of the water, backs arched like tautened bows, grotesque in convulsive crucifixion: men lying dead in the water, insignificant, featureless little oil-stained mounds in an oil-soaked plain: and a handful of

fear-maddened men, faces inhumanly contorted, who saw the
Ulysses and knew what was coming, as they frantically thrashed
their way to a safety that offered only a few more seconds of
unspeakable agony before they gladly died . . .

On board the *Ulysses*, men for whom death and destruction had
become the stuff of existence, to be accepted with the callousness
and jesting indifference that alone kept them sane – these men
clenched impotent fists, mouthed meaningless, useless curses over
and over again and wept heedlessly like little children. They wept
as pitiful, charred faces turned up towards *Ulysses*, and, alight
with joy and hope, petrified into incredulous staring horror, as
realization dawned and the water closed over them: as hate-filled
men screamed insane invective, both arms raised aloft, shaking
fists white-knuckled through the dripping oil as the *Ulysses*
trampled them under: as a couple of young boys were sucked into
the maelstrom of the propellers, still giving the thumbs-up sign:
as a particularly shocking case, who looked as if he had been
barbecued on a spit and had no right to be alive, lifted scorified
hand to the blackened hole that had been his mouth, flung to the
bridge a kiss in token of endless gratitude: and wept, oddly, most
of all, at the inevitable humorist who lifted his fur cap high above
his head and bowed gravely and deeply, his face into the water as
he died. Suddenly, mercifully, the sea was empty . . .

The Chapmans read the book clean through before easing sweated
palms and exchanging a look which passed its own verdict on this
first-time manuscript. Alistair MacLean went off to Gallowflat
School next morning little knowing what activity his literary effort
had sparked off.

Ian Chapman hastened to the office and dispatched the manuscript with a memo to William Collins, the chairman in London, to
whom his own name was little better known than MacLean's. Three
days later, his phone rang. The chairman was on the line. In a burst
of doubt, Chapman embarked on an apology for having bothered
him.

'No, no,' said the chairman. 'I would like to publish it. But how
did you get hold of this manuscript?' Chapman explained. 'Go and
tell him I'll pay him an advance of a thousand pounds.'

It was a lot of money in 1954. Ian Chapman looked at his watch.

MacLean should just about be home from Gallowflat School. He would drive straight out to King's Park Avenue to break the news. Once again he was kept on the doorstep, but as the story unfolded, a puzzled MacLean said, 'Oh ay. Well, I suppose you had better come in.' He tried to explain to Gisela, who had nappies strewn around the room as she attended to baby Lachlan.

Amidst the confusion and excitement, she went off to make a cup of tea and Alistair sat down to absorb the news and to hear exactly what it meant. 'A thousand pounds of an advance. What does that mean?'

Ian Chapman explained the technicality that publishers usually offer an author a guaranteed sum in advance of publication. It was an advance on royalties, meaning that the author's subsequent earnings from his percentage of sales would take into account that he had already been paid a portion of the money due. Clearly an innocent in the world of publishing, Alistair did have one practical question, albeit another naïve one. 'Will I make enough from this to put a down-payment on a house? You see, Gisela wants a place of our own and we have our eye on a house being built in Clarkston [another suburban district on the south side of Glasgow].'

Ian Chapman had his own ideas about the potential earnings of the book, but even without building up hopes it was plain enough that the author was already guaranteed not just a 10 per cent deposit on the detached bungalow but nearer 40 per cent of the total asking price, which in 1954 was a mere £2,750.

Alistair permitted himself a wry smile and shook his head in disbelief. So many things were going through his mind. It was much too early to contemplate a life outside teaching but it was certainly time for something stronger than a cup of tea.

When Ian Chapman left, he broke the news to Mrs Isobella McAllister, their widowed landlady, who had grown very fond of the young couple now keeping her company in the small semi-detached. Then he went next door to tell the Joneses at number 341 and to thank them for the use of their typewriter.

'When he sat down to write *HMS Ulysses*, he didn't have a type-writer at all so he borrowed our old Remington,' Pamela Jones recalled. She had always found him quiet and moody and was pleas-antly surprised to see the change in his attitude that night.

Still finding it hard to take in, Alistair repaired to the little back

bedroom where he had written the book and looked out on the back
garden of Mrs McAllister's house. There hadn't been much to
inspire him in the view from his window, just a wartime air-raid
shelter which became a feature of many a city garden. (The one
next door is still there). As a symbol of refuge from German bombing
attacks, the shelter must have grated a little on Gisela.

What grated more on Mrs McAllister's niece, however, was the
fact that Alistair made a habit of apologizing in front of Gisela for
the fact that she was a German.

'It both hurt her and annoyed me – and I told him so,' said Elma
Nairn, who regularly went across from Pollokshields to visit her aunt
in King's Park. Young Elma would take issue with him on many
subjects, none more so than his attitude to his German wife. 'After
all, he knew she was German when he married her. He had a
cruel tongue and I felt heart sorry for Gisela, who was a pet.' Mrs
McAllister remonstrated with her niece for talking to Mr MacLean
like that. Both knew that the young couple were fairly hard-up and
felt delighted when they broke the news of the book.

Elma Nairn, who is now Mrs Corkill from Fenwick, near Glas-
gow, was one of the first to notice that all was not well in the
MacLean marriage; and on pram-pushing expeditions to the King's
Park shops, Gisela had also conveyed her unhappiness to Mrs Jones.

More recently, Gisela looked back on those early days and told
me, 'Of course, Alistair and I fell in love when we met at Godalming
but when one falls in love one wears pink glasses. Very soon after we
were married I noticed that things were not what they had seemed to
be and the marriage became extremely painful for me. But Lachlan
had just been born and, because of my upbringing in Germany, I
felt compelled to stay for the child's sake.'

In the semi-detached bungalow at King's Park Avenue, Alistair
and Gisela had only two extremely tiny rooms to themselves. There
wasn't even enough space for erecting a cot so the baby had to stay
in his pram.

Once he had made his decision about trying his hand at a novel,
Alistair came home from school and started writing after an early
tea. Then, when it was time to take the pram to the bedroom,
they manoeuvred it past the hallstand and changed ends, as Alistair
continued his writing in the front room. Much as they liked Mrs
McAllister, he had decided the accommodation position could not

be tolerated for much longer. If they could not afford a deposit on that house in Clarkston, he would pursue a teaching post in Wigtownshire, where there was a house with the job.

Whatever problems were threatening to develop in their marriage, Alistair and Gisela at least shared a sense of relief that they could now afford a substantial deposit on a house of their own, and resumed their interest in the property at Hillend Road, Clarkston.

Meanwhile, Collins were generating excitement about their new author, planning to launch him in the early autumn of 1955. Keeping up the Scottish connection, Robert Clark, boss of the Associated British Picture Corporation and himself a Paisley man, bought the film rights of *HMS Ulysses* for £30,000, and that memorable magazine *Picture Post* paid £5,000 for the serial rights.

The book itself went into print with hardly a change, except for the removal of the middle 'S.' in the author's name. 'Alistair MacLean' sounded better. Ian Chapman crossed his fingers as Collins arranged a London launching party for their brand new author, of whom so much was expected, with a guest-list which included names like Lady Edwina Mountbatten, whose husband had conducted that memorable ceremony of Japanese surrender which Alistair attended in Singapore exactly ten years earlier.

Though little known outside the Glasgow office until then, Ian Chapman had been promoted to the London editorial base of Collins as a result of his MacLean discovery, and it fell to him to arrange for the author to be there on the big night. He would, of course, be anxious to come.

That was where Chapman ran into his first experience of the obstinate Highlander. The chosen date would mean a day off school, he was told, and unless they changed it, they wouldn't be seeing him at any fancy party in London. But the party was for him; it would be pointless without him. He made it plain that, however much he disliked teaching, his duty was in the classroom and the only available date was the Monday of the September weekend.

The date was duly changed and Alistair and Gisela travelled down by train from Glasgow for the big occasion. For all his native thrawnness and reluctance to admit pleasure, there is evidence from an early scrapbook that Alistair was nevertheless taking a quiet pride in his thrust to prominence. There was much pasting of headlines to show that 'CITY TEACHER WRITES £50,000 BESTSELLER'; there were press photographs of Alistair and Gisela, with baby Lachlan, having moved into their new home, and a cutting to show them boarding that train for London.

The party to launch *HMS Ulysses*, due in the bookshops a week later, was hosted by the Book Society in its London headquarters at Grosvenor Place. In the customary manner, literary and social London turned up to congratulate the author, not the most natural recipient of Belgravian gush but managing nevertheless to cope with effusion in a delightfully off-hand way.

Shorter of stature and speech than most of the guests had expected, Alistair had quickly learned that useful art of limiting individual engagement to two or three minutes, which meant he was able to circulate widely in the course of the three-hour party. Everyone wanted a word. Sir Alan Herbert, himself a successful novelist and librettist, encouraged him with a pat on the back. Tom Driberg, journalist and politician, wanted to give him solid advice. Lord Jellicoe told him who he was and Mr Ivliev, the Russian naval attaché, apparently did his best in his own language, mixed with English, to say he thought the book was wonderful.

Gisela stood back in a corner with friends, stealing none of Alistair's limelight but surveying it all with not a little wonder and making it plain that she wouldn't have missed it for worlds.

Unexpected colour was brought to the occasion with the arrival of the actress Mary Ure, wearing a crinoline frock, pink dust-coat and larger-than-Ascot black velvet picture hat. As one Scot come to congratulate another, she was fresh from the first rehearsal of a new production of *Hamlet*, in which she was playing Ophelia to Paul Scofield's prince.

The inevitable gossip-columnists were there, faintly cynical and amusing as ever about such events. One scribe wrote:

At length we said our goodbyes but, as I moved away, my sleeve was plucked. 'Can we meet Phyllis Calvert?' whispered Mrs MacLean. 'She's supposed to be here.' Through the milling crowd I elbowed, elbowed and elbowed without finding Miss Calvert but, when I last looked over my shoulder, Mrs MacLean was looking the happiest successful novelist's wife on record. The commission could be forgotten. I could slip away with a picture in my mind of one novelist who was keeping his head amid the champagne of success.

Alistair and Gisela caught the night train home and he was back in the classroom at Gallowflat School next morning, the flattery of Belgravia receding in the new light. A dawn with a difference was breaking that September morn.

10

It is now a matter of publishing history that *HMS Ulysses* turned out to be one of the most successful British novels of all time. Ian Chapman, by then general sales manager of Collins, found himself caught up in a truly dramatic experience in the selling of books. Even by publication day it had an advance sale to the shops of 134,000 hardback copies, and by the spring of 1956 it had sold 250,000.

Within a very short time, as a result of the combined income from royalties, film rights and serials, Alistair MacLean had grossed £100,000. Enough to make a down-payment on that house in Clarkston? Enough to buy the whole length of that suburban street! The public were soon acclaiming a masterpiece of the sea and attuning their ears to a new name, which would be mentioned in the same breath as Nicholas Monsarrat, the English novelist whose *Cruel Sea* had appeared four years earlier.

It may have been no more than the Scottish penchant for keeping her famous sons in check, but Alistair MacLean could have been excused, that autumn day of 1955, for thinking he had committed some heinous crime. On opening his *Daily Record*, a popular tabloid newspaper produced in Glasgow, he was confronted with a headline which said 'BURN IT!' Yes, they were talking about *HMS Ulysses*.

'Here is a book for burning,' screamed James T. Cameron (not to be confused with the better-known James Cameron), whose by-line box revealed that he, too, had served on the Russian Convoys and had taken part in intercepting the notorious *Tirpitz* when she came out to raid a convoy:

For it seeks to garb the gallantry of the Royal Navy in a boat-cloak of black burning shame with one of the most fantastic, the most unbelievable tales of the sea I have ever come across. And I have heard a few unbelievable tales of the sea . . .

No doubt Mr MacLean has drawn on his escort experience but he has drawn more on his imagination and on the tales told about the fleets spread across the world's ocean. He leaves no horror undescribed. Blood and entrails splash almost every page. Death and destruction stroll skull by skull through this eight-day story of a cruiser that led a navy force escorting a convoy from America to Russia. If Mr MacLean had sustained the atmosphere and tension of the first thirty-two pages I should have had no complaint.

But from then on, he allows his tale to drop down into drivelling melodrama that makes *Sweeney Todd* and *Maria Marten of the Red Barn* read like Shakespeare. It makes *Mutiny on the Bounty* look like a United Free Church of Scotland choir outing on a hot June afternoon . . . His book becomes a horror comic strip, viewing life aboard a warship through a fairground distorting mirror.

So it went on till Mr Cameron concluded:

The Sea Lords are going to be very angry about this book. Very, very angry. For it seems the book is a success. A first print of 135,000 has been ordered. The serialization and film rights have already brought in £50,000 . . . and the impression it leaves on the mind of the reader . . . is that the Royal Navy is no bloody good. That I deny. I served in the Royal Navy.

Mr Cameron, remembered by colleagues as a rather waspish sub-editor, was right in at least one point. The book was a success. Within the same Kemsley building in Hope Street, Glasgow, there were others who had served in the Russian Convoys and who took a different view of MacLean's first novel.

One of the ablest journalists of his generation was Angus Shaw (father of the Wimbledon tennis player Winnie Shaw), who worked for the *Daily Record*'s sister paper, the *Evening News*. Shaw had been a lieutenant commander during the war, on a ship escorting the tragic convoy known as PQ17. As a man who had been through it all himself, he wrote in this vein:

Many grim books have been written about the war at sea. I have read most of them, including *The Cruel Sea*. They are Sunday School reading compared with *HMS Ulysses*. It will appal. It will repel. It is a picture of almost unrelieved torture, mental and physical. There is an almost clinical detachment in the manner in which MacLean analyses by sentence and chapter the psychological reaction of a ship's company to the torturing strain of incessant 'Action Stations'. It becomes almost an exercise in mental flagellation, stunning in its repetitive effect, nauseating in its impact.

Occasional flashes of humour, a macabre incident, or a character's smile-provoking idiosyncrasy lightens the scene momentarily only to focus in fresh perspective the loathsome ferocity of sea warfare in latitudes where nature itself is allied with the forces of darkness.

But let there be no mistake about it: this first novel is a best-seller. MacLean has taken a theme that no writer has yet touched – the Allied convoys to Russia. The neglect of this field is perhaps understandable. Far too few survived the ordeal; those who did have tried to forget a living nightmare.

Subjected to Arctic gales of incredible fury, attacked by submarine packs and exposed to incessant attacks by dive-bombers – annihilation by German surface raiders was just an incidental hazard – the poorly defended convoys struggled to their Russian destinations. For the crews of the attacked and maimed ships there was little hope. Unless picked up immediately, those who escaped on rafts and lifeboats died a quick death from the intense cold. Tankers carrying aviation spirit disintegrated in flashes of searing flame; the heaving seas became burning wastes and men human torches. Those who struggled in the fuel oil died in agony, their lungs and stomachs burned within them. Men who die in raving agony seldom qualify as heroes; men silently prayed that the cup of lingering death in the loathsome oil slicks would pass from them and there would be some semblance of decency in their dying. Little wonder the story of the Murmansk convoys has not been told. There was no romance in it; its heroes were unsung. MacLean tells it as it happened; he glosses over nothing.

Shaw went on to give hint of his own appalling experience in escorting the PQ17 convoy, when word came that the German *Tirpitz* had appeared – and the convoy escorts were ordered to withdraw, leaving the PQ17 to its fate. He recalls:

> Then followed brutal, calculated annihilation. Twenty-three ships were sent to the bottom by submarine and aircraft. Was this one of the gigantic blunders of the war? MacLean has little doubt about it. Controversy will rage on this issue alone. Against the background of this terrible calamity at sea, the author introduces the Arctic seasoned cruiser *HMS Ulysses*, a 'lucky ship', manned after successive northern convoys by a battle-exhausted crew; an admiral driven mad by his own tactical mistakes; a crew openly mutinous to cold-blooded, unimaginative control from London . . .
>
> MacLean's writing style is impeccable. Knowledge of the sea, allied to Conrad-like prose, makes memorable his description of the storm which struck *HMS Ulysses* . . . This is the story of the Russian convoys that had to be told. It is not for the squeamish.

Angus Shaw, who lives in retirement on the Clyde coast, has since recalled to me how those daring convoys which did manage to reach Murmansk were disillusioned by the reception. Evidently the Soviets were less than hospitable, so brain-washed as to be suspicious even of their allies who had sacrificed so much to come to their rescue.

But Shaw's approval of MacLean's book, in contrast to his colleague's view, was no more than a confirmation of what was said by another man with first-hand experience, one of the most distinguished writers of his day, Godfrey Winn, who, for all his genteel, effeminate manner, was one of the surviving heroes of that PQ17 convoy. Winn burst into print in *Picture Post* with an article which began like this:

> I want to tell you one of the strangest experiences of my life. It happened on a day when the barometer had soared into the

eighties. But I was unconscious of the sweating heat for I myself
was ice-cold: my mind, heart, all memory lay imprisoned in the far
wastes of the North and the Barents Sea. I was *en route* for Murmansk again. This time I wasn't in my own ship, *HMS Pozarica*,
which somehow survived the massacre and holocaust of PQ17,
officially described as the worst convoy of the war. Instead, I was
on board another light cruiser, *HMS Ulysses*, a younger ship than
ours but one which had already grown old in the Russian convoys
and on the Arctic patrol.

So far she had been a lucky ship. And only those who have
spent much time at sea in wartime know what that reputation
means. 'A lucky ship and a ghost ship and the Arctic was her
home.' That is how her young Scottish creator, who has in my
opinion – but maybe I am prejudiced – written the finest war
novel yet, describes the heroine of his story.

Godfrey Winn went on to analyse and marvel at the perception
and writing skills of Alistair MacLean before revealing, as only Winn
could have done, the circumstances of how the two men met. It says
much about the respective statures of the established English writer
and the subservient young Scot, still wondering if he is going to
make it as a professional. Winn continued his eulogy:

Moreover, as the hours passed and I read on with parched throat,
I was lost in admiration for the professional skill of the author,
who assuredly is as good as Forester and as convincing in his
technical detail. And what higher praise can one give than that?

A first novel? It seemed utterly impossible – and then the bell
of my flat rang, just as I reached the last page of the biting,
bitter Epilogue, and into the peaceful summer atmosphere of my
living-room came a quiet, compact figure who, with his high
cheekbones and raw colouring, I think I would have recognized
as a Scot before he opened his lips.

At ease, we sat for an hour and yarned about 'far off things and
battles long ago'. And my guest told me how his literary career
had started with his winning a short-story competition in a Glasgow paper for a hundred pounds – 'needed the money badly' –
and how Collins had had the vision to commission a novel and
take a blind chance: and how, working in the daytime as a school-

master, teaching English, he'd finished his book in three months, at night, sitting at a typewriter, set on an old card-table . . . and how he'd stopped for a fortnight in the middle, when his son and heir was born: and how, when he'd finished his story, 'it didna seem so good' to him, but his young bride, like so many other wives before, had reassured her man, telling him to be of good cheer.

They discussed the book in detail and Winn became more and more enthralled by what he had read, when setting it in the context of the modest young man who had written it. As MacLean got up to say goodbye, he said, deprecatingly, 'Of course, it is only a novel. It's fiction.'

Winn was having none of that:

In his eyes at that moment was the look of someone who had sailed those seas himself and knew, as we all knew, what the price of Admiralty could be. This book will be a fresh bond between us all: this book which is the finest epitaph that any ship could wish to have. As for myself, I am very proud to have my copy signed by its creator, 'With best wishes from an apprentice.' An apprentice indeed!

Those early comments continued to be pasted into a scrapbook, with all the touching innocence and quiet pride of the beginner. On balance, the professionals had been kind to him.

11

Long before they knew anything about the book, the Gallowflat staff-room began to suspect that Alistair's short-story triumph had inspired some greater literary effort, judging by the number of school jotters disappearing from the cupboard. He was seen in deep conversation with his friend Frank 'Pinny' Robb, the head art teacher, who had taken to drawing ships.

So it was no surprise when the news of *HMS Ulysses* broke over Rutherglen. The parsers and analysers cast their sideways looks, drew heavily on their pipes and passed a variety of opinions on their colleague's much-publicized arrival on the literary scene. In a generally euphoric mood, celebrating as if Alistair had just won the football pools, most went out to buy a copy and have it signed, in anticipation that a humble fellow master might soon be soaring out of their reach.

As head of English, Willie Murray had long since decided that MacLean could write. Willie Hamilton, principal maths teacher and himself no slouch in the literary sense, took a more critical view.

'I don't see what the fuss is all about,' he informed the staff-room. 'He certainly has action and excitement in his book but you can't remember the characters.' Willie, whose comments were not without validity, wasn't inclined to pay good money for his own copy. Some pulled knowing expressions and thought they detected the influence of Robert Bridges in his writing. Most conceded, however, that while they might be sitting in fireside judgement, the one who had gone out and done it was Alistair MacLean. Good luck to him. And fifty thousand quid? Who could argue with that?

Along King's Park Avenue, the MacLeans' former landlady proudly showed her autographed copy to friends and neighbours. It said: 'To Isobella McAllister, with best wishes and many thanks for the loan of the wee back room where this book was written – Alistair MacLean, 17th November, 1955.'

Between receipt of the £1,000 advance in the autumn of 1954 and publication day a year later, the MacLeans had realized their dream of a house to call their own. Those Clarkston bungalows were being built by the Glasgow firm of MacTaggart and Mickel on the southern edge of the city's suburbs. The house which Alistair and Gisela had earmarked was in Hillend Road which, even to this day, remains the very last street before the greater Glasgow conurbation gives way to the green belt of Renfrewshire farmland. Built into a steep slope, the houses on one side are reached by a flight of steps, giving them a clear view to the south, over the rooftops of the neighbours across the street.

Their choice of number 16 was a five-room detached bungalow, with lounge, dining-room and one bedroom downstairs and two bedrooms upstairs. The slope from street-level to the house continued steeply up the back garden to a substantial garage opening on to a back lane. The purchase price in 1955, perhaps stirring disbelief a generation later, was £2,750, against which the Collins advance went down as a sizeable deposit before Alistair and Gisela moved into their brand-new home in the early summer.

With the obligation of first occupants to put the garden in order, there are photographs of the time showing the young husband, complete with baggy trousers, pausing for a word with a passing neighbour and resting on his spade, thoughtfully stroking his chin.

A passing word was as much as the neighbour would get, for Alistair MacLean is still remembered in the street as the quiet man, not given to much conversation. Standoffishness was not in his nature; it was just the reticence of rural Scotland as viewed against the matey ways of gregarious Glasgow.

Feeling all the more a stranger in a foreign land, Gisela made little contact with her neighbours. They were just the couple with the little boy who kept themselves to themselves, remembered by their next-door neighbour, Ian Carlaw, a leading motor-trade figure in Glasgow, as having a garden as unruly as his own. The Sandersons across the street can recall little about their presence and were

among those in later years who found it difficult to reconcile the
anonymity with the heights of fame and fortune.

Beyond Hillend Road lies pastureland stretching towards the picturesque village of Eaglesham. Within that landscape (though the
German-born Gisela would have realized little of it as she looked
out from her lounge window) the farming folk still jealously guarded
their moment of history. For it was upon those fields, one night in
1941, that Rudolf Hess came crash-landing on his solo flight, allegedly to plead for a negotiated Anglo-German settlement of the
Second World War. It was the occasion which prompted Winston
Churchill to say 'The maggot is in the apple,' as a prelude to the
Führer's deputy spending the rest of his long life in Spandau Jail,
Berlin.

Alistair MacLean looked out towards Hess's landing-place as he
stood at the window of the front room and contemplated the progress of his next literary venture. His publishers had been in touch,
keen to nurture his career and anxious to know his plans. 'You are
making a lot of money, Alistair,' was the point made by Ian Chapman. 'Are you going to give up teaching?'

With typical Highland caution, he had replied, 'It could all be a
flash in the pan. I'll see what happens next.' Meanwhile he had
replaced the 1939 Hillman, his very first car, which had been
wrecked by a drunk driver while parked outside the house in King's
Park Avenue. From the greater distance of Clarkston, he still drove
daily to Gallowflat School, giving some hint of his thoughts to the
staff-room when he grumbled about working like that just to throw
it all away on tax. He would make a final decision if and when a
second book was accepted.

Towards that end, he was now hard at work in the front room of
16 Hillend Road, when there was still no more than bare boards on
the floor. Propped up by a cushion on a dining-room chair, Alistair
MacLean spent long evenings at his portable typewriter, which
rested on a cross-legged card-table, and battered away with two
fingers of his right hand and one of his left in an attempt to prove
that *HMS Ulysses* was something more than a flash in the pan.

Who would have imagined that the words which came spilling on
to virgin paper in that cheerless little room in a Glasgow suburb
would blend into what the world came to know as *The Guns of
Navarone*, famous not only as a pulsating novel but as a memorable

film, produced by Carl Foreman and with a cast which included Gregory Peck, David Niven, Anthony Quinn, Richard Harris, Anthony Quayle and Gia Scala?

Although he didn't know it then, Alistair MacLean was on his way to his first million, no longer needing to worry about the security of a future outside teaching. He had drifted into the profession without ever having been happy in it, but now, with Collins accepting that crucial second novel, he knew precisely what he was going to do when he left for Gallowflat School that spring morning of 1956.

Little Willie McIntosh and his classmates were hardly prepared for what was coming when Mr MacLean came round the front of his desk and called for attention. 'I presume,' he said, 'you know I have written this book. As a result, I have decided to leave school and concentrate on writing books. I shall not be here next week.'

When he wrote *HMS Ulysses* he had handed round a bag of sweets, and boys were nudging each other and saying was this all they were getting out of his fifty thousand. But now the class was stunned into silence. Gallowflat may not have been a shrine of academic excellence but the boys had grown close to their Highland schoolmaster.

Though they could not articulate it at the time, they knew he had opened their eyes to a wider world and they knew, in their individual hearts, that they were going to miss him. When the day arrived, he bade them goodbye and walked out of their lives for ever; except that they followed his career with special interest and were to be found heading the queue at the local Rio cinema when films like *The Guns of Navarone* came to town.

The staff were sorry, if not surprised, to hear that he was leaving. The good old Glasgow banter had been maintained to the end, Willie Murray demanding to know when Alistair was going to use his talents to write a real book.

'Other than yourself, Willie,' he would reply, 'I don't know of anybody who would read it.' There would be no money in it anyway. While already embarked on a lifelong habit of denigrating his own work, he would end up by making just one claim for himself: that his grammar and punctuation, drummed into him by Miss Mackintosh at Daviot, were precisely correct.

The teachers took up a collection and bought him a barometer as a parting gift. George Bradford wished him 'fair weather' in his writing career, the ladies on the staff made tea and Alistair gave a short speech of thanks, promising that he would be back to see them. He kept his personal friendship with Dougie Seggie but never did reappear at the school. Willie Murray and Frank Robb had hoped he might endow a prize at Gallowflat but nothing came of that either.

Fellow teachers watched his departure with a mixture of memories: the sight of Alistair cutting snippets from newspapers to store away ideas for his plots; the fact that he had brought Gisela to just one Christmas party, the only time many of them saw her. There was the impression of a dedicated, regimented writer, who could shut himself away when necessary. And always the banter. When he wrote *Ulysses* and moved to Clarkston, he took a copy of *Picture Post* to the staff-room, with photographs showing him digging the garden. He was told it was the first real work he had ever done.

So Alistair had taken his farewell of Gallowflat, said goodbye to teaching, and was now assured of a living as a fulltime writer, slipping through to that front-room typewriter for his day's work instead of driving off to a classroom, the escape from which brought a relief that was palpable.

While avoiding the limelight, he had inevitably become a celebrity, not least on his own doorstep, where journalists were beginning to seek him out. At Kemsley House, Glasgow, a senior executive of the *Evening News*, Angus Shaw (the man who wrote his paper's glowing review of *HMS Ulysses*), decided it was time for a series on this up-and-coming Scots author. Who would he get to write it? As it happened, one of his reporters, Bill Knox, lived in Craighill Drive, just round the corner from the MacLeans.

Knox knew little about the new author except the location of his house and the existence of *Ulysses* but he knocked at the door in Hillend Road and introduced himself as the journalist who was to be writing the series.

It was the start of a friendship which spawned yet another novelist. 'You should try writing a book yourself,' was Alistair's advice one night to Bill Knox, whose reply that his interest had been limited to short stories carried echoes of MacLean's own conversation with Ian Chapman.

'Ach, any idiot can write a book,' said Alistair. Bill Knox took the advice, dividing his summer between digging his garden and rushing in to write a little more of his detective story. His final effort was too short. 'It will have to be sixty thousand words,' said Alistair. 'Stretch it.'

Bill Knox stretched it, had his story accepted by Hutchinson of London – and was on his way to becoming a thriller writer, now with sixty books to his name and sales of around five million. It turned him from a journalist who wrote a book in his spare time into a novelist who did some journalism.

MacLean took great pride in his protégé, envying that connection with journalism which enabled Knox to meet people and recharge his literary batteries, a privilege denied the solitary author who closets himself in his den without the fresh air of outside contact.

Bill Knox and his wife thus became friendly with Alistair and Gisela, remembering them as a pleasant young couple gathering their first pieces of furniture and getting used to the fact that they had some money in the bank. Alistair seemed to be enjoying that fact in a rather cautious way.

There was now a bedroom for the baby, but he would recall his teaching days in furnished rooms when he had hung up a blanket to deaden the noise of the typewriter for the sleeping infant.

Despite his newfound fame, Alistair was leading a very quiet life in Clarkston, much in the style of a schoolteacher, no more, popping down to the local shops or round to visit the Knox family. Always the handyman, he went to help Bill erect a sectional garage and narrowly escaped serious injury when the latter dropped a section, just missing him.

For all the intricate plots and splendid stories, Bill Knox was among several observers who knew Alistair from the early stages but would not have anticipated the heights of success, fame and wealth he was to attain. What they did know was that the sheer intellectual enjoyment of a good-going argument was meat and drink to him, when he would round off a rough-and-tumble by telling his adversary that he was talking rubbish. Knox would annoy him by refusing to engage in controversy, and observed that Alistair had the temperament of the black West Highlander, often brusque with strangers in particular, putting up a kind of protective shell around his real self.

From long nights in the privacy of that room in Clarkston, *The Guns of Navarone* was destined to become an even more familiar title than *HMS Ulysses*, if only for the fact that it was the first of MacLean's books to be turned into a film – and a fabulously successful one at that. He was later to tell interviewers that, after careful thought in working out everything in advance, he wrote his stories straight on to the page and hardly bothered to reread them, giving the impression of getting it all right first time.

He may well have come close to achieving that ambition, at least in his own judgement, but his confidence could hardly have benefited from the early reception of his work at Collins, where some literary men took a different view of MacLean's achievements.

12

Any notion that bestselling authors, having delivered their manuscripts to the publisher, can simply await their transfer into print, unaltered, unchallenged, is seriously dented when you examine the experience of Alistair MacLean.

Publishing houses are bristling with literary luminaries who scan manuscripts with a finely critical toothcomb, questioning everything from style of writing to credibility of story and character, often raising the hackles of an author to the point of an enquiry about who this person can be, this genius of whom nobody has ever heard. In fairness, these people have an essential job to do, as literary tasters and first readers, whose reactions are a valuable sounding-board.

When MacLean submitted to Collins the manuscript of *Navarone*, the one which would decide his future as novelist or schoolteacher, it landed by chance in the hands of Milton Waldman, a highly respected adjudicator of literary standards, who would submit to his chairman a frank assessment, upon which acceptance or rejection would be largely dependent.

Waldman's report of 21 February 1956 began with the explanation that he had not yet read *HMS Ulysses* and could therefore make no comparison between that and the manuscript now in his hands. He found MacLean a born writer of adventure stories, with the gift of slipping in a mass of technical information to give plausibility to the task his characters were engaged upon. Indeed, he felt he could be too inventive, piling up too many incidents until the tension, instead of mounting, began to relax through the sheer strain imposed on the reader's nerves. The reading became no longer compulsive and some of it even ended up as boring, with MacLean labouring nearly all his points too hard.

Amid further criticism of characters, Waldman went on to something which was more hurtful to MacLean, the English scholar who prided himself on his use of language if nothing else. Not as natural a writer as a story-teller, MacLean frequently didn't know the meaning of the words he used, Waldman claimed. Throughout the manuscript, he evidently confused 'of' and 'off', as for example, 'he slipped of the rock'. That this was no casual error was shown by the fact that it was uniformly so through the whole manuscript. His dialogue was an even more difficult matter.

Mr Waldman conceded that this was perhaps not the type of book that should be subjected to so critical an analysis, but if MacLean intended to go on writing successfully, he had to be subjected to this treatment to induce him to impose a certain amount of discipline upon himself.

Unnecessary words and sentences had to be pruned away and the rest subjected to the ordinary rules of syntax, lexicography and punctuation. He found it tedious when sentence after sentence went without conjunctives, somewhat in the Peter Cheyney manner – 'he took up the object, looked at it, set it down, turned away, lit a cigarette' etc.

Mr Waldman's literary grilling, seeming more fitted to a rejection slip than a manuscript which would soon take the reading public by storm and lead to one of the most popular films of all time, left the Glasgow schoolteacher feeling very much like a pupil under severe pressure from his English master, who thought he could do much better. Only that earnest desire to break away from the classroom and establish himself as a fulltime writer could explain the compliance, almost subservience, with which MacLean responded to Waldman.

Within three weeks of that criticism having reached the Collins chairman, MacLean had reconstructed *Navarone* and returned it to Waldman from his home in Clarkston. In a covering note, he said he had carried out all the major changes and most of the minor ones suggested.

He added:

Navarone, in its present version, is still no imperishable work of art . . . but I can see that it is a much better-knit, faster-paced and considerably more convincing book than it was originally. For all this and for all the care and trouble you have taken, my very sincere thanks.

Whatever his reactions would be at a later stage, MacLean certainly knew his humble place in 1956. If taking guidance from a man like Waldman would help to open that escape hatch from teaching, then so be it; some pride would have to be swallowed and confidence regathered over the technical criticism about the tools of his trade.

It was certainly surprising that so many errors of basic English were allowed to creep into his original manuscript, but it was all taken as a salutary lesson from which MacLean's work would surely benefit in the longer term. Like a good and encouraging teacher who had had the satisfaction of improving the essay, Waldman responded with congratulations on the speed and skill of the revision. He now felt sure the book was going to be an enormous success, as indeed it turned out to be.

Apart from the mechanics of creating a book, it is always fascinating to discover the process of thought which leads an author to the writing of a particular work. MacLean was not the most communicative in that or any other direction but, once *Navarone* was on its way to spectacular success, he did give an insight into his thinking when, in 1958, he wrote for the broadsheet of the Companion Book Club.

It would be thought that a writer should be able to state, quickly and lucidly, why he chose for any given book a particular plot and setting for, after all, readers had a right to expect the author would devote a considerable amount of time and thought to these matters before he even approached the writing proper. He wrote:

I believe I did that for *The Guns of Navarone* but when it comes to the business of analysing the actual whys and wherefores I do not find it at all easy: there are so many reasons, of varying weights, and there are the seemingly trifling but really imponderable ones. An instance of a reason in the latter category is the fact that I like and admire the Greeks: if I didn't, I'm quite sure I wouldn't have written the book. But that thought didn't occur to me when I was writing it.

That, however, is a negative reason. On the positive side, I wanted to write a war story – with the accent on the story. Only a fool would pretend that there is anything noble or splendid about modern warfare but there is no denying that it provides a great abundance of material for a writer, provided no attempt is made either to glorify it or exploit its worst aspects. I think war is a perfectly legitimate territory for a story-teller. Personal experience, I suppose, helped to play some part in the location of this story. I spent some wartime months in and around Greece and the Aegean islands, although at no time, I must add, did I run the risk of anything worse than a severe case of sunburn, far less find myself exposed to circumstances such as those in which the book's characters find themselves.

But I did come across and hear about, both in the Aegean and in Egypt, men to whom danger and the ever-present possibility of capture and death were the very stuff of existence: these were the highly trained specialists of Earl Jellicoe's Special Boat Service and the men of the Long Range Desert Group, who had turned their attention to the Aegean islands after the fall of North Africa. Regularly these men were parachuted into enemy-held islands or came there by sea in the stormy darkness of a wind- and rain-filled night and operated, sometimes for months on end, as spies, saboteurs and liaison officers with local resistance groups. Some even had their own boats, based on German islands, and operated throughout the Aegean with conspicuous success and an almost miraculous immunity to capture and sinking.

Here, obviously, was excellent material for a story and it had the added advantage for the writer that it was set in an archipelago: I had the best of both worlds, the land and the sea, always ready to hand. But the determining factor in the choice of location and plot was neither material nor the islands themselves: that lay in the highly complicated political situation that existed in the islands at the time, and in the nature of Navarone itself.

There is no such island as Navarone – but there were one or two islands remarkably like it, inasmuch as they were (a) German-held, (b) had large guns that dominated important channels and (c) had these guns so located as to be almost immune to

destruction by the enemy. Again the situation in the Dodecanese
islands was dangerous and perplexing in the extreme, as it was
difficult to know from one month to another whether Germans,
Greeks, British or Italians were in power there – an excellent
setting for a story. So I moved a Navarone-type island from the
middle of the Aegean to the Dodecanese, close in to the coast of
Turkey, placed another island, filled with trapped and apparently
doomed British soldiers, just to the north of it, and took as much
advantage as I could of what I had seen, what I had heard, the
fictitious geographical situation I had arranged for my own benefit, and the very real political and military state of affairs that
existed in the Dodecanese at that time.

By now, MacLean had not only committed himself to a life beyond
the classroom but was beginning to earn such unthinkable sums of
money as to consider the wisdom of remaining in Britain when there
was an already established practice of moving abroad to avoid the
punitive taxation.

Gisela still remembers his relief and pleasure when he was able
to stop teaching. Then later, in their Clarkston home one day, he
suddenly said to her, 'How would you like to live in Switzerland?'

'To me it seemed wonderful,' she enthused, 'not through the
aspect of the money but because I would be closer to my homeland.
The Scottish people were friendly but I always felt a foreigner there.
So we made plans to move to Switzerland, to a small place called
Wilen, near Sarnen.'

Thus Alistair MacLean uprooted himself from his homeland,
departing with such haste that the selling of number 16 Hillend
Road, Clarkston, was left to an agency, with the result that Alan and
Joan Moorhead, an English couple moving north, never met the
previous owners. (The widowed Mrs Moorhead remained in the
house until 1991, only later discovering that *The Guns of Navarone*
had been written in her own front room.)

Alistair, Gisela and three-year-old Lachlan would now make their
home in the Bernese Oberland of central Switzerland, where they
rented a flat until they built a house of their own, an attractive
chalet-style villa overlooking the lake.

Before leaving Glasgow, MacLean had completed his third novel,

South By Java Head, plunging his readers dramatically into the last hours of Singapore before it fell to the Japanese in February 1942. As people scurried to escape the clutches of the invader, whose brutality was already known, Brigadier Foster Farnholme, complete with casual cheroot, becomes the central character of a motley collection who join the last ship out. The Japs have a special reason for wanting to block his escape: he is carrying the complete, stolen plans for their intended invasion of Australia. How they are intercepted and face the full horror of enemy tactics gives MacLean the chance to show himself in dialogue and to describe the changing character of human beings when faced with ultimate cruelty. Even at the distance of the Far East there is a whiff of the homeland in the ever-spunky Corporal Fraser of the Argyll and Sutherland Highlanders.

Once again, however, he was running into the literary net of Milton Waldman, who was even more critical than he was of *The Guns of Navarone*. Even on a second version of the manuscript, he had a damning report for the chairman. MacLean may have got rid of the more glaring inconsistencies, but there was still no more story than before and no more objective.

'I cannot but feel,' Waldman concluded, 'that MacLean has expended enough of his time and talent on this particular novel, without getting anywhere. I very strongly recommend that he consider putting it aside and getting on with another book, preferably one having nothing to do with the war.'

Ian Chapman became the buffer in this kind of dilemma, keen to further the relationship between his protégé and Collins yet knowing his responsibility as a publisher. In retrospect, he believes that Waldman, a highly respected reader for the company, was judging MacLean by classical standards and would not have been the first to recognize a commercial success.

Some of Waldman's comments certainly left the impression of a nit-picking pedant, though, equally, some of MacLean's flaws as revealed by Waldman were truly inexcusable. William Collins was inclined to take Waldman's advice, and the task of breaking the bad news would fall to Chapman, by now MacLean's close friend as well as the company diplomat. He dreaded his mission.

Arranging a family visit to the MacLeans in Switzerland, he dispatched his wife and young son in advance and would follow them to Wilen, via Scandinavia, where there was other business to attend to. Boarding the plane at Heathrow, *en route* to Sweden, he was given an evening paper which told of that day's air crash at Munich, in which the famous Busby Babes of Manchester United Football Club were all but wiped out. The whole nation was in shock.

As the engines revved up and the plane was speeding down the runway for take-off, it suddenly shuddered, screeched and spun round, to the accompaniment of an apology from the pilot, who said he would try again. Amid the palpitations, the publisher pondered which was the more frightening thought – an aeroplane emergency or trying to tell Alistair MacLean that his latest manuscript was not good enough.

On the flight to Scandinavia he summoned all his powers of tact to work out the least offensive form of words. It was a good book . . . yes . . . but not the right one to follow *The Guns of Navarone*. So how about putting it in a drawer for the time being and applying his undoubted genius to something slightly different? (Heaven alone knew what he would have thought if he had seen Waldman's report).

Marjory Chapman was already settled into a warm reunion with Alistair, Gisela and Lachlan when her husband arrived in Switzerland. 'There's some mail from London,' she told him. 'Oh, and there's a telegram too.' Ian Chapman went up to the bedroom and tore open the telegram. It came from William Collins, the chairman, and read: 'HAVE JUST SOLD FILM RIGHTS OF JAVA HEAD TO DANNY ANGEL. WONDERFUL! TELL ALISTAIR IT'S A GREAT BOOK!'

He swallowed hard, regained his composure and went downstairs to say, 'Well, is there champagne in the house, Alistair? I have great news. Let's celebrate!'

The story had indeed been sold to Danny Angel, a distinguished British director who operated from a wheelchair. Like so much else in that unpredictable industry, of course, the film was never made, but Chapman's embarrassment was averted and Waldman's advice was quietly put aside.

His tenacious snapping at the author's heels was scarcely relaxed as the manuscripts continued to flow roughly at the rate of one per year. In fairness, Waldman was merely adhering to his own high standards of judgement. There were others in the Collins camp who might have sniped at MacLean from more dubious motives, unable to forget that he had been discovered by some lesser light in Glasgow who should have been sticking to the revelations of his Bible department.

Though Waldman's criticism continued, MacLean was gaining in confidence, even in truculence when necessary, more ready to assert himself now that he had two major successes under his literary belt. He did not hesitate to tell his publishers, 'Get that man off my back. I've had enough.'

The chairman needed little reminding of MacLean's growing commercial stature and the fact that they could easily lose him if the two were not kept apart. His name was already big enough to start a scramble at other publishing houses if there were a hint of his dissatisfaction.

Despite the internal criticism, he still believed that his manuscripts needed no revision and that he should be able to wash his hands of them the moment they left his IBM golf-ball typewriter. He had no interest in making changes or correcting proofs, though he did take an interest in the jackets of his books and the accompanying blurb material. Indeed, that gave him an opportunity from time to time to release his biting sense of humour. Studying two possible versions of an intended blurb, he sent a gently phrased note to Collins to say that, if they used either in their present form, would they also be kind enough to send him the address of Heinemann, the rival publisher.

At a later stage, when he ran his toothcomb over the promotional material prepared by someone at Doubleday, his American publisher, for his book *When Eight Bells Toll*, he converted his disbelief into a few well-chosen caustic comments. He wrote:

Covers are frequently drawn by artists who have not read the book but it must be a bit unusual to have the blurb-writer prepare himself in the same fashion. Briefly, the complaints are these: the cover depicts a bloke in a scuba suit caught in a searchlight. The artist must have been thinking of some other book. Doesn't happen in mine.

In the second paragraph, reference is made to an incredible pursuit at sea. The only incredible thing is the blurb-writer's imaginative power. No pursuit in my book.

In the third paragraph, Calvert is alleged to have boarded the

Nantesville in the Irish Sea. Somebody must have transferred the Hebrides down there when I wasn't looking.

In the fourth paragraph, the criminals are said to be busy hi-jacking ships off the Western Highlands of Scotland. The ships were all hi-jacked in the Irish Sea or off the Irish coast.

Continuing the catalogue of errors, he concluded: 'And if all the foregoing is not enough, the whole blurb is written in a kind of mental shorthand. The bloke uses even more clichés than I do. Anyway, as we used to say in Toonheid, it's diabolical, i'nt it?'

As MacLean settled into his new Swiss home at Wilen, he discovered Paul Townend, mine host at the local hotel and himself a splendidly well-educated English gent, fluent in German and fascinated to find that such a celebrity had come to settle on his doorstep. Paul was also a writer *manqué* with at least one published book, *Man on the End of a Rope*, which was based on the real-life story of a climber who had been left just like that. But there were drinking sprees, and Gisela felt her husband was being devoured and diverted from his writing. Whereas he had once been a modest drinker who enjoyed a pint with the lads, there were now signs of a developing problem, hastened by the wealth which made alcohol more readily available.

It was a problem which, in time, would turn him from a prompt and reliable deliverer of his manuscript to one who would fall behind his deadlines and engage in a late scramble to catch up.

The MacLeans were limited for friends at Wilen and Alistair was soon issuing invitations to his old pals in Scotland to come over and keep him company. He had kept in touch with Bill Knox, his writing protégé in Clarkston, by means of a recording tape which carried messages back and forth between Scotland and Switzerland. Finally, Bill, his wife Myra and their two children boarded the family Ford Consul and drove off on their first adventure abroad. It was 1960. Alistair was out to greet them as they swung into the driveway of the villa. All travel thereafter was by the MacLean Mercedes, the two families driving off on local adventures, Alistair taking a childlike pleasure in putting them all on a steamer at one pier and driving to the next stopping place, where he was waiting with a welcoming wave.

Bill Knox thought Alistair's den did not exactly reflect the prosperity that had followed the Clarkston days. It was just a plain little upstairs cupboard of a place, furnished with a very ordinary desk, no drawers, and a kitchen chair. There was no appearance of reference books or even a waste-paper basket; and beyond that, nothing but his typewriter.

Most of all, Alistair kept in touch with Dougie Seggie at Gallowflat School, his old sailing friend to whom he had handed over total ownership of their beloved *Silver Craig* when he gave up teaching. (Dougie later sold it to an Irishman for £200.) That bond among people whose companionship is forged under sail was strong as ever and soon there was an invitation not only to Dougie and Violet and their daughter, Helen, but to his brother Tom – and the indispensable Willie Campbell, big, solid, likeable Willie who had been with Alistair that day the *Silver Craig* broke down while carrying passengers on the Clyde.

They all flew to Switzerland for three weeks with the MacLeans, landing at Basle Airport, where Alistair, forever mindful of courtesies, was awaiting them at an unearthly hour of the morning, complete with the Mercedes which was his pride and joy.

His Scottish guests were instantly impressed with the house and its surroundings as they mounted the stairway which led from the garage into the hall. Violet admired the split-level ground floor with its dining-room, sitting-room, kitchen and bedroom with en-suite bathroom; upstairs on the first floor there were four more bedrooms with bathroom while Alistair had his den on the second floor, with its magnificent view over Lake Sarnen.

After a week of catching up with the news and recalling different days on Clydeside, the four men went off camping, Dougie Seggie privileged to drive the Mercedes, albeit on the unfamiliar roads of Switzerland. While the girls stayed at home and went on shopping sprees, the lads were careering through central Europe on their staggish adventure, the Scots complaining only about the vile smell of dung which rose from the continental fields. There was a fine camaraderie between Alistair, Dougie, Tom and big Willie as they drove on by the German border. Dougie drove through a red light on a single track which snaked its way downwards, and when he reached the bottom his raucous mates were landing him in deeper trouble.

'He's only a Scotsman, he won't understand you,' Alistair was

calling. 'Ach, he disnae speak onything but Glesca!' big Willie was
shouting to the Polizei from the back seat. The police were having
none of it. Dougie was ordered to reverse the Mercedes all the way
up the hill again, a hazardous operation he didn't relish.

Alistair did keep a small boat on Lake Sarnen but he preferred
the open sea and the conversation was largely about good fun and
friendship on the *Silver Craig*, as well as their nightmarish voyage
down the west coast when they bought it, trying to negotiate the
locks of the Crinan Canal with no reverse power to stop the boat.

All this was in contrast to the MacLeans' lifestyle now – and in
the future when they would come again to the Clyde, this time with
a boat called the *Ebhora*, berthed at Ardbeg on the Isle of Bute, and
collect the Seggies for a visit to the latest craft, all palatially fitted
out and sporting fancy gadgets. All very posh, Dougie thought, but
maybe not so much fun.

When the MacLeans invited their guests out for dinner, Tom
Seggie and big Willie volunteered to stay behind as babysitters for
Lachlan and Helen Seggie. It was when he went to check that the
children were all right that Willie Campbell encountered a scene
which tested his unflappable nature. Lachlan's bed was saturated in
blood and he was haemorrhaging badly from the throat.

Willie used his wartime experience of first-aid to clear the boy's
throat with his fingers and restored some semblance of normality
before sitting down to contemplate what could have happened. It
was a frightening experience. When the MacLeans came home, they
apologized for not warning Willie that this sort of thing was liable
to happen; he was surprised at their nonchalance. It was also an
early sign that Lachlan was developing an ailment of the skin and
blood vessels which was to dog him through his youth and into
adulthood, resulting in a succession of operations which seemed to
do little to alleviate a distressing condition.

The immediate emergency was over, however, and Lachlan and
Helen scampered happily about the house next day. To the adults,
Alistair seemed like an interested and caring father, though to little
Helen Seggie he gave the impression of a man who didn't have
much time for children. She remembered, too, that he was a devotee
of the singer Pat Boone, especially for his recording of 'Peace in the
Valley'.

Though three weeks is a long spell to entertain guests, Alistair was in his element with his Scottish visitors, the kind of people with whom he could relax and feel completely at home.

His visitors in turn were coming back after the holiday of a life-time, sensing nevertheless that Gisela, in her quiet way, had felt a little out of things. Violet Seggie, who regarded Alistair as a good friend without pretence in his nature, also felt uneasy that he was drinking too much. One evening by the lakeside he had surprised her by becoming very drunk.

It was just a step in the developing pattern of his life. Success had no doubt brought its own strains, its opportunities and its loneliness. Soon there would be another dimension to his career as a bestselling writer.

13

Alistair MacLean's emergence as a bestselling novelist in the mid-fifties coincided with the biggest revolution the world of popular music had ever known: the arrival of Rock 'n' Roll. But the gyrations of Elvis Presley and Bill Haley were innocent matters compared to other happenings in the United States at that time.

A great many people were becoming the victims of an extraordinary character called Joseph McCarthy, a Wisconsin man who became a state judge in 1939 and a Senator in 1945, taking his seat in defiance of a Supreme Court ruling that, as a serving judge, his election was contrary to the Constitution. Exploiting a public unease in the United States over the treason trials of people like Klaus Fuchs, Nunn May and Alger Hiss, he began laying about him with accusations that the Truman administration was soft on communism and that the State Department was harbouring more than 200 prominent Reds.

In 1953, his obsessive zeal landed him the chairmanship of the powerful Permanent Sub-committee on Investigations, as he began his witch-hunt against all sorts of people, most of them innocent, putting them on trial in the full glare of television and ruining many a reputation in the process. The fact that he ran headlong into trouble, himself accused of financial irregularities, and that he was dead by forty-six, remembered only by Truman's description of a 'pathological character assassin', did little to help his victims.

Almost inevitably, these included a number of Hollywood's better writers who, even if their politics would have been regarded as pale pink in the United Kingdom, were branded as rampant Reds on

Sunset Boulevard, condemned to plying their trade elsewhere. Many came to the comparative sanity of Britain, among them Carl Foreman, who even had to work under a pseudonym before resurfacing under his own name in the role of writer-producer. It was in that capacity that he came to *The Guns of Navarone*, MacLean's second book and the first to be filmed. So how did that come about?

It was the legendary Mike Frankovich, head of Columbia Pictures, who happened to read the book and handed a copy to Carl Foreman, asking him to read it and suggesting he might consider making it as a film. Foreman's initial reaction was negative. First, there was the question of *amour-propre*, the fact that all film-makers prefer the thrill of discovery to be their own.

Perhaps more to the point, he had only recently written one war film, *The Bridge Over the River Kwai*, and written and produced another, *The Key*, as Jan de Hartog's novel *Stella* was renamed for the cinema.

Foreman had had his fill of war stories and feared that Frankovich was type-casting him as a writer and maker of war films. Greatly respecting the judgement of the Squire, as Frankovich was called, Foreman at least read the book, at one sitting, and recoiled from the manifest difficulties involved in translating it to the screen.

He reported that it was too big, too difficult, too potentially time-consuming and too expensive to consider as a film, at least for him. He wanted to do something smaller, more intimate, more socially realistic. But Frankovich was not easily diverted. He persisted gently and made it clear that, while he appreciated the difficulties, he would listen to a realistic approach about the cost of a film based on this vast adventure story.

Foreman took the hint, read the book again, agreed to try it – and the rest is cinematic history of the epic variety. As he had feared, it was a tremendously difficult film to make, needing two full years of effort by many people. But, as he conceded, it was magnificently worth it in the end, a huge success which was to change the lives of everyone connected with it, not least that of Alistair MacLean.

When Foreman finally met the author he was taken aback. He said later, 'My image of the man who had written so robust, so dynamic and so vast an adventure story was on the same scale. Instead, I met a rather small man, quiet, reserved, modest, his charm and erudition hidden, at least to me, behind an almost impenetrable

Glasgow accent. Later I learned that his shy exterior belied unbounded courage and tenacity.'

Alistair MacLean made it clear from the beginning that he had no intention of becoming involved in the writing or making of the film, a wise decision which might have served him better if he had stuck to it for the rest of his career.

He told Foreman he felt his child was in the hands of a kind and intelligent foster parent and that he would stand by with his fingers crossed until it grew into a film. He was even more flattering when the film was made and he asked for a copy of the script for his own analysis and study. It was a particular writing skill he knew very little about.

Conversely, as Foreman embarked on the screenplay, he was to find that what appeared as deceptively simple and all too easy to write was, in reality, the result of a masterly control of construction and consistently rising tension and suspense, leading from one breathtaking climax to another.

He was discovering what several literary editors at Collins already knew, despite the criticisms: that Alistair MacLean was gifted with a finely honed and quite remarkable craftsmanship. His admiration was such that, when preparing the credit titles for the film, he went beyond the contractual requirements and, instead of saying the film was 'based on a novel by Alistair MacLean', emblazoned in the main title the words: 'Alistair MacLean's *The Guns of Navarone*'. It was the kind of recognition which super-stars of the cinema are known to demand and was all the more meaningful coming from a man who was sometimes accused of hogging credits to himself.

MacLean, said Foreman, had developed the question 'What happens next?' into a fine art, and when you opened his adventure stories it was like leaping on the back of a swift, strong, thoroughbred horse, a veritable Pegasus, and embarking on a breathless ride through a countryside made magical by almost unparalleled imagination and inventiveness.

'I believe that Dumas, if he could, would read MacLean with pleasure, with admiration and, quite often, with a touch of affectionate envy,' he added.

This was praise indeed from the man who had already written *High Noon* and who, having acquired the film rights, decided to write the screenplay of *The Guns of Navarone* himself, as well as producing it.

If the truth be known, he even wanted to direct it, but Columbia drew the line at that. If they wanted American stars in the film, they also wanted a British director, and that assignment went to Alexander Mackendrick, a native Scot like MacLean, who was even a former pupil of the novelist's old school, Hillhead High in Glasgow.

Mackendrick, who had gone south from the Glasgow School of Art in the thirties to work for the J. Walter Thompson advertising agency, turned to making animated cartoon films and then, after the Second World War, joined Michael Balcon at Ealing Studios. He first came to public attention when Balcon gave him a Compton Mackenzie story and asked him to go off and make a second-feature movie on location. This was *Whisky Galore*, an enduring classic which led to other Ealing comedies, like *The Ladykillers* and *The Man in the White Suit*, before Mackendrick was spirited away to America to prove that he could do it there as well. His reputation was greatly enhanced by his *Sweet Smell of Success*, which appeared in the same year as *Navarone* became a novel.

He returned from Hollywood in time to be briefed for the film version, setting out with Jeff Drake, the distinguished production designer, on the preliminary reconnaissance, which included the finding of locations. They went to places like Cyprus and Rhodes and spent six months on the planning of *The Guns of Navarone*.

A man of great depth, Mackendrick had his own, rather quirky, ideas about how *Navarone* should be done. 'I wanted to take what was essentially a typical, action-packed wartime melodrama and give it some pretentious overtones,' he was to tell me later. His interest in Greek mythology enabled him to find a symbolic significance in MacLean's twin guns of Navarone, but classical allusions were not in Foreman's plans.

Together with other matters, it led to a fall-out between the two men. With little time left before production was due to start, Mackendrick was paid off and the task was offered to another director of Scottish background, J. Lee Thompson, whose family had moved from Perth to London, where the young man established himself in the thirties.

Indeed, Thompson was just eighteen when he wrote the play *Double Error*, which went on at the Fortune Theatre and was subsequently bought by British International Pictures, for whom he went to work as a screenwriter at Elstree Studios in 1935. Having written a second play, *Murder Without Crime*, a big success which reached Broadway, Thompson later directed it as a film for the Associated British Picture Corporation. He was also writing the screen version of Ivor Novello's *Glamorous Night* and the 1940 production of Ian Hay's *The Middle Watch*, which starred one of his own relatives, the legendary Jack Buchanan, whose Helensburgh family were connected to the Thompsons from Perth.

J. Lee Thompson, who took a leading part in the 'kitchen sink' drama of the fifties, used that decade for films like *Yield to the Night* (it starred Diana Dors and was credited with having helped to abolish capital punishment in Britain after the hanging of Ruth Ellis), *No Trees in the Street* and *Tiger Bay*, which introduced us to Hayley Mills.

He had also gained attention for his direction of *Ice Cold in Alex* (called *Desert Attack* in America) before the call from Carl Foreman to take over *The Guns of Navarone*. Though *Navarone* was produced from a British base, Thompson regarded it as a Hollywood film, and indeed it proved to be the major event of his professional life, converting him into a resident of Beverly Hills, a status he retained into the nineties, when he could claim to be Hollywood's oldest active director, in his late seventies and with fifty films under his belt.

When Mackendrick was paid off, Gregory Peck was already in place as one of the big names about to shoot the picture. He had recently seen Thompson's *Northwest Frontier* (or *Flame Over India* in America) and expressed his preference for this director. Stars can have that kind of influence.

Arriving at such a late stage, Thompson had little time for preparation and was so wrapped up in working out the technicalities of his film that, unlike Sandy Mackendrick, he couldn't have the time for arguments with Carl Foreman. That would come later, when he made *McKenna's Gold*.

'I think I was the only director who ever made a second film for Foreman,' he told me later. 'He was an excellent producer and an excellent, if lazy, writer but he did interfere with directors as well as being obsessive about credits.'

Never having dealt with such a galaxy of international stars before,

Lee Thompson was hoping to ease himself into the shooting sched-
ule, but that luxury was not an option. His very first day on camera
involved the full array of Gregory Peck, Anthony Quinn, David
Niven, James Darren, Gia Scala and Richard Harris. At that level,
the big names are not averse to suggesting changes in the day's
work, and Thompson was soon running into his first experience of
it. 'Would it be okay if I did it this way instead of that?'

Small in stature, he was being put to the test. 'I had carefully
worked out every shot in my own mind and I knew that, on this
occasion, I couldn't be flexible. I had to be firm and simply say,
"No, let's do it my way."'

At the end of the first day's shooting Gregory Peck put a hand
round Thompson's shoulder, broke into a smile and told the rest of
the cast, 'Folks, we're in good hands.' Thompson knew then that
any flexibility would have been taken for weakness and that they
would have walked all over him.

From then on, it was some wonderful teamwork which produced
The Guns of Navarone. Any strain at the beginning was removed by
Anthony Quinn when he introduced a chess tournament to alleviate
the boredom which inevitably creeps into film-making.

'They used to play chess between shots,' said Thompson, 'and
all the tension was poured into that, leaving an atmosphere in which
it was a pleasure to film.'

The cliff scenes of *Navarone* were shot on the island of Rhodes,
by the town of Lindos, where they spent the four months from April
to July of 1960. The rest of the filming took place at Pinewood
Studios, built originally as Britain's answer to Hollywood and still
there today, twenty-four miles into the Buckinghamshire countryside from London.

There, by clever simulation, the big guns of Navarone were placed
in an open field, seen as if they were at the other end of Europe,
embedded in the cliffside rock of a Greek island.

Some wartime activity was nevertheless required on Rhodes, and
David Niven junior has one abiding memory from his schooldays,
of visiting his father on location there. With the mainland of Turkey
so near to Rhodes – and the Turks having no special love for the
Greeks – there was evidently a day of panic when an observation of
events on the island sparked off an alert that Greece was preparing
to attack its neighbour!

When the sweat had been shed, the tedium endured and J. Lee Thompson had wrapped up his marathon adventure, there was only the uncertainty of public reaction to be declared. Would Frankovich be vindicated in his original hunch?

In the spring of 1961, a loud boom of publicity preceded the world première of *The Guns of Navarone*, billed to take place in London at the Odeon, Leicester Square, on Thursday 27 April, 'in the gracious presence of Her Majesty the Queen and His Royal Highness, the Duke of Edinburgh'.

Ten million dollars and more than two years of meticulous effort had gone into what was undoubtedly one of the most ambitious films ever undertaken from a British base. Columbia Pictures were releasing Carl Foreman's Open Road production in CinemaScope and Technicolor and much was made of the fact that the Greek government had pulled out all stops to facilitate the smooth completion of the film.

Carl Foreman burst into print to say:

It seems to me more than literary coincidence that Alistair MacLean's story is set on the same stage as the *Odyssey* and the *Iliad*, Jason's search for the Golden Fleece and Theseus' grim contest with the minotaur in the awesome labyrinth. [Foreman was sounding as if he had been listening after all to the classical allusions of Alexander Mackendrick, the original director.] For like so many of these epic tales of adventure born on the blue waters of the Aegean, this story tells of men who dare even the gods as they struggle towards their goal with dedicated courage.

Through all this dramatic publicity, Ian Chapman was struggling towards a goal of a more immediate nature – to persuade Alistair MacLean to turn up for the big night in Leicester Square. Having come up against the customary mulishness, in which MacLean was refusing to come from Switzerland for the première, Chapman wrote him a pleading letter:

I am not exaggerating when I say Carl Foreman will be upset and very hurt if you and Gisela do not come over for the première. From his point of view, he feels it is very important that you be

here and from your own point of view and from that of the future,
I do really urge you to come.

The film was scheduled to run in Leicester Square for eight
weeks after the première, which was then the longest ever run
immediately after an opening. All the performances were what the
business called 'hard ticket performances', which meant they were
not continuous programmes. It was also to be on a bookable basis
all over Britain.

Chapman felt he was winning the battle until he ran into the
schoolboyish antics of his famous author. Their exchanges reached
the comical level of explaining that he would need to wear a black
tie on the night, since it was a full-dressed occasion – and MacLean
questioning if this was a celebration or a wake.

Now fully aware of the big royal occasion, to be attended by the
Queen, his next question was, 'Can my mother be presented to her?
She is coming down from Glasgow and would love to meet the
Queen.'

With all the line-up of stars and dignitaries, Chapman knew it
was quite out of the question but tried to be as tactful as possible.
'I don't think that would be possible,' he wrote.

'Why not?' MacLean demanded.

'Because it has really nothing to do with your mother, Alistair.'

'It has everything to do with my mother. I wouldn't be here
without my mother. I'm not coming.'

Whatever gamesmanship was at work, Chapman had to employ
all his powers of persuasion (he also enlisted MacLean's brother
Ian) to bring peace to the situation – and Alistair to the première.

Mrs MacLean was duly met at Euston Station and taken to Ian's
house at Ewell in Surrey, where family and friends gathered for
pre-film drinks, consumed stealthily in an upstairs bedroom since
Alistair was still so wary and respectful of his formidable mother
that he didn't dare drink in front of her. She had long since signed
the pledge and Alistair could recall, not so many years before, when
he had appeared at her home in Carrington Street, Glasgow, on a
Hogmanay Night, and been forbidden to give a drop of that stuff to
his brother Gillespie, who was all of twenty-four. Disapproval of
her late husband's fondness for a dram would have been greatly
compounded if she had known the full extent to which drink bccame

a problem for both Alistair and Gillespie. Having seen the evils of the demon in Glasgow and the islands, she no doubt had some good reason for her stance.

That night in London, however, it was all fairly innocuous, a celebration of a royal occasion in which her beloved son was the most vital figure. Nevertheless, while she sat in dignified temperance downstairs, guests were taken quietly upstairs before a fleet of limousines arrived to speed them across London.

It was a truly glittering night, crowds gathering for the royal occasion and a buzz of excitement electrifying the foyer. Throughout the show, Alistair sat mumbling that this was a terrible film but, once again, with the quirkiness of his nature, he was enjoying it just the same.

Along with stars like Gregory Peck, Anthony Quinn and David Niven, the MacLeans lined up for presentation to the Queen. There was Alistair, diffidence written all over him, chatting to Her Majesty and looking rather neat in his dinner jacket and black bow-tie. Gisela stood erect by his side, looking gorgeous in her off-the-shoulder evening gown and immaculate coiffure.

For her there was the mixed emotion of being the wife of the author and a member of the German race which formed the enemy in so much of her husband's writing. She can rationalize the situation quite happily and even brought some humour to the situation when she told me, 'In *The Guns of Navarone*, Alistair had this German kicking someone and kicking him again and again. I got him to drop the third kick!'

When his fellow novelist James Leasor asked him how he reconciled marital harmony with the number of Germans killed in his novels, Alistair told him that, at the end of each book, he counted up the number of dead and that the British or the Allies invariably suffered more heavily than the Germans. Leasor wasn't sure if he was joking or not.

So *The Guns of Navarone* became a screen classic which keeps on running more than thirty years after it was made, giving people like J. Lee Thompson not only their greatest success in films but a continuing income which helps maintain a life-style in Beverly Hills and elsewhere.

Thompson gained the impression that, for whatever reason, Carl Foreman didn't want him to meet Alistair MacLean, and indeed there was some delay before he did. But they met up eventually and got on well together.

In fact, Thompson was in line to turn more of MacLean's books into films, including *HMS Ulysses*, when the rights were held by Robert Clark of Associated British Pictures. Nothing came of that. Then he was going to direct *The Golden Gate*, and there was a lengthy conference in Charles Bronson's dressing-room at the Warner Brothers studios in 1975. That was dropped when they failed to get a script. There were also plans for him to direct *The Way to Dusty Death*, the motor-racing story which was very close to Alistair's heart and which had much to do with his friend, Jackie Stewart. That came unstuck, but Thompson was glad that some of these plans did not proceed since he was not overimpressed by some of the later books.

'Unfortunately, poor Alistair was ill served by the film industry,' he said. 'You could list *The Guns of Navarone*, *Where Eagles Dare* and possibly *Ice Station Zebra* and say they were good films. The others seemed to lack something.'

But J. Lee Thompson speaks warmly of Alistair MacLean and is grateful for that break which took him to Hollywood. His introduction to Sunset Boulevard found him staying in one of the luxury bungalows adjoining the Beverly Hills Hotel – and discovering it was the one in which Marilyn Monroe had had one of her steamy affairs. From there he managed to catch the tail-end of that colourful era, in which he would join people like Sam Goldwyn for the Power Breakfast in the Polo Lounge of the Beverly Hills, that early-morning institution where so much of Hollywood's destiny has been carved out.

Whatever criticism is levelled at the dictatorship of the big studio moguls, Thompson still regrets their passing, giving them credit for knowing a talent when they saw it and standing by a director even when he had made a bad film. He had gone to California to promote *Navarone*, through which he formed a close friendship with Gregory Peck, for whom he stayed on to direct his next picture, *Cape Fear*.

As for Alistair MacLean, he never came to terms with the film world and its mystique. Much as he had flattered Carl Foreman over *The Guns of Navarone*, and however much the producer may have added to his fortunes, he came to lose all taste for him in subsequent dealings.

MacLean was neither sufficiently aware of the intricacies of the cinema business nor possessed of the temperament to accept one fundamental fact about that genre which escapes many writers: that the making of a film has very little to do with the creative talent of a single mind, however talented and sensitive that human being might be. It has everything to do with the team effort of a group, often filleting the writer's skills to such practical proportions that he will scarcely recognize his own genius.

Film scripts, it could be said, are not so much written as rewritten, six or seven times, and often as late as on the director's chair, with a whole crew waiting to shoot the next scene. The sensible novelist is one who leaves the filming to the professionals, grabs the cheque and walks away, even if it means some gnashing of teeth all the way to the bank.

14

However much Alistair MacLean tried to keep the internal critics at Collins off his back – and whatever damage had been inflicted on his ego – he was still fighting a rearguard action when he reached his sixth book, *Fear is the Key*, a tale of revenge set against the sub-tropical background of Florida and the Gulf of Mexico.

Milton Waldman was still catching the chairman's ear with forceful opinions, and this time, it seemed, MacLean had well overstepped the bounds of probability and would forfeit readers' confidence. There were others, including the bosses of both Collins and Doubleday in New York, who seemed to agree.

In June 1960, Alistair replied from his home in Switzerland, regretting that 'once again, they're all out of step except our Johnny'. He was at pains to explain that he was trying to create a new style for himself, writing to his publishers that:

> The old alleged technique that carried me so miraculously through *Ulysses* to *The Last Frontier* has had its day. Moreover, it bores me to tears and beyond. What I'm trying to do is develop a technique of completely impersonal story-telling in the first person (which, says he bitterly, is heaven only knows difficult enough without all those characters in London and New York jumping on me with both feet as soon as I try).

He was really trying to tell a story as the eye of a camera would see it, and this needed a first-person narrator to create a constant interplay. 'Without it,' he said, 'I might just as well go back to writing rubbish like *Navarone* or *Java Head*.' That, of course, was more a device to assist his argument than a serious criticism of his previous stories.

'What I am trying to do I may not be doing very well; but at least I know what I am trying to do and I have the lonely feeling that as yet I'm the only person who does,' was the cry from the wilderness.

MacLean's correspondence would range from warmly phrased letters to Ian Chapman to salvos of sarcasm about those people at Collins who were so clever at telling him how to write his bestselling novels while they seemed otherwise incapable of writing their own names. Why couldn't they write the damned things themselves? Bouts of overreaction would be followed by profuse apologies; always there was the hint of the dour Highlander with his mixture of mock aggression and dry, biting humour, teasing and provoking.

All the time, however, he was building up towards a crisis, and he was never more serious than the day he confronted his publishers with a proposition which set them back on their heels. Alistair MacLean had decided he wanted to write under another name.

After those first few years when his fame had burgeoned profusely, he was now into a phase, not uncommon among authors, when he felt he was being taken for granted at Collins. Setting aside the critical reports on his manuscripts, his first complaint was that he did not feel they were handling his foreign-language sales as well as for other authors.

Then one evening, revealing the secret doubt of many successful writers, he challenged his friend, Ian Chapman. 'I know what you think – and you have got it all wrong,' he began obliquely. 'You think my books now sell only because of the name I've established with *Ulysses* and *Navarone*. If I wrote under another name, you think I wouldn't sell.'

Chapman, who had not been thinking anything in particular, was now goaded into an assessment. 'Well, with another name, I doubt if you would take off in the same way as you did with Alistair MacLean. You need a bit of luck for that kind of thing and it might not happen a second time.'

The eyebrows went down in a silence of thought and no more was said. But a few weeks later, Collins received a letter which made them more furious than they had ever been with MacLean.

The gist of it was that, after years of depending on Collins to guide his affairs, he had signed a contract with Curtis Brown, the London literary agents, who would represent him on all matters to do with his new name. 'I'll show you what I can do under another name!' was his challenge. 'I'll show you what Curtis Brown can do with selling my subsidiary rights to foreign countries.'

Collins would still be the publisher, albeit working through a third party, but MacLean compounded the blow by revealing his choice of pen-name. Mischievously rubbing salt into the wound, he had plumped for Ian Stuart, the forenames of Ian Chapman's young son – except that he had chosen the wrong spelling of Stewart.

Chapman had to contain his anger and frustrations. The matter had reached crisis point and would have to be sorted out. That opportunity would arise at the festive season of 1960, when MacLean was back home for Hogmanay in Scotland for the first time since he moved to Switzerland.

He motored up from Surrey in his green Mercedes saloon, with its Swiss registration plates, enjoying a warm reunion with his mother in front of her blazing fire at 57 Kersland Street, Hillhead, Glasgow, to which he had financed her move from Carrington Street, which had taken on a decidedly rundown appearance. He had just spent Christmas with Gisela and six-year-old Lachlan visiting friends in England and taking the opportunity of that clear-the-air discussion with Collins.

They had had little option but to go along with his plan to write under the name of Ian Stuart, and Chapman's task became no easier when he was handed the first manuscript from his 'new' author. Starting from scratch, Mr Stuart hoped to entice a worldwide audience with his very first title, *The Dark Crusader*, the story of a Secret Service agent's last assignment – a job in Australia concerning eight scientists who have disappeared without trace.

Knowing that he would be suspected of bias against this venture, Ian Chapman had nevertheless written to MacLean in Switzerland to confess that he had never felt at such a loss about what to say. The plot was complicated, characters were wrong, some of the action was hard to accept and some of it was too drawn out and too technical. His embarrassment shone from every sentence.

In his reply, MacLean was soon in full flight, having assured Chapman that he appreciated his detailed analysis but adding sarcastically:

You will now appreciate the feelings of a surgeon who labours far into the night trying to save a case he knows to be doomed even before he starts operating ... From our talk and your letter, I gather, without I may say much difficulty, that you regard this as a thoroughly bad book. Look at the criticism. (1) The faults in it are basic and can be eliminated only by a complete rewrite. (2) The plot is overcomplicated, at times unconvincing, at times downright incredible. (3) The relationship between the two principal characters is wrong. (4) Some of the characters leave much to be desired. (5) At times boring and overburdened with technical detail. (6) Carelessly and hastily written. (That was the one that really got me.)

Why then, in heaven's name, do Collins want to publish this rubbish? Nobody's *asking* them to publish it, nobody's even *wanting* them to publish it. I certainly never asked nor wished that this book should be published by Collins. On the contrary, very strong pressure was brought to bear on me to ensure that this book *should* be published by Collins and not by any other publisher.

Ah, you may say, that pressure was brought to bear in the expectation or at least hope that I had written a half-decent book. The old firm [his name for Collins], your argument may go, wasn't to know that it had bought a lemon. Well, if you have, there's a simple remedy: let me have the lemon back and I'll try to find a publisher who will show slightly more interest and a degree more enthusiasm and not give the unfortunate impression of dragging their feet, as Collins appear to be doing. You are under no compulsion or obligation to publish this bad novel merely because you asked for it: I would be delighted to release Collins from what is, anyway, a purely imaginary obligation. And I most certainly don't want it published because you consider you're doing me a favour or out of some misguided sense of pity. Not, I may say, that I can ever conceive of a firm of Collins's unparalleled astuteness and business sense ever printing a book for those reasons.

Why, then, do you want to publish it? ... Merely to see that I don't establish a connection with another publisher? To have control of it and handle it in such a way as to see that it doesn't conflict with your admittedly major interest in the books under my own name? In spite of promises made, to underplay and soft-pedal – by the perfectly legal tactic of treating this simply as just another first novel – the promotion and publication of this book, which may not be as bad as you maintain, in what you may regard, although I wouldn't, as a justifiable attempt to discourage me in this latest venture and encourage me to give up this nonsense of pseudonyms and agents?

How, anyway, can you now expect me to believe that Collins is the firm best fitted to handle the book? If the book is as bad as you say and if you so obviously lack faith in it, can you genuinely imagine that I believe you will honestly and sincerely get behind it in promotion, publicity and selling?

Apart from the fact that a keen awareness of the demerits of the book is bound to act as a severe psychological brake on those responsible for handling it, would your publishing ethics really permit you to go all out in foisting off this rubbish on an unsuspecting public?

On the other hand, I do believe that I *might* just possibly find a publisher who would regard it with a less biassed and jaundiced eye and who *would* be prepared to get behind it . . .

MacLean wasn't pulling a punch. While hurt that Collins were taking such a critical stance, he knew the worth of his name to any other publisher in the land, who would be rushing to sign him up and feeling that the gods were in benevolent mood. Whatever their misgivings about the manuscript, Collins were in the dilemma of knowing that they had to go along with his demands if they didn't mean to lose him altogether.

Once tempers had cooled, the correspondence shows that each side pulled back from the brink, with MacLean indicating that he was trying to make changes in *The Dark Crusader* after all, and Collins indicating they weren't really looking for changes now and were more thinking about getting down to publishing plans.

For the record, *The Dark Crusader* was published later that same year, 1961, under the name of Ian Stuart, and MacLean proceeded to write a second book under his pseudonym, *The Satan Bug*, the following year. Collins were to claim figures which showed that the books suffered under the unfamiliar name. MacLean's pride compelled him to maintain the opposite view, but perhaps the proof of the matter was that these books later appeared under his own name and certainly fared none the worse for that.

MacLean felt his Ian Stuart books couldn't have been all that bad when *The Satan Bug* was bought up for its film potential and appeared as a 1965 Hollywood production, with a screenplay by James Clavell, who would later produce novels such as *Shogun, Noble House* and *Tai-Pan*. It was a typical MacLean (alias Stuart) story, of a traitorous scientist and the stealing of a deadly virus for use by a mad millionaire. The critics thought it was no more than 'slow-moving, portentous and gadget-filled, looking good but seldom stimulating'.

He would have had a wry smile in 1991 when *The Dark Crusader* was one of four of his books bought for filming by Simon Lewis, an enterprising Cambridge graduate making his way in Los Angeles and striking deals with big studios.

MacLean had had his fling with a second name, and whatever frustrations were released or doubts resolved, the exercise proved nothing of significance. He had made his point and went quietly back to the more comfortable existence under the name which had made him famous.

Shortly after the *Navarone* première in London, there were rumblings from Switzerland that Alistair was thinking of bringing his five-year tax exile to an end and returning to live in Britain.

However much they may have wished at times to see him at the other end of the earth, his publishers were genuinely pleased at the prospect of having him back. They had felt for some time that he was living in an intellectual wilderness and needed contact with a world that was closer to reality.

In the absence of another child to follow Lachlan, who was now seven, Alistair and Gisela decided to adopt a baby, and Collins put them in touch with an agency in Britain. Whatever Gisela's dissatisfaction with the marriage, she had decided to make the best of it; another child might cement the relationship.

There were difficulties with a British adoption, but all was resolved when they found their little boy in Germany. Alistair announced it in the final paragraph of a letter to Ian Chapman in October 1961, in which he said, 'He's like myself, a kindly, tolerant and well-behaved child who never cribs about anything.'

The rich humour was always lurking, even in the body of that same letter, which shows that he had not finished with Collins over

The Dark Crusader. 'Do you have on your staff at present,' he asked, 'an ex-illustrator from a horror comic who was kicked out for overdoing things? If you have, I know who was responsible for the cover design of *The Dark Crusader.* I think it's ghastly beyond words.'

The new baby was called Michael, believed to be the child of a hotel receptionist and a salesman but a German, like his new mother, and warmly welcomed into the house at Wilen. Ian and Bunty felt Gisela had a special affection for the child of her own nationality and that Michael could do no wrong thereafter. As so often happens after an adoption, Gisela then found herself pregnant almost immediately, a further change in the domestic structure, which would now include a move back to Britain.

'I realized I had to do what I was told,' she claimed later, with an air of resignation which hinted again at that determined streak in MacLean when he had made up his mind.

Gisela conceded that, after those few years in Switzerland, Alistair needed more contact with people. The social life was restricted, with only the Townends at the Waldheim Hotel living nearby, and the deficiency had to be made good by a stream of visitors from Scotland.

Ian's wife, Bunty, managed to find them a house at Lower Bourne in Farnham, Surrey, where they could stay for several months until they decided on a more permanent home. Though taxation would become a problem once more, they sold up at Sarnen and returned to Britain. In October 1962, Gisela gave birth to Alistair Stuart MacLean who, with exactly the same name as his father, now completed the trio of sons.

From their temporary abode at Farnham they moved briefly to Ireland before returning in 1963 to a splendid residence called Sunbiggin at Haslemere in Surrey, the biggest and most sumptuous residence they would ever own.

Sunbiggin was a Georgian mansion standing in two acres of ground, with its own tennis court, a rose garden and an orchard. A pond in the garden had to be filled in since Alistair was still a toddler, but there was plenty of space for the children to play in safety. The grounds abounded with rich foliage, which included a fig tree and a cedar of Lebanon.

The house itself had a conservatory and a granny-flat, intended

for Alistair's mother, but she refused to move from Glasgow, prefer-
ring to be near her friends and her Gaelic culture. A large hallway
greeted you at Sunbiggin, leading off to a sitting-room, dining-room,
kitchen, laundry and maid's room. You could reach the granny-flat
from downstairs or the first-floor corridor, where there were also
four bedrooms and two bathrooms; there were two more bedrooms
on an upper floor and sundry features like the butler's pantry and a
large garage which housed the Lancia.

The furnishings matched the grandeur of the house and one
would have guessed that the MacLeans had found themselves a
residence which could become home for the rest of their lives, a
perfect setting for the upbringing of the three chidren, Lachlan,
then aged nine, two-year-old Michael and the year-old Alistair, who
came to be known as Ali.

In his new den at Sunbiggin, Alistair had completed another
book, the title of which now rolls off the tongue with ease; but it is
interesting to find how difficult it can be to arrive at a suitable title.
It was something he never mastered. For his latest book he was
offering Collins suggestions like Polynya, Beyond the Barrier, The
Ice-Bound Desert, No Sun, No Moon, No Stars, Burning Ice, The
Shrieking Wasteland and The Lifeless Land.

He regretted that such eminently suitable titles as *Darkness at
Noon* and *The Moon Is Down* had already been used, and said his
own preference was No Sky Above. There was just one other
suggestion he could offer – Drift Ice Station Zebra – 'unusual but
too long, too obvious and anything but mellifluous,' he said. Well,
knock off the 'Drift' and it was amazing what could commend itself
to the public ear.

Ice Station Zebra it became, the story of an American atomic submarine which leaves the Holy Loch, on the River Clyde, on a stormy
night, with orders to take a certain Dr Carpenter under the North
Polar ice-cap and to bring him to the surface near a burned-out
weather station called Zebra. Who is he? What has happened? And
what are they after?

Though he continued to have no interest in proof-reading or
revisions, Alistair MacLean did take an imaginative interest in the
jackets of his books and came up with some lurid ideas for *Ice Station
Zebra*. Some were too crude and he confessed that he didn't like
any of them anyway.

'I think something much simpler and more graphic is called for,' he told Collins. 'What I would like is the dim and dark representation of a submarine in, say, a greenish sea, with the ice-cap close above it – as would be seen from the side, not from above or below. Not blindingly original but it ties in well with the title I have in mind. I have in fact a lot of titles in mind, most of them uniformly useless.' It was the same letter which listed his title suggestions and finally arrived at *Ice Station Zebra*. The jacket artist paid some attention to his thoughts on the front cover, which ended up with a submarine enclosed by ice in a sea which was blue, not green.

Alistair MacLean had written one of his better stories and there was much excitement when it became the Book Society choice, enthusiastically welcomed by Lee Barker at Doubleday, his American publishers. There was much hopping with excitement of a different kind in Washington, where the Pentagon wanted to know how he had acquired such precise knowledge of the US nuclear submarine. It was simple. He had bought a submarine kit from an American toy-shop, read a few articles in *Time* magazine and used his fertile imagination. Apparently, with that combination, he was deadly accurate.

But the time for shocks was not over.

15

Now restored to life in Britain and delivering the manuscript of *Ice Station Zebra* to the Collins office in 1963, Alistair MacLean treated Ian Chapman to another of his cryptic comments.

'Well, that's it,' he said ominously.

'What do you mean, "That's it"?' queried Chapman.

'I mean, "That's it" – that's the last book you are getting out of me. I have achieved all I wanted to do. I've never enjoyed writing and was doing it only to make money. Now that I have made the money, I'm giving it up and am going to become a businessman. I have bought the Jamaica Inn, down on Bodmin Moor, and plan to develop a chain of good-class hotels, after studying the business in Europe and America.'

Alistair had indeed bought the Jamaica Inn, made famous through Daphne Du Maurier's novel of the same name, and he proceeded to buy two others, Bank House, near Worcester, and the Bean Bridge at Wellington in Somerset.

Now well settled in his stylish home at Haslemere, he kept travelling across to the Jamaica Inn to establish his presence as the owner and to collect samples of the local water, determined to analyse its suitability for the brewing of his own beer. He was full of fancy notions like that, spurred on by his real interest in science, a subject pursued since those prize-winning days at Hillhead High School, Glasgow, and one which could have given him a successful career.

Proof of this enthusiasm for the hotel project was discovered, to his surprise, by Robert Pitman, the distinguished book critic of the *Sunday Express*. MacLean was not the type to consort with journalists

but he developed a particular affinity with Pitman, who had no
sooner arrived in the middle of the Cornish moor that August day
of 1964 than he found himself roped in to sell souvenirs in the shop,
which was a minor fringe activity at the large and ancient inn.

The author himself was leaping to and from the cash register,
attacking the keys with all the controlled passion of a Dame Myra
Hess performing the 'Emperor' Concerto.

'Laddie,' he was saying, wrapping up an ornamental corkscrew,
'I've been more in contact with real life in the last hour than during
nine years of writing novels.'

Beyond the souvenir shop, barmen and pretty bar-girls were ring-
ing up further cash registers in the Stable Bar, Mary's Bar and Joss's
Bar, names taken from Daphne Du Maurier's novel. Mary was Mary
Yellan, heroine of *Jamaica Inn*. Joss was Joss Merlyn, the leading
man in Miss Du Maurier's company of smugglers and wreckers.

But the Jamaica Inn itself was no fiction, for there it stood on the
moor, with 400 years of history and now a gold mine among the tin
mines, or so it seemed. MacLean left Pitman in no doubt that this
was where his future lay; this was to be his chief interest, relegating
authorship to second place. He was fascinated by the history.

Progress in the twentieth century may have turned the A30 road
into a tourist highway but the Jamaica Inn had managed to retain a
sense of total isolation, standing high on Bodmin Moor, lonely and
bare in winter but strikingly beautiful when the sun shone. In the
warmth of the interior, it was easy to see the attraction of the
place.

Standing on that road from Launceston to Bodmin, the Inn was
built in an impressive Cornish granite, dating back to 1547. Over
the years, many people had timed the horse ride from the inn to the
coast to prove its connection with smuggling, back in stagecoach
days when it was a meeting-place for rogues.

In the warmth of a roaring log-fire, you could still sense the
atmosphere of the highwaymen warming themselves with a hot
punch after a night of nefarious deeds. Surrounded by tales of
mystery, landlords had sworn they had heard footsteps in the bar,
said to be those of a stranger who was murdered on the moor after
being summoned from the Inn. His spirit is said to return to finish
the ale he left before being slain.

Swords, muskets, lanterns and brass ornaments hung from ceiling

beams in the stone-flagged Smugglers' Bar. With its Daphne Du
Maurier room, it became a tourist attraction, within easy drive of
the quaint fishing villages with their smuggling legends.

Alistair MacLean was in his glory. As he and Robert Pitman sat
beneath aged rum casks hanging from the ceiling, he explained his
motives. 'Let's be frank about it. I'm not a born writer. I know it
and you know it. I don't enjoy writing. In Switzerland I wrote each
book in thirty-five days flat – five weeks for seven days a week; plus,
of course, time for preliminary research. Two days! I wrote like that
because I disliked it so much I just wanted to get the darned thing
over.'

Like many other novelists, MacLean received dozens of letters
from people who thought they had a brilliant idea for a story and
were prepared to go fifty-fifty if only he would write the book. It
amused him that somehow they always hit on the figure of fifty-fifty.

'I have a standard reply,' he told Pitman. 'I say, "It so happens
that I also have a brilliant idea for a story. I'll give it to you, you
write it up – and we'll split the proceeds fifty-fifty." I never hear
from them again.'

For all that, MacLean did receive many of his ideas for books
and films from other people – he was never too proud to turn them
to his advantage – but the story does underline the extent to which
he regarded the actual writing of a book to be a chore.

In contrast to all that, he was surveying the customers pouring
into the Jamaica Inn and extolling them as real people. 'Sitting
writing fiction in an attic room in Switzerland wasn't real at all.' He
was now in full swing. 'You know the value of most novels published
today, including mine. It's not really a moral way of earning money.
Now I can afford to be moral. This may not earn as much, hour for
hour, as writing books but at least it's doing something solid.'

Taken aback by this diversion in MacLean's career, Pitman wrote:

The frank words rang out in startling contrast to the views of
most writers and indeed most would-be writers. Every evening,
in every big city, there are men and women returning from business who shyly take up a notebook in the train and make notes
for the great novel which they some day intend to write. They
yearn to escape from what they regard as the drab, immoral prison
of commerce out to the free, true, outer world of books. But here

I was listening to an escapee from books relishing the freedom
and truth of commerce.

MacLean was pointing out that one of his books was different
from the others. In *Fear is the Key*, he felt he had characters and
dialogue which clearly pleased him. But in terms of sales, he found
it had been the least successful so he had gone back to the old stuff,
which had sent him in search of a business career.

Jamaica Inn was the 112th hotel he had inspected in his
search and he confessed his attraction to the whole romantic idea
of it.

'Look at that table over there,' he pointed. 'It's older than the
inn, something like six hundred and fifty years old. But the romance
is only part of it. I'd buy the Taj Mahal or the Tower of London if
I could – but only if they were showing a clear profit. Francis
Chichester said a sensible thing in his book. He said writing about
doing things was a paltry substitute for actually doing them. A paltry
substitute.'

In his quick Scottish voice, MacLean licked over the words, and
Pitman was left hoping, on behalf of his millions of readers, that he
could one day be persuaded to sit down again at his typewriter for
another thirty-five-day stint.

There must have been something about the hotel trade which
appealed to the MacLeans, surely something more than becoming
their own best customers. His younger brother, Gillespie, gained
his diploma at the Scottish Hotel School in 1952 and was manager
of the Lochboisdale Hotel on South Uist. After recuperating at his
brother's home in Switzerland, he had gone on to manage the
County Hotel, Forfar, and the Balavil Hotel at Newtonmore, where
he would play host to shooting parties from New York and to people
like Prince Bernhard of the Netherlands.

As an example of Alistair's warm generosity, a cheque arrived for
Gillespie one morning. It was the total sum required to buy a hotel
of his own – the Roy Bridge, near Spean Bridge, twelve miles from
Fort William. Gillespie could never have afforded to buy a hotel
from his own resources and was duly appreciative of his brother's
generosity. He went on to own the Commercial at Balintore, in
Easter Ross, and the Tarradale in the northern village of Muir of

Ord, which he sold in 1984, before settling to semi-retirement and a part-time job at the local golf club.

On hearing of his brother's business intentions in the south of England, Gillespie, a taller version of Alistair, though just as reserved, was ready with the benefit of his own experience. He thought it was a bad move and told him so, thinking particularly of the difficulties of keeping an eye on staff. It was bad enough watching one establishment but when you had three, as Alistair now had, it became a major problem, unless the chain was sufficiently large and organized that there could be no fiddling. Alistair wasn't even enough of a businessman to have a proper stock-taking.

His high-flying plans to produce his own beer came to nothing, as did his entire ambition to be the smart owner of his own chain. As it dragged on through the sixties, the venture was such a financial flop that he called on the help of his brother Ian and his wife to take over the running of it, forming a company in which they became chairman and director respectively. The Bank House at Worcester had been a particular disaster.

Ian was working his way to the top of the Shell organization, having kept his connection with the sea and ending up as director of operations for the company's entire tanker fleet. He did, however, take on the added responsibilities of Alistair's hotels and was appalled at what he found.

It confirmed his view that his brother had two blind spots – that he was God's gift to the business world and that he was a judge of character. Ian reckoned that he was neither and that his talent was much more for surrounding himself with parasites and hangers-on, a criticism which could well have been extended to his more prosperous writing career.

If anyone could hire the wrong manager, it was Alistair. As a result, he didn't make a penny from the Jamaica Inn. Stories abounded. There was at least one employee of the MacLean hotel enterprise who arrived with nothing and left with enough to buy a business. Another had a habit of washing his dog in the bath.

Alistair was not beyond seeing the funny side of his business failure, as shown in a letter to Ian Chapman in which he revealed some teething troubles with the Worcester hostelry, where he was already going down for the third time in a sea of trouble.

I mean, what would you do with a chef de cuisine who, preparing a tasty snack of duck and glazed orange for Chief Constable, Town Clerk and divers other citizens of repute and finding that he has forgotten to order oranges, boils a pound of Silver Shred and pours it over the unfortunate fowl? The same as I did, no doubt. But it makes life no easier in these days of increasing staff shortages.

The whole disastrous venture lasted from 1963 till 1969, though one of the hotels wasn't actually sold until 1976. There came a time when Alistair was seldom seen near his hostelries, a habit which Ian encouraged with vehemence.

The fact that he had turned his back on the writing career, after those eight years of remarkable success, was no reason why he should lose contact with Ian Chapman, whose friendship and under-standing went far beyond the professional level. Ian and Marjory, who had moved into their own home at Cheam, continued to visit Alistair and Gisela at Haslemere, as family friends would do.

The connection between the two men was maintained on a more regular basis of a monthly lunch in London. At first they met at Madame Prunier's famous fish restaurant in St James's, and later at Overton's nearby.

Whatever else they discussed over the medium-rares, Ian Chapman never once raised the subject of another book from MacLean. No question about whether he was missing his writing career was allowed to pass his lips; he was too good a psychologist for that. He knew that dour Highlanders took a pride in their independent stance, a position which could sometimes make them strangely vulnerable.

Chapman's avoidance of the subject didn't mean he was unconcerned about his friend's welfare or what he was doing with his time; it had become patently clear that he was making no progress with his business life and that he was drinking more than was good for him.

A full three years had passed before the forbidden subject was allowed to surface, and it arose, you could be sure, because Alistair wanted it that way. Gathering his brows in an ominous posture one lunchtime at Overton's, he studied his dining companion at an angle before launching into it.

'Do you know this?' he began. 'Since I delivered the manuscript of *Ice Station Zebra* to you three years ago, you have never once asked me to write another book.'

'Why should I, Alistair?' asked Chapman. 'You told me you had given up writing and that was that. It was a considered judgement; you had made your money and your purpose was achieved. I accepted that and wouldn't have insulted you by asking for another book. But what brings this on?'

MacLean scowled. 'Everybody else is after me, you know. The film people are after me.'

'Really?' Chapman played along. 'Well, I'm delighted.'

'Have you ever heard of a man called Kastner? Elliott Kastner? Well, he's a big producer-director in the film world and he's pressing me to write a screenplay and make a big movie.'

'That's wonderful. Will there be a book along with the film?'

'Yes, of course. Will you publish it?' asked MacLean.

'Well,' Chapman smiled. 'We'll have to see if you can still write, Alistair. I mean, you've been away from it for a long time.'

It was the conflict needed to spur him into action. This man Kastner had indeed been pursuing him, emerging as one of a number of key people to be found at milestones along the route of Alistair MacLean's twisting and turbulent life. So who was he?

16

Elliott Kastner, the man who had suddenly appeared in Alistair MacLean's life, was brought up in the Harlem district of New York, a working-class lad who started as an errand boy for a theatrical agency in Manhattan before landing a job in the literary department of the Music Corporation of America. That company bought Decca, which owned the Universal film studios, and young Kastner found himself working there and becoming more and more bitten by the cinematic bug.

Having brought in the scripts for *Midnight Cowboy* and *The Graduate* – and having watched them both being rejected! – he decided it was time to move out and open a little office of his own. Elliott Kastner, film producer, was in business, with $10,000 in savings. Normally film producers don't dip into their own pockets, using the big studios and financial institutions instead, but Kastner had little option. If he couldn't afford the Philip Marlowe creator, Raymond Chandler, he would stay within his own limits and pay an obscure writer called Ross Macdonald $1,000 for his story *The Moving Target*. To write the screenplay he hired a little-known novelist, William Goldman no less, paying him $5,000 – and had the audacity to approach Paul Newman about playing the lead. Newman read the script and said, 'Yes, I'll do it.'

Kastner took it to the legendary Jack Warner, presented a budget of $3.3 million and said he wanted a cut of $500,000 for himself. Warner fumed but, when Kastner threatened to take it across the road to Mr Fox, he signed the deal – and Newman did indeed star, along with Lauren Bacall, Shelley Winters, Robert Wagner and many more in what was known as *Harper* in America and *The Moving Target* in Europe.

Elliott Kastner had definitely arrived in films, destined to succeed in the role of the tough-talking, shrewd-minded, rough-diamond American producer, kicking asses and bawling down the telephone with expletives to paralyse your maiden aunt, before slipping into a more gentle and understanding and humorous mood.

He came to Britain in the mid-sixties to make *Kaleidoscope* (later reissued as *The Bank Breaker*), liked the country so much that he decided to make his base here – and opened an office at Pinewood Studios, ambitiously taking up a lengthy residence at the prestigious Connaught in London. He has been at Pinewood ever since and was later to find himself a popular subject for the gossip-columnists over his long-standing association with Tessa Kennedy, mother of his two children. (Tessa Kennedy captured the international head-lines in the late fifties when she and Dominic Elwes figured in a society elopement which rivalled that other runaway romance between Jimmy Goldsmith and the heiress Isabel Patino.)

Soon after arriving in Britain, Elliott Kastner happened to read *HMS Ulysses* and *The Guns of Navarone*, loved the adventures and the theme of courage and resolved to track down the author.

The first Alistair MacLean ever heard of him was in that call to his home in Haslemere, for which Kastner had managed to acquire a telephone number. This American was identifying himself as a film producer and a keen admirer of his, regarding *HMS Ulysses* as his favourite book of all time. What's more, he wanted to meet him.

Wary as ever, MacLean explained to the stranger, in a thick Scottish accent Kastner found hard to understand, that all six books he had written up to that point had been sold for films. So why did he want to see him? There was nothing left.

Kastner said it wasn't a book he wanted to talk about.

'I don't want to be wasting my time,' MacLean replied bluntly. 'And, in any case, I don't fancy myself as a writer. I'm a business-man.' To Kastner's plea that he wasn't good on the phone so could they meet, he said impatiently, 'If you can't tell me now, I'm not interested.'

'Okay, okay,' said Kastner, 'I want to talk to you about writing an original story directly for the screen.' There was a long pause at the other end before MacLean said, 'Hmm. Nobody ever asked me that before.'

The persuasive American had won his point and found himself with an invitation – 'Come after lunch' – to the Haslemere residence, where they spent two hours getting to know each other.

'What makes you think I can write a screenplay?' Alistair wanted to know.

Kastner explained that the dialogue in his books was highly cinematic and that, with the economy needed in writing for the screen, he was sure MacLean could do it faster and have some fun in the process. Knowing that this would be a new departure, he had brought two screenplays, one by William Goldman and one by Robert and Jane Howard-Carrington, from which he could study the technique.

What did he want him to write about? Kastner was quite specific. He wanted an adventure story that would sweat. He wanted it set in the Second World War, with five or six guys overcoming enormous obstacles to rescue someone. MacLean would know the territory. He wanted a woman or two if possible but, basically, he was looking for sweat. 'I want the clock ticking,' was how he summed up what was in his mind.

Alistair was deep in thought. 'What will you pay me?' he asked, showing that, for all his alleged conscience about making money too easily, it was never too far out of mind.

Kastner agreed on an initial $10,000, then $100,000 with a fifty-fifty deal on profits. And, whereas producers usually own the rights, he was giving him the publication right so that he could turn it into a book if he wanted. They struck a deal on the spot.

Alistair said he couldn't start on a screenplay until January 1967 – because he was writing a book for Collins. That would have been interesting news for his publisher but it revealed that he was, after all, working quietly at a book, in anticipation of some Collins coaxing. It turned out to be *When Eight Bells Toll*, a book which later, by coincidence, would involve the same Elliott Kastner.

As to the project in hand, they agreed on a delivery date of eight weeks from 15 January 1967. Kastner was invited back to Haslemere in December, this time for lunch, after which Alistair took him through to his den and gave him a magnifying glass and an atlas with the map of Germany. He pointed to an obscure dot and said,

'Here is where the action will take place. A castle called the Adler Schloss.' It was all the information he had to give away at that stage.

Eight weeks from the starting date, a parcel containing the screenplay arrived on Elliott Kastner's desk at Pinewood Studios. 'My palms were sweating as I read it,' he said. 'It was wonderful, rich, full, exciting. The only problem was that it had a shitty title.' MacLean's titles were not improving. 'I asked him what Adler Schloss meant and he told me it was "The Eagle's Castle".

'I remembered my Shakespeare and thought of a title from *Richard III* – "where eagles dare not perch". I simply cut off "not perch" and we called it *Where Eagles Dare*.'

Kastner had provided the inspiration and the title but the rest was Alistair's. He had made a deep impression on the American film producer, who found him to be a highly intelligent, skilful writer, a character with wonderful imagination. He could also detect the country schoolteacher, protesting he didn't want to be part of Hollywood or anything posh like that.

Even at that stage MacLean was openly contemptuous of the film-world, yet Kastner found a transparency through which he saw a man longing to be part of it nevertheless.

'It began to penetrate that the real Alistair MacLean was a gentle, generous, naïve kind of fool,' he said. 'He kept on about being "a businessmaun" but, for all his bluster about being so clever with bricks and mortar, he was really an asshole in business. I thought at first it was genuine but, over the years, I could see it was just his way of covering embarrassment about calling himself an artist.'

On reflection, Kastner believes MacLean was exploited down the years. While conceding that Carl Foreman had made a good film in *The Guns of Navarone*, he thought they had stolen it from MacLean, paid him in peanuts. 'This crusty little man was a sucker. He seemed shy yet he took enormous pride in his work. He also allowed himself to be seduced by people, some good, some bad.'

Despite such criticism of others, Kastner himself was to incur the wrath of MacLean over money he alleged had not been paid, a later episode which would lead to a hostile scene.

Meanwhile, having persuaded Alistair MacLean to write his first screenplay, Elliott Kastner now faced the monumental task of turning it into a film. To direct *Where Eagles Dare*, he engaged a young man from his own American neighbourhood, Brian Hutton, an actor who had done a little directing.

He would also need a big-name actor to give him financial protection through the minefields of film production. If the up-and-coming Kastner had managed to persuade Jack Warner to back his earlier venture, he was not so lucky this time. Warner refused. That made Kastner all the more determined to succeed. Who was the biggest British star around? He mulled over names like Peter O'Toole and Michael Caine before setting his sights on the biggest name of all: Richard Burton. That's who he would get, dammit!

Arranging a meeting through Burton's agent, Hugh French, he set out for Nice, where the actor was shooting a movie. French was extremely doubtful about his chances but the streetwise Kastner would not be readily diverted.

He met Burton and told him the time was propitious and that he could bring the same class and dignity to this film as Gregory Peck had given to *Navarone*. He promised that the film would be cast around him, with wonderful actors like Michael Hordern, Patrick Wymark, Donald Houston, Peter Barkworth, Robert Beatty and Mary Ure.

Hugh French raised doubts over the director being unknown but Kastner paved a glorious path for the young man and told Burton that, if you put Brian Hutton and two actors in a room, there would be sparks on the screen. Burton agreed to do the part. Kastner was then in a position to go to MGM with the news that he had an Alistair MacLean screenplay, a cross-plot, a budget – and he had Richard Burton. It was a seductive mixture and they made a deal.

He was also keen to give a leading role to an actor who was making a name for himself in the mid-sixties. But the sound of Clint Eastwood did not convince MGM that he was worth the $350,000, plus share of profits being asked for. They were finally persuaded, however, and Eastwood was still collecting income from *Where Eagles Dare* into the nineties.

Kastner beavered away at everything from casting and music to locations in Austria and managed to hire that remarkable stunts director, Yakima Canutt, who was then in his seventies.

Alistair MacLean was not the kind of author to hang around the film-set but, when the cast came back from the Austrian castle to Shepperton Studios, Richard Burton was climbing a wall, as part of a scene, when he spotted him in the watching crowd below. Burton stopped the scene, climbed down to discover that MacLean had just dropped in for a brief visit and took him to his caravan for a chat. It extended to about an hour and a half, during which time the actor consumed five large vodkas. To MacLean's astonishment, he then returned to the set and took up where he left off, climbing the wall with more alcohol inside him than seemed safe.

It cost $6.2 million to produce *Where Eagles Dare*, a triumph of the cinema which satisfied the customers, made a lot of money for MGM, and gave Elliott Kastner the most exciting adventure of his film career, as well as a good financial reward.

'That film really lifted Alistair,' he claimed. 'I could have given him half the money I offered and he would still have been as happy as a pig in shit.'

Kastner then had time to assess people like Burton and MacLean, having closely observed both men through their involvement in *Where Eagles Dare*. They had much in common. Both were heavy drinkers, but he was surprised to find that Burton, the apparent extrovert, was as shy of meeting MacLean as he was of meeting Burton. In some ways, he reckoned, MacLean was the writer Burton wanted to be. Their similarities may also have been the root of their differences.

When the filming of *Eagles* returned from Austria, MacLean was due to take a party from his Collins and Fontana publishing house to spend a few hours at the Shepperton set. An in-house memo at Collins warned that, while the Welsh actor was due to be filming that day, there could be no guarantee that they would see him.

'A further complication,' said the memo, 'is that Richard Burton and Alistair MacLean are not speaking.' Alistair, who reluctantly agreed to take the party there nevertheless, later gave a friend his graphic description of how he and Burton had quarrelled and come to blows in an inebriated state at the Dorchester Hotel, London, ending with a right hook to Burton's nose which sent him sprawling on the floor.

Kastner was finding Burton a deeply complex man, with feelings of guilt on the one hand about the money he was making yet flaunting his wealth on the other. MacLean, too, was racked by guilt about what he was making and wanted to give it away generously; at other times he would boldly state that writing had become no more than a business and that he was doing it only for the money. Contradictions.

Burton carried the further guilt complex of having sold out from his real art, which was the theatre, although he was not prepared to acknowledge the fact.

Barry Norman, the film critic, who knew both men, put it to Burton that he should have been the great stage actor of his generation but had gone instead for the easier option of Hollywood. He got no admission but was convinced that much of the man's drinking was a form of self-contempt, arising from the fact that he had never fulfilled his promise.

With Burton, therefore, it was a wasting of the talent which led to drink. With MacLean, Barry Norman felt, it was the realization that he didn't really possess the talent he would have liked. 'Alistair was a good story-teller but he was ambitious to be a much better writer than he ever became. His novels became pot-boilers and so did his films.'

The similarities between the two extended to that feeling for the written word. Despite his own gift for the spoken word, Burton admired writers more than any other group of people. He wanted to be one himself but lacked the discipline to be an actor, never mind a writer, and although he kept his diaries, he had neither the self-control nor the confidence to do something for publication.

In further examining the friction between them, one can speculate on whether Burton envied MacLean his writing talent or perhaps felt he could have done better himself.

Whatever the attitudes, Richard Burton saddened Elliott Kastner with the way he would qualify films like *Where Eagles Dare*, never admitting that he was proud of his involvement. Kastner claimed to know that Burton had never made so much money in his life as he did from *Eagles*.

His conclusion on MacLean was that he was hell-bent on self-destruction, always trying to do himself down. 'As far as business was concerned, he didn't know his ass from his elbow and some of the deals he entered into were preposterous. There were many people who made a career out of massaging him.'

Kastner knew Billy Collins, chairman of the publishing company, but didn't feel Alistair's deal with Collins was a good one. For a writer of his commercial stature, especially after the success of *The*

Guns of Navarone, he felt he should have been renegotiating his terms. That, however, was none of his business.

While delighted to have struck a major movie success with *Where Eagles Dare*, he made no bones about the fact that Alistair MacLean was by no means as good a screenwriter as he was a novelist. That first screenplay may have sweated his palms with the events of Alder Schloss, but it had been far too long and needed much refining as well as cutting.

'His story-line and characterization were brilliant but, frankly, his screenwriting was clumsy,' he says now. 'It is usual that novelists are not as good at that as screenplay writers but, on balance, I prefer to have a novelist because you get a better story. Whatever the flaws, you can always put that right.'

Barry Norman supports the point. 'It is not running Alistair down if we say he wasn't a screenwriter. It is a different technique altogether. One of the reasons the British film industry is in its current state is that we don't have screenwriters. It can be much harder to write for the cinema, cutting down a long book to perhaps a hundred pages of script.

'There is a lot of slack writing in novels and I suspect Alistair was writing his screenplays in much the same way.'

The chairman of Collins generated much excitement about the forthcoming première of *Where Eagles Dare* in a letter to Lee Barker, boss of Doubleday in New York, who, as usual, was publishing the book in America. Having seen an advance showing, he thought it was streets better than *The Guns of Navarone* and was bound to be a tremendous success. It is in the nature of publishers, however, all things being equal, to enthuse more about the next book than the last one.

'I told our Fontana people,' wrote Collins, 'that they should sell at least two million in paperback and should out-sell any Ian Fleming.'

It all built up to another royal première in Leicester Square, a glittering night for filmland with the crowds greeting Richard Burton and Elizabeth Taylor and Princess Alexandra lending royal dignity to the occasion.

As the film was shown, Ian Chapman sat beside MacLean, feeling increasingly uncomfortable as he took to his mumblings once more, audible this time, with comments like, 'This is terrible! I didn't kill as many Germans as this. I was writing an anti-war film.' It was all part of the ritual.

After the pomp and protocol, they were driven off to the Savoy, where they sauntered through to the River Room, overlooking the Thames, to join in the celebration dinner. If Alistair MacLean had any illusions about the status of the film-writer in those days, they were to be promptly shattered.

While Richard Burton and Elizabeth Taylor were already holding court, Ian Chapman tried to pinpoint which table had been reserved for the author. He soon found out. There was none. What nonsense was this? It was Alistair MacLean's night. Without him there would have been no film, no première, no dinner.

Barry Norman confirms that that was how it happened as recently as the late sixties. 'There was a time when they stood so far down the credit listing that they had to share the screen with a dozen other people in the film. Yet the writer is the most important person of all.'

The status of the screenwriter has been enhanced in recent times and at least Alistair MacLean was never lacking in due prominence where the credits were concerned.

As for the dinner at the Savoy, if the film-world was not exactly recognizing Alistair MacLean as the central star of the evening, his publishing friend, Ian Chapman, was going to make sure he at least had a table to call his own. Making his way to the store-room, he slipped two workmen a tenner and helped them roll a large circular table on its perimeter, through the assembled guests, to be set up in the heart of the gathering.

Those sons of the Scottish manse were damned if they were going to be upstaged by any prima donnas from Hollywood. Burton and Taylor eventually joined MacLean's party and, whatever the depth of difference or the shade of bloody nose, that evening went down as one of the more memorable of show-business celebrations.

Alistair had bounced back from the wilderness with a vengeance, hitting the cinema screen with a spectacular success to match *The Guns of Navarone* of eight years earlier. Together, these two films would join that élite band of celluloid classics guaranteed, through the demands of television and video, to be seen in perpetuity.

The silent years of the mid-sixties were now behind him and he had broken new ground by writing directly for the cinema, as opposed to writing books, like *Navarone*, which would be translated into screenplays by someone else. Whether or not it would be to the long-term benefit of the author's work became a matter of serious doubt for people like Ian Chapman, who felt the medium of cinema was changing MacLean's whole approach to writing. The requirements of the film world were so vastly different that some would say his books were seldom so good again.

'From then on, he was writing visually,' said Chapman, 'writing with the screen in mind and neglecting to build up the atmosphere and description a book requires.'

In retrospect, he might have done better to stay within the bounds of his own undoubted talent instead of dabbling in screenplays, where his own undoctored work was of inferior quality.

Because of the time it takes to make a film, Collins had already published the book of *Where Eagles Dare* well before it reached the cinema. Even before that, they had also published what MacLean had been quietly preparing in anticipation of Collins's overtures. Having delivered the manuscript of his first novel in three years, he was still agonizing over a title for it. He wrote to Chapman:

> From the following list of feeble suggestions, you will draw the inevitable conclusion that I have not been racking what passes for my brain. Cross my heart, I have. Titles just aren't in my line.
>
> *Beul nan Uamh* would have been exactly the right and aptest title. Unfortunately, it's almost totally unpronounceable and the English equivalent, *The Mouth of the Grave*, is too morbid even for me.

So he went through a list of twenty possibilities which ranged from Hebridean Harbour, In the Still of the Storm and The Misty Islands to The Dark Skerry, They Never Came Ashore and Full Fathom Five.

'A fine ring to that last one, I think,' he wrote. 'Another quotation, admittedly, but what was good enough for Shakespeare is good enough for me.' Threatening to produce a second list of twenty, which would presumably be worse than the first, he did include one title which commended itself to the people at Collins.

That book of 1966, marking his return from the disastrous flirtation with business, became known as *When Eight Bells Toll*, taking him to the western shores of his native county of Inverness, with stormy waters beating upon those scattered islands which lend so much romance to the Hebridean legend. Writers down the generations have found it irresistible.

When eight bells tolled in the head of Alistair MacLean, however, they rang out with a realism which had less to do with romantic visions of western sunsets than the scything winds and driving sleet which cut you to the quick in that north-west shoulder of Scotland. It was out there, between islands ranging from barren bleakness to breathtaking beauty, that Secret Service agent Philip Calvert set out in pursuit of modern-day pirates, who were plundering ships on the west coast of Britain. In particular he was after a gang of bullion-snatchers who had gained control of a ship weighed down by its multi-million cargo of gold ingots, reserves being called in by the United States Treasury.

Instead of heading from Bristol to America, it had been diverted northwards to MacLean's native land. As it veered round the seaward side of the Mull of Kintyre (within sight of Paul McCartney's farm, as it turned out), Calvert took his own vessel up the landward side of the peninsula, into Loch Fyne and through the Crinan Canal to rejoin the hunt. There were real-life names and routes, well-known to anyone familiar with the Scottish archipelago. MacLean was indeed in home waters as he sent Calvert to track down the callous killers who had come to disturb the gentle tenor of West Highland ways.

After that break from writing, he showed that he could slip naturally back into his inimitable style. His native country had produced great prose, from Walter Scott to Grassic Gibbon, poetic power from Robert Burns to Hugh MacDiarmid. Patent honesty wouldn't have allowed him to insinuate himself into that level of literary Scots; but he had set a new post-war fashion for modern writers of adventure, not only in Scotland but around the world, where his books were selling by the million and turning him into an extremely wealthy man.

Great Scots had done similar things in previous generations. John Buchan comes to mind, another son of the Scottish manse, brought up in Perth and Glasgow before going on to Oxford and the diplomatic service, ending up as Governor-General of Canada, the man who signed that country's declaration of war against Hitler. Buchan

had given us *The Thirty-nine Steps* and so much more, a highly
acclaimed figure who died in 1940, when the Second World War
was scarcely into its stride.

That era had gone by the end of hostilities and now the post-war
period had produced a Rutherglen schoolteacher. MacLean was
fortunate in the timing of his discovery inasmuch as there was still a
thriving film industry of the fifties, ready to turn his kind of gripping
adventure into cinema. Even when that industry struck leaner times,
his name was well enough established to give him an advantage over
newcomers. In that respect, there had to be sympathy for writers
like Brian Callison from Dundee, highly regarded by MacLean and
perhaps a comparable talent, whose later arrival put him out of
season for film treatment.

Having given MacLean a major movie success with *Where Eagles
Dare*, Elliott Kastner was now lining up a film version of *When Eight
Bells Toll*. The big film producer would privately have preferred
another screenwriter but decided against usurping MacLean's position. He reckoned that, for all his bluster against the movie world,
he had thoroughly enjoyed the experience of screenwriting.

On this occasion, the big Hollywood studios were not involved.
Kastner wrote a letter to a wealthy gent he once met casually and
gave him the chance to be the financial backer of the next Alistair
MacLean film. Back came a cheque for $1.85 million, just like that,
proving that there are always wealthy individuals around the world
prepared to risk their money on a precarious investment like a film.
The rewards can hardly extend beyond the fulfilment of a romantic
notion.

This violent story of pirated gold and hi-jacked ships was filmed
on the island of Mull, just off the Scottish mainland from the town
of Oban and right in the heart of MacLean's ancestral base. Again
with a nose for an up-and-coming actor, Kastner hired Anthony
Hopkins and gave him his first leading role in a film, alongside
experienced hands like Jack Hawkins, Robert Morley and Derek
Bond. The film, released in 1971, was not exactly a box-office hit,
described by film critic Leslie Halliwell as 'an acceptable kill-happy
thriller; humourless James Bondery graced by splendid Scottish
landscape'. At least it washed its face financially.

Backed by Nat Cohen and his EMI company, Kastner kept the
MacLean bandwagon rolling with an earlier novel, *Fear is the Key*,

set in Florida and the Gulf of Mexico. While still giving him full authorship of his films if he wanted, Kastner found MacLean was too busy to write the screenplay and willingly switched to Robert Carrington, by whom he laid much store. The cast included Barry Newman, Suzy Kendall, Ben Kingsley and Ray McAnally.

17

If Alistair MacLean was back on song, artistically speaking, he was running desperately off-key in matters of finance and taxation. Carl Foreman had certainly boosted his income with the spectacular success of *The Guns of Navarone* but MacLean was flirting with a scheme to form a partnership, the purpose of which would be to handle the production of his films.

In particular, the idea was to exploit the rights of a sequel to *Navarone*, and his associates in the venture were to be a couple of newfound acquaintances who need explaining. Geoffrey Reeve was a young Englishman seeking to move upwards from promotional films to more ambitious levels of his profession. The fact that he had been introduced to Alistair MacLean and was planning to collaborate with him was a highly attractive prospect for a budding director with ideas and enterprise. He would later suggest the plots of two MacLean books, *Puppet on a Chain* and *Caravan to Vaccares*, and introduce him to Amsterdam and the Camargue, which would provide the background to these two stories. He also suggested the basic thinking for that sequel to *The Guns of Navarone* and travelled with MacLean to Yugoslavia, the country which would provide the setting.

Geoffrey Reeve owed his MacLean introduction to the third part of the triumvirate, a London wine merchant called Lewis Jenkins. The arrangement was that MacLean would write outlines, Reeve would direct the film and Jenkins would act as chairman of the company which became known as Trio Productions. Reeve was already steeped in films, but how, one has to ask, does a London wine merchant become involved in the tortuous dealings by which films are made?

Jenkins was the son of a London stockbroker, of Welsh background and English public school overtones, a large frame of a man with good connections, the sort who will move heaven and earth to put you in touch with whoever you need to be put in touch with. Taking a different tack from his father, he went early to the wine trade, through the firm of B. B. Mason, and extended his business interests to boat and caravan building. An underwriter at Lloyd's, he was a man of some style but not an obvious candidate for friendship with Alistair, who lacked those easy graces. The introduction was initiated by Lewis Jenkins, who read in the papers one day the terms of a film deal involving MacLean – it was *Ice Station Zebra* – and reckoned the man was being taken for a ride.

Alistair's curiosity was aroused by his letter, which came through Collins, so he phoned the stranger to see what was on his mind. They arranged to meet in London and went for lunch at Sweetings, a very old fish restaurant, where there were gulls' eggs on the menu. Alistair remembered gathering eggs like that as a boy in Scotland and couldn't get over the price they were charging.

His financial affairs were immensely complicated and Jenkins listened with some horror to the extent of his tax problems before giving advice and arranging to put him in touch with a chartered accountant in the Channel Islands. The aim would be to save tax in relation to his films.

That was how Alistair came into contact with Dr John Heyting, a brilliant international tax lawyer, based in Jersey, who worked out a plan for consideration. A New Zealander, Dr Heyting had appointed another solicitor of New Zealand background, David Bishop, as his London agent and it was suggested that Mr Bishop, then in his early thirties, should look more precisely at the suitability of Dr Heyting's proposals in relation to Alistair's needs.

In fact, David Bishop had to report that they would not produce the benefits required. Visiting the MacLean home in Haslemere to discuss the plan, he had to confess he had never read any of MacLean's books and knew very little about him. Having advised against the scheme, it seemed his involvement was now at an end.

Ironically, it was just the beginning of a significant business and personal relationship which would last for the rest of the writer's life, with an involvement which persists to this day, when Bishop, as literary executor, has a major influence on how the copyrights are exploited and on what happens to the continuing royalties.

Ian MacLean believes that the two biggest breaks in his brother's career were when he had the good fortune to catch the eye of Ian Chapman and the good sense to engage David Bishop.

Though cordiality is not the keynote of the relationship between the solicitor and some members of the MacLean family today, Alistair took a liking to Bishop, a square-cut man in the rugby-playing mould of New Zealand, son of a First World War hero who decided to settle in England, as a small farmer in Hampshire. David Bishop, who now lives near Winchester, read law at Cambridge and worked for Shell in North America before discovering his aptitude for private practice. He eventually became the senior partner at Baileys Shaw and Gillett of Queen Square, London, building a sound knowledge of the laws relating to copyright, tax and entertainment, a combination which made him an ideal adviser to a man like Alistair MacLean.

When Bishop arrived on the scene in 1967, the new partnership of Jenkins, Reeve and MacLean had embarked on its plan to produce a sequel to *The Guns of Navarone* and he was invited to act on their behalf in negotiations with Columbia Pictures. The deal would include Geoffrey Reeve becoming associate producer.

Early in 1968, Reeve reported that he had discovered Carl Foreman rather jumping the *Navarone* gun by registering a title for the sequel without telling anyone and before the title of the book had even been settled (his title was to be *After Navarone*). A furious MacLean rang up Bishop, fulminating about 'this rogue Foreman' and issuing instructions to take action.

Bishop raised the protest quite sharply with Foreman, who conceded that his action had been premature, though he claimed that, having made *The Guns of Navarone*, he was trying to protect the position of the sequel and was protecting MacLean's interests as well. If only he had told him.

By now MacLean was firmly in his triumvirate, having cemented the friendship over lunch at Jenkins wine cellar in Upper Thames Street, London. The highly talented David Lean, who had directed films such as *Dr Zhivago* and *Lawrence of Arabia*, was interested in tackling an Alistair MacLean film and was invited to join them for lunch. As it turned out, he was so fully committed for the following three years that nothing came of it.

Though the row with Foreman was settled amicably, MacLean was not over-anxious to have anything more to do with him. His preference now was for a younger director, like Geoff Reeve, who would listen to what he had to say. Though Foreman was the big name, he never did direct that sequel, which came many years later, under the title of *Force Ten from Navarone*, the same as the book which Collins had published in 1968. The film was produced by the late Oliver Unger and turned out to be a financial flop.

From that moment of confronting Carl Foreman, David Bishop became firmly established as Alistair MacLean's legal man-of-business, getting to know more and more about his financial affairs and not particularly liking what he found. During his years in Switzerland, MacLean's copyrights had been vested in a company called Gilach AG, but on his return to Britain in 1963 they were transferred into a scheme run by a London tax adviser, Stanley Gorrie of Cavendish Square, who specialized in the affairs of high earners in the entertainments industry.

The scheme involved a number of commercial trusts which would hold and handle the money earned by artistes, who signed away their earnings for a number of years in exchange for an annual salary plus, it was hoped, a substantial tax-free sum at the end of the day. Bishop was surprised to find that the Crewe Organization, through which Gorrie operated the scheme, took a third of earnings for its trouble and that, in a period when MacLean was earning around £300,000 a year, he was being paid a basic £10,000 by the organization. If he wanted a new car, he had to go cap in hand to Gorrie, who was not himself an accountant, though he employed accountants, but more of an ideas man, a business-getter.

'If I had been introduced to Gorrie independently and asked if I would do business with him,' said Bishop, 'I would have said no. He was certainly the wrong man for Alistair.'

Through the scheme, much of the money from MacLean's writing was finding its way into ventures like the Jamaica Inn, part of that ill-fated attempt to be a hotelier.

In 1968, Bishop advised him the Gorrie scheme was doing him no good at all and that the sooner he was out of it the better. MacLean totally agreed but wondered how it could be achieved.

Bishop's advice was that he should consider going back to live in Switzerland and that he would try to negotiate a way out of the Gorrie connection. The more he saw of it the less he liked it; not only were his existing copyrights vested in the scheme but they had a hold on all future books and films as well.

Lewis Jenkins, too, so disliked the scheme that, on one occasion, he vented his displeasure by using his full height to pick up the smallish Gorrie by the scruff of the neck. Bishop chose the more orthodox course of skilfully extracting his client from the scheme, a mission which took six months and cost over £100,000 to achieve, involving as it did borrowing money from the bank and selling the film rights of two books cheaply in order to raise the cash to buy back all of MacLean's rights.

It was a bruising episode but at least MacLean was now clear. The break with Gorrie was finally achieved in 1969, but for stamp-duty reasons the assignment had to be undertaken outwith the United Kingdom. Bishop executed it during a ski-ing holiday at Zermatt, when the notaire blinked in disbelief at the sight of a London solicitor arriving hot-foot from the slopes, complete with ski clothing and complicated legal documents, seeking to release Alistair MacLean from the Gorrie scheme and give him back the copyright of his own books.

Like many others, Bishop found it hard to understand why a man like MacLean needed to become involved in fancy investment schemes at all. From now on he would be master of his own destiny, in control of his own copyrights, without any intervening companies or trusts, a situation which remained until shortly before his death, when he settled them on his family.

MacLean had now gained enough faith in Bishop to offer him power of attorney over his business affairs, but that was refused. If the author didn't want such a close involvement himself, there was another financial arrangement which could work to his benefit should he decide not to return to Switzerland.

His fellow author and the creator of James Bond, Ian Fleming, had run into tax problems two years before his death and did a deal with Booker McConnell, the international traders, whereby they paid a lump sum for 51 per cent of his copyright company. In that way, Fleming had a sizeable payment plus 49 per cent of his copyrights retained.

MacLean could have done a similar deal and Bishop's proposal might well have been accepted – if only he had refrained from mentioning the name of Ian Fleming. The very sound of Bond's creator was anathema to MacLean, who said, 'Fleming relies on sex, sadism and snobbery. I don't want to do anything which is associated with him.' So that was, irrationally, that, however much it smacked of cutting off his nose to spite his face, and Bishop now found himself very much responsible for what was happening to his client's money.

For all their ambition, the Trio Production company of Jenkins, Reeve and MacLean got nowhere with their plans to make a sequel to *Navarone*, nor any other film for that matter, though that did not mean the association was finished.

The large, genial, quiet-spoken Jenkins clearly enjoyed rubbing shoulders with the bestselling novelist, who was just as intrigued by the style of a man who could take a phone-call from Prince Philip with such consummate ease or casually introduce him to his friend Pietro Annigoni, the famous Italian painter. Jenkins opened up a different world for MacLean, who went to wine-tastings at his cellars and met an interesting variety of people. Through that, he became a member of Lloyd's. He would visit the Jenkins family at Totteridge and they would go to parties at Haslemere, where they in turn would meet people like Bill Travers and Virginia McKenna and Robert Pitman, the journalist.

Having had no more than a little outboard runabout on Lake Sarnen, Alistair decided to buy himself a proper boat again, now that he was living within thirty miles of the English Channel and with the kind of access to the open sea he had known during his days on the Clyde. With his enthusiasm for the sea still outstripping his knowledge or aptitude, he called on his brother Ian to inspect the vessel he was thinking of buying, a sixty-foot Irish fishing boat, based at Malahide, the seaside resort near Dublin. Ian took along one of his top-notch marine experts from Shell, Jock Main, and the pair of them immediately rejected the vessel as not being seaworthy.

The sellers had to put it right and Alistair eventually sailed his latest boat, all varnished pine, white paint and tricolor, across to Penzance in Cornwall and then to Shoreham-by-Sea, near Brighton, to which he could drive with ease from Haslemere. Once a month or so he would venture out in his pride and joy, which was called the *Ebhora*. It was really like old times when Dougie Seggie and Willie Campbell arrived down from Scotland and the three mus-keteers set sail with bold plans to reach France. Alas, the weather closed in on them and, with North Sea ferries crossing their path, it was time to turn around and head back for the English ports.

The lure of the Clyde was never far away, and for a time Alistair berthed the *Ebhora* at Port Bannatyne on the Isle of Bute, where once again his old mates from Glasgow could join him. On one particularly memorable voyage through the Crinan Canal, up to Oban and across towards Tobermory on the island of Mull, Alistair was pleased and proud to play host to his beloved mother. The Seggie family were on board, along with Lachlan and other members of the clan MacLean, and for all it was a testing time for the nervous system when a gale blew up and they headed for the Bay of Aros. But the wind changed and, without radio communication, they ended up swinging at the end of an anchor and heading for the rocks. They were lucky to escape from serious consequences.

Alistair's mother kept her calm, and for some the lingering memory of that experience was the sound of her beautiful Gaelic intonations as she spoke to fishermen on the quayside, once they had reached the safety of Tobermory.

Alistair found great satisfaction in entertaining the family in the luxurious setting of the *Ebhora*. While berthed at Port Bannatyne, he sailed up the west coast of Scotland to collect Gillespie and his wife Margaret at Fort William. Once again, they sailed down Loch Linnhe by Ballachulish for a wonderful day out amidst Highland scenery, royally entertained by their host, who made sure that fresh salmon was on the menu.

Back at Haslemere, Alistair became godfather to Lewis and Caro-line Jenkins's son Philip and was in cracking form when they held a celebration party at the Post Office Tower Restaurant in London. He had a double portion of caviar and was so relaxed and enjoying the company that he and Gisela missed their last train to Haslemere. They ended up with an expensive taxi-ride home, complete with a bottle of brandy and two glasses from the restaurant.

Lewis Jenkins came to know what others would also find out: that there were two different people inside Alistair MacLean. He could be the kindliest man in the world and he could also turn nasty.

Richard Burton was not the only one to be the object of a swipe, many of them off target for obvious reasons. Few were now in any doubt that drink was at the root of the personality change.

Slight of build, Alistair could consume vast quantities of alcohol and become blind drunk yet surprise everyone by appearing at the crack of dawn, bright as a button, as if nothing had happened.

'He would drink anything,' Lewis Jenkins confirmed. 'I remember one occasion when he came to lunch at my cellars with Richard Burton and Robert Shaw. I couldn't believe the amount and variety of alcohol consumed over that lunchtime.'

But if drink had become a major factor, there were other problems developing in MacLean's life from which that fondness for the bottle could not be separated.

18

Members of the MacLean family were beginning to see that early doubts about the compatibility of Alistair and Gisela were not misplaced. When they were living not far from each other in Surrey, Alistair would arrive for a planned visit to his elder brother's home in East Horsley, obviously embarrassed at having to apologize for Gisela's absence. She would be feeling unwell, or there was some other excuse, but Ian and Bunty felt there had either been a row or she wasn't in the mood for company.

At that period of the late sixties, while preparing to take David Bishop's advice on living once more in Switzerland, Alistair was deeply upset that his close friend, Robert Pitman of the *Sunday Express*, was dying of leukaemia. He visited his bedside at St Bartholomew's Hospital in London, where Pitman was undergoing the unpleasant process of blood replacement, known as plating, and was distressed by the puncture wounds in his friend's chest, where the tubes had been fitted. His hair had fallen out, but through all the distresses Robert was maintaining a courageous and cheerful attitude, continuing to write his weekly column for the *Daily Express* and his books column for the *Sunday Express*, all in the stir of a public ward – there were no private wards at Barts – something he achieved by pulling the sheets and blankets over his head so that no one would hear him dictating into a tape-recorder.

Even more than most novelists, Alistair had little to do with other writers, but his firm friendship with Robert Pitman brought him into contact with James Leasor, the well-known journalist and author. Leasor went up to Oxford in 1946, edited the *Isis* magazine and met Pitman, a friendship which developed through their days in the Beaverbrook stable of bright young men.

In happier circumstances, Alistair met them at a London party given by the American writer Ronald Kirkbride, whose alleged connection with the CIA would have intrigued him. Their subsequent meetings were mostly at St Bartholomew's, where Alistair was giving Robert Pitman the encouragement of a writing project which they would embark upon together.

All this was coinciding with the MacLeans' departure for Switzerland, marked by a memorable farewell party at Haslemere. Amidst the jollification, Alistair told James Leasor he would have felt better if he had been leaving Britain for health reasons. It was ironic, he said, that he was perfectly fit whereas Robert, with no wish to leave England, was dying.

Bob Pitman's death was a shattering blow, to which, however, Alistair reacted positively. He and James Leasor became two of the trustees for a fund which Robert had set up for his children. Alistair wanted to do something more to help and sent David Bishop to see Robert's widow, Pat, at their home in Shepperton by the Thames, offering to undertake a project in her husband's memory, from which the money would go entirely to her and the family. Bishop thought he met with a cool reception, Pat Pitman expressing her appreciation of the kind thought but declining the offer with thanks.

The emotions of that period were further complicated by the fact that Gisela believed Alistair was showing an interest in Pat Pitman. She didn't want her at the farewell party but Alistair invited her just the same, and when it was all over she unleashed her wrath.

The vibrations of the accusation filtered through to the children, and Michael, who was eight at the time, has vivid memories of the ensuing row. 'That was when I remember seeing my father punch my mother,' he recalls, confirming the suspicion that violence had already entered the marriage.

There had indeed been suggestions of Alistair's interest in Pat Pitman – there was no suggestion of any reciprocal interest – a side of his nature little known even to his closest friends, who to this day will protest that, whatever else, he was not a womanizer. They are almost certainly wrong.

There were domestic rows about lipstick on his collar and reports of seductions. Though Alistair had given the impression of being a loving and caring father in the earlier part of their marriage, there was now a pattern of behaviour which his children should most certainly have been spared. While Lachlan and Ali have refused to meet me on this or any other question, Michael speaks frankly about childhood memories of his father being drunk and squabbling with his mother.

His views have to be weighed against the fact that he was the adopted child, without genetic affinities, and that his Germanic origins would place him more on the side of Gisela, herself a German and inclined to show favour to Michael, balancing up Alistair's clear preference for young Ali. Yet Michael expresses great compassion for his father and talks about him intelligently, lending validity to his criticisms. 'If you didn't establish your rights with my father,' he said, 'he simply got worse. The more he saw he could step all over my mother, the more he did. She was practically a slave. It took a certain kind of character to stand up to him and my mother didn't deserve to be with a guy like that. But he was her husband and she respected marriage and, despite all the horrible things that happened, she still harbours an affection for him to this day.'

That affection is beyond doubt, and Gisela was naturally reluctant to enlarge upon the more unpleasant side of her life with Alistair. But she did confirm the general accuracy of the child's observations when she told me, 'Our marriage was certainly in a bad state and I felt more or less paralysed. I also had a feeling that something was going to happen.

'David Bishop had persuaded Alistair to go back to Switzerland and I thought finally that maybe this was best. I was extremely concerned about the children. The two younger ones were still small and I believed they needed two parents.'

She refused to be drawn into discussion about her husband's immoral pursuits but cast her eyes to the heavens and left little doubt that she had a tale or two which would shatter the faith of his defenders. In that stimulating decade of the Swinging Sixties, there is little doubt that Alistair was finding the blatant sensualities more to his taste than the cooler dignity of his German wife.

For now, however, with the farewell party over, the MacLeans bade goodbye to their magnificent home in Haslemere and headed once more for a fresh start in Switzerland, after an absence of six years, this time singling out Geneva as the place where they wanted to live.

Having largely sorted out the financial mess, David Bishop teamed up with his Geneva agent, a leading Swiss banker and tax lawyer, Henri-Paul Brechbuhl, to negotiate a simplified tax arrangement with the Swiss tax authorities. Now that a famous author was returning to live in their country, they were happy and flexible enough to accept a fixed annual payment, irrespective of his earnings.

With the legal work completed during his adventures on the ski-slopes, Bishop joined the MacLeans at Versoix, where they had found temporary accommodation before settling on a permanent home of their own. Alistair seemed delighted to be back in Switzerland, as relaxed as Bishop had ever seen him. Bishop helped them look at a number of houses and from that point onwards the relationship between solicitor and client developed into a much closer personal friendship.

Just as people like Lewis Jenkins and Geoffrey Reeve were enjoying their contact with MacLean, Bishop too was benefiting from the company of such a well-known figure. He had several distinguished clients but this was his first experience of a bestselling author and he found it stimulating, not to mention lucrative, without in any way diminishing the quality of friendship.

The MacLeans moved from the Motel de Founex at Versoix to a house at chemin Degallier, still in Versoix. 'It is literally on the wrong side of the tracks,' MacLean wrote, 'but it is quite a nice villa for all that, with a splendidly stocked wine cellar which the owner, an otherwise sane man, is entrusting to my care. We shall certainly be there for the minimum of a year, the least time I can expect to elapse while I obtain permanent accommodation, owing to the fact that Collins don't often pay any royalties.' (That was MacLean's way of preparing his publisher for a later request, seeking an advance of £50,000 to buy the new house!)

Through all the upheaval of removal, the books continued to flow from his typewriter, the latest being *Puppet on a Chain*, an idea which took root during that visit to Amsterdam with Geoffrey Reeve, when they happened to pass a warehouse near the docks and spotted a puppet hanging by the neck from a chain, a piece of innocence which MacLean quickly turned into a sinister plot, about which the *New York Times* later wrote:

> It's a top-drawer effort, filled to bursting with murder and mayhem, grit and gore as Major Sherman, an Interpol narcotics sleuth, tracks down and breaks up a tough, resourceful and ingenious-minded gang of smugglers operating in and around Amsterdam. If you have any red corpuscles in your blood you will find your heart pumping triple time as Sherman moves in for the confrontation. The writing is as crisp as a sunny winter morning and MacLean has provided a travelogue for a part of Amsterdam the ordinary tourist is not likely to see – and a good thing too. He has also included a pagan rite that will send the amateur anthropologist back to his books and the rest of us cowering in our Morris chairs. It's not good, clean or funny but you won't quickly forget it.

If the publishers, reviewers and reading public were managing to mount some excitement about the book, it goes without saying that it didn't take the film-world long to upset MacLean's blood pressure. Having got nowhere with his associates in their proposed sequel to *The Guns of Navarone*, he more or less handed over the film rights of *Puppet on a Chain* to Geoffrey Reeve, who had been doing so much to help, with little or nothing in the way of reward.

To convert the book into a film would involve all the usual hot-and-cold reactions, optimistic noises and disappointments with which MacLean was already learning to live. Robert Clark of the Associated British Picture Corporation, who had bought the film rights of *HMS Ulysses* and never made it, was now interested in *Puppet*. He wrote a letter to Maurice Silverstein of MGM Pictures in New York reminding him of a conversation they had while standing at the Savoy Hotel, awaiting the arrivals from the première of *Where Eagles Dare*:

> We fell to talking on the possibility of doing something by way of a joint production and I said an excellent opportunity seemed to present itself for us to do business, in that we had acquired an interest in Mr Alistair MacLean's latest novel, *Puppet on a Chain*. This seemed to interest you and I sent round to you the following

morning a copy of the first rough script. Have you made up your
mind . . . ?

Back came Silverstein's reply:

> In my opinion there is a familiarity of plot and theme that cannot
> be disguised, even though there is quite a bit of cleverness in
> MacLean's script. Thanks ever so much for letting us have a look
> at the script. Best wishes . . . [Aren't there some curious ways of
> saying 'no thank you'?]

Associated British Productions were also negotiating to the point
of coming close to a deal, on the basis of a £30,000 payment, which
included MacLean's own screenplay and the services of Geoffrey
Reeve as producer or director – if they decided to accept him. While
MacLean had every faith in Reeve, the company evidently didn't
know enough about him to confirm his appointment. They would
consider giving him a chance to direct, with a number of safeguards,
including the right, after the first week of rushes, to consider replac-
ing him if his work was not deemed up to standard.

In the event, the film was actually made by the Big City company
of the Israeli film producer, Kurt Unger, son of Siegfried Unger, a
distinguished producer in Germany before the war. Kurt Unger,
once production boss for United Artists in Europe, had branched
out as an independent in 1960, making films like *Judith*, with Sophia
Loren, Peter Finch and Jack Hawkins; he happened to be looking
for an action story when he came across MacLean's latest novel.

They did a deal and Unger accompanied MacLean to Amsterdam
to be shown some of the locations which could be used. Filming
was soon under way and MacLean, who normally spent very little
time on the sets, did turn up in Amsterdam, to be joined by brother
Ian and his wife Bunty, Ian and Marjory Chapman and David
Bishop, who happened to know the local Chief of Police, Piet
Cleveringa, with whose cooperation they managed to film those
thrilling boat chases on city canals (albeit at speeds which certainly
were not authorized). The production team was no doubt preoccu-
pied with filming difficulties but there was some ill feeling that no
one had taken time to thank Cleveringa for his assistance. The
visitors also gathered that production problems had resulted in

Geoffrey Reeve being replaced as director in the middle of shooting
and that the more experienced Don Sharp had been brought in.
Kurt Unger played down that aspect, saying, 'It was Geoff Reeve's
first film on this scale and there were some things not right. We
brought in Don Sharp as a second-unit director, responsible for
such scenes as the motor-boat chases.'

Unger had bigger problems with Alistair MacLean's script. 'He
was a good writer but he was not a screenwriter,' he told me. 'And
what he wrote as a screenplay for *Puppet on a Chain*, I'm afraid, had
to be rewritten.'

The more experienced Paul Wheeler was engaged to put right
the flaws, and such were his alterations that, once MacLean saw the
early version of the film, a state of near-apoplexy was induced. In a
memo to Unger at the Dorchester Hotel, demanding changes, he
was soon in full flight:

> Who does this fellow think he is? If he can improve on practically
> everything I write and is clearly of the opinion that he is so much
> the better writer, why is it I have never heard of him? Or why
> doesn't he go write his own screenplays?

MacLean had had books and screenplays hacked around before
but he had never been so angry as with 'this rubbishy travesty of
what I wrote'. Professionally, it was the most intolerable insult ever
to come his way, he said:

> I feel like a doctor who has been called in after a group of myopic,
> first-year medical students armed with hacksaws have completely
> misdiagnosed and performed major surgery on a previously
> healthy patient who is now, understandably, in extremis. Whether
> the patient can at this stage be saved is a matter of conjecture of
> the most apprehensive kind – and I should hate to see the kind
> of odds Ladbroke would offer on it.

With pride severely hurt, he was of course seriously overreacting
to the film-writer's treatment, which necessarily upsets the smooth
narrative of the story-writer. He had the grace to acknowledge that
some of the individual scenes were actually very good, which indeed
they were. *Puppet on a Chain* was a much underrated film which

stands the test of more than twenty years. He also had the grace to
take his own share of blame:

> I don't entirely blame Wheeler, except inasmuch as he appears to
> have been the actual perpetrator of this cinematic crime, the
> assassin who went to work on a perfectly viable screenplay. But
> Wheeler did not go to work without consent and encouragement
> and those who permitted or connived at this assassination and
> gave it their approval on its completion are equally guilty. Very
> probably I'm the most guilty of the lot.
>
>   I was supposed to be a co-producer; I had a more than vague
> idea of what was going on but I sat back and did nothing. Had I
> troubled to exert myself in the early days, no doubt I could have
> exerted a modifying influence on the final shooting script. I didn't,
> and that's that. *Mea culpa.*

He went on to dissociate himself from any film credits – and
enclosed a copy of his complaints to Ian Chapman, with a covering
note in characteristic style, saying: 'You will gather perhaps that I
was not in the best of humours when I put those notes together . . .
and I feel that I won't be forgiven.'

Kurt Unger did order some reshooting, which lasted for several
weeks, and claimed that MacLean eventually told him that *Puppet*
ended up as the best movie from any of his books. Perhaps his
conscience was troubling him. Good though the film was, it is doubtful if he rated it more highly than *The Guns of Navarone* or *Where
Eagles Dare.*

In view of MacLean's diatribe, Kurt Unger, Paul Wheeler and
company could reasonably have pointed out that he could have
exerted a greater influence if he had not been so much under the
influence.

With much public attention on some highly visible filming in
Amsterdam, he was due to give a press conference but disappeared;
nobody knew where he was. Ian Chapman had been on the point
of informing the police when he spotted the bold fellow coming
through the swing doors of the Europa Hotel, slumped against the
glass and in no state to be seen by the press or anyone else. Chapman
swung a limp arm over his shoulder and supported him to his room,
then told the newspapermen, who knew MacLean was there, that

that he was having a sleep after a drink too many and that he would guarantee to have him there next day.

Among the waiting journalists was the writer and broadcaster Barry Norman, who remembers that, when Alistair did finally appear for their interview, he was disarmingly frank about what had happened and was most contrite – as well as suffering, unusually, from a hangover.

It was to the credit of the journalists of those days – as well as some indication of the respect and loyalty which MacLean could inspire in those who met him – that they confined themselves to the business on hand, which was to discuss the film and other aspects of his career. In all his years of erratic behaviour, sometimes in public, there was not a whiff of his drinking to be found in the gossip-columns. The tabloids of a later date might have decided to have a field day.

As it was, Barry Norman was given an earful of MacLean's disenchantment with the film industry – and this before he had seen the version of *Puppet on a Chain* which strained his arteries. The Scotsman in him was deeply offended by so many people sitting around a film-set apparently doing nothing. So to cut himself off from this distressing sight, he planned to revert to his original practice of writing the books and leaving the film-making to others. (That was an intention he didn't quite fulfil.)

He was prepared, as a matter of fact and not as a boast, to place himself among the top four popular writers of the day, the others being Harold Robbins, Agatha Christie and Georges Simenon. With *Puppet on a Chain*, he thought he had changed his style of writing from the earlier books. 'If I went on writing the same stuff, I'd be guying myself,' he said. 'As it is, I can hardly keep a straight face sometimes when I'm putting the words down.'

19

At last, in 1970, the MacLeans found what was intended to be their permanent home, the charming Villa Murat, set on rising ground close by the village of Celigny and within easy reach of Geneva, just fourteen miles away.

They had been searching desperately for well over a year in an area well-known for extortionate prices, and although Villa Murat was little more than half the size of Sunbiggin at Haslemere, it cost nine times as much to buy. By most people's standards, however, it was still a large and handsome residence, a box-like rectangle of three storeys, with cavernous cellars, gate-lodge and garage, spacious hallway with the staircase rising in wood-panelled dignity. The main gateway led off a lane at the back of the house so that the walk round to the front patio was rather like coming on stage in a vast theatre and surveying the auditorium as it spread across the parterre stalls to Lake Geneva and upwards to the dress circle of the French Alps in the High Savoy. Even behind the villa there was an unobstructed view of the Jura mountains, which were four miles distant.

All this was certainly an improvement on the furnished rooms of a Glasgow suburb, but it was a measure of the standards to which Alistair MacLean had become accustomed that he did not regard it as the dream-house he had been anticipating. He had visualized something more along the lines of a modern, sprawling, ranch-type house, largely made of glass, à la the late Frank Lloyd Wright. He had cast an eye on the lakeside itself but realized that only the financial whizz-kids of the day, like Bernie Cornfeld, could afford the £100,000 per acre on which to build the dream-house.

Alistair was at least impressed by the thickness of the walls at the
sixty-year-old villa – 'clearly designed by the ghost of the architect
of Edinburgh Castle,' he wrote, 'rendering this what must be the
only atom-bomb-proof residence along the shores of Lake Geneva.'
He could also look back with humour at 'the rented shack we had
for eighteen months before that, which was no better than a converted rabbit hutch that would have had any self-respecting rabbit
shouting "Rachman" at the top of his voice.'

Surveying his new home, he found that the purchase included
seven unwanted acres, four of them growing a splendid crop of
sweetcorn and three acres of untamed grass that had seen neither
scythe nor sickle. 'Perfect for my field of operation,' he said. 'I can
just see me sitting there in my summer deck-chair, the top of my
head barely visible above this splendid crop of hay.'

David Bishop felt relieved that the financial situation had been
largely resolved, though a considerable amount had to be found to
buy Villa Murat, including that £50,000 advance on royalties to
which Collins had agreed. By now he had had time to assess his few
years of contact with MacLean and came to the conclusion that, of
all the elements in this enigmatic figure, the most noticeable was his
solitariness. For all his string of acquaintances, he had very few
friends. Indeed, as a couple, he and Gisela had not formed many
friendships in their Swiss connections.

Ironically, one of their neighbours just down the road was none
other than Richard Burton, for whom MacLean still had no liking.
Despite the proximity, there was absolutely no contact between the
two men. Having missed the Savoy Hotel party which followed the
première of *Where Eagles Dare*, Gisela had never been introduced
to Burton. While dog-walking, she would meet him out exercising
his Pekinese on that country road at Celigny, where he would pass
her by without any inkling that she was the wife of Alistair MacLean.

Wherever he went on his travels, Burton always returned to
Celigny, where he felt most at home in the house he had owned
since 1957. He even called it Le Pays de Galles, which meant Wales.

As another tax exile taking refuge in Switzerland, Alistair
MacLean would think of his homeland too, though there was some
surprise that he failed to appear at his mother's funeral back at
Daviot. Word was that he had used up his permitted quota of visiting
days to the United Kingdom for that tax year, but there was also a

suggestion that he was on a heavy drinking bout at the time.

Mrs MacLean had moved from her original Glasgow home in Carrington Street, first to Kersland Street and then to better property in Falkland Place, Hyndland. Since her son's rise to fame, she had wanted for nothing. But she suffered a stroke in the year of Alistair's return to Switzerland and was taken south to the home of Ian and Bunty, where she died at the age of seventy-eight, having been a widow since she was forty-five. Ian and Gillespie arranged the funeral back home in the Highlands, at her beloved Daviot, while Alistair mourned privately in Switzerland.

When he did manage to re-enter Britain, he would occasionally stay with David Bishop in his mews flat in Kensington, Bishop having been in no hurry to surrender his bachelor status. They would drop round to the local pub for a drink and a snack, the kind of atmosphere in which Alistair seemed relaxed and happy. He would tease Bishop as a bachelor about being a lucky man and, in that frame of mind, he had a very fine sense of humour. He still disliked the limelight and revelled in the simple things of life. Disliking the fancy or pretentious or anything that smacked of vulgarity or showing off. He would go out and buy a Rolls-Royce, on the basis that it was the best; but he detested people who were intellectually phoney.

He could have existed on a diet of sausage, bacon, egg and kippers, with some red wine and a Raymond Chandler book. Even when he dined at the famous Carlton Hotel in Cannes, he would stick to the plain grilled sole and was liable to add a copious dressing of HP Sauce to whatever he happened to be eating. He had a weakness for ice-cream and amused David Bishop in Geneva one day when they were coming from a complicated and serious meeting with lawyers. Passing a paddle-steamer which served as a restaurant-café, he bounded off with boyish enthusiasm, saying, 'Come on, let's have a knickerbocker glory.' And there he was, like a kid, spooning up an enormous sundae.

Having by then read his books, David Bishop became fascinated by Alistair's intelligent approach to things and his complete mastery of all those technical details in his stories.

People like that, the creative brains who provided the cinema with some of its best and most exciting stories, were also of special interest to Barry Norman, in his authoritative role of writing about the film world.

As a preliminary to a major profile for world syndication, starting with the *Observer*, he and his wife Diana had dinner with Alistair and the Chapmans at the London Dorchester, where plans were made for Norman's visit to Geneva. Alistair sat next to Diana at the table, became increasingly drunk and caused her considerable distress with his account of his son Lachlan's illness, which he declared to be leukaemia. Diana relayed the story to Barry when they went home and, anxious to clarify a situation he had not fully appreciated, he took it up with family contacts next day. It was then he discovered that the leukaemia story was totally untrue and that Alistair had been blethering in his cups.

Lachlan was certainly suffering from a distressing disorder of blood and skin, which was at the least related to acne but had complications which led to a series of costly operations in top London hospitals. Alistair was greatly upset and would have done anything to alleviate the situation. But it wasn't leukaemia, and when Diana Norman heard the real version she was furious with Alistair for having gained her sympathy under false pretences, vowing she would have nothing more to do with him. She never did.

Barry Norman kept his professional appointment in Geneva and spent two days on the interview. Gisela was away from home so they dined out, Alistair enquiring if Barry would care to drive them in the Rolls.

'I got pleasure in driving the Rolls and he got pleasure out of seeing my pleasure,' he recalls. 'So there was a kindliness in the man. He said he didn't drive at all because his eyes were so bad. In fact he said he was virtually blind.' That was another exaggeration.

The *Observer* article gave a flavour of Alistair as he settled into his new home:

On the Friday night I drove with Alistair MacLean to dinner by the shore of Lake Geneva in his Mercedes and, on the Saturday, we drove to lunch in his Rolls-Royce. On the first occasion, he said, 'I'm an arrogant bastard and you can quote me,' and on the second, he said, above the uproar of the Rolls-Royce clock, 'I don't belong in this class. It's ridiculous.'

The statements are contradictory and neither is wholly true. If he is now in the Rolls-Royce class, he has earned the right to be there. At the latest reckoning his books have sold nearly 23 million copies and continue to sell at the rate of two million a year. His earnings from books and films can hardly be less than £200,000 a year and his latest and sixteenth novel, *Bear Island*, had an initial print order of 100,000 copies and will move automatically to the top of the bestsellers.

The above revelations, though more or less public knowledge already, will annoy him intensely for he loathes publicity. He regards it as self-glorification and he sees little glory either in himself or his work.

'I'm an extraordinarily ordinary man,' he said. 'Basically I'm a person who tells stories – and what does that mean? How much is it worth?' The clue to this self-deprecation lies possibly in the fact that, sixteen years after publishing *HMS Ulysses*, he still doesn't regard himself as a writer, at least not a natural writer. It was something he drifted into. Until his first novel made him rich, almost literally overnight, the idea of earning his living as an author had never occurred to him.

'I spent the war years in the navy with a spanner in my hand,' he said. 'And when it was over, I tired of mechanical things and having dirt under my finger-nails. So when the chance came to go to Glasgow University, I read English literature because I could do that without getting my hands dirty.'

He explained to Norman how he had carried on teaching after *HMS Ulysses* and had needed *The Guns of Navarone* to convince him he could safely become a fulltime writer:

'I wrote it with more method than inspiration,' he revealed. 'First, I drew up a list of the characters, then I drew a diagram of the plot. There were a number of squares to represent the chapters and in the squares were circles to show where the characters came in – and red crosses to show where they died. Then I looked at it again and said, 'MacLean, you've got the balance wrong; too many crosses in the middle and not enough at the end,' so I rearranged it until there were crosses all the way through.'

He thought for a moment over what he had just said and then shook his head. 'By God, that was cold, wasn't it? That was calculating and cynical. I've never written a book that way since.'

He lives comfortably but without ostentation in a charming villa overlooking Lake Geneva. The only signs of real affluence are the two cars and he has them not for their value as status symbols but because he believes simply that they are the best cars in the world.

'Last year,' he said, 'an English newspaper wanted to do an article about all us drop-outs in Switzerland – the jet-setters – and they asked if they could include me. I fell about. Me a jet-setter? My idea of a big day out is to go to the local café and play table football with my two young sons.'

He is a very private person with a very few, very close friends and hardly any acquaintances.

'I have a bad name for being unsociable,' he said. 'I don't mix with other celebrities. I don't like the company of the famous. And I don't like being a celebrity myself.'

A small, thin, greying man of forty-eight, MacLean is a son of the manse, and though he has lived in Switzerland off and on for the last fifteen years, his Scottish accent is as powerful as ever. Ian Chapman believes this Scottishness, and particularly his Calvinistic background, is responsible for the obvious guilt he feels about his huge success.

'Alistair started writing to make money,' he said. 'That's a fact. But now he's made it, he has a conscience about it. It seems to him sinful that he should earn such vast sums for doing something that comes so easily to him. All the time he is trying to ease his conscience. He's always trying to help people, to look for something to justify what he is doing.'

That he does help people I know for a fact and he does it by stealth and not for self-advertisement. He is an extremely kind and likeable man and also surprisingly vulnerable. A man in search of a cause.

At present he has a cause, although it would be cheap and unfair to imply that he pursues it simply to salve his over-demanding conscience. He is writing a book about cancer and since all proceeds are going to cancer research, he stands to gain nothing from it. Even so, he has an unreasonable fear that he will be castigated for doing it.

'I'm on a hiding to nothing,' he said. 'People will say, "Oh,

MacLean's just doing this for publicity or money," but it isn't so. I'm doing it because, in Britain alone, 15,000 people died unnecessarily of cancer last year. They were too scared and too late to seek help. If I can get through to people like them and help just one of them to save his own life, the book will be worth doing.' Again a pause to reflect on his words. Then, 'God, that sounds pompous.'

He has, in fact, another more personal reason for writing the book – the hope that it may turn out to be the book he has wanted to write for at least ten years, the book he talks about when he says, 'Look, I'm a bestselling author and I'm not good enough. Not good enough for me, anyway. But one day I'll write something that will come as close as possible to pleasing me.'

MacLean then sought to analyse what he thought to be the reason for his success:

'It's not a get-rich-quick formula; it's more complex than that. But the basic secret, if there is one, is speed – keep the action moving so fast that the reader never has time to stop and think, "But this is impossible." That's why there is never any sex in my books; it holds up the action.' Actually, there's another reason for the absence of sex. 'It's probably the Calvinist in me,' he said, 'but I don't approve of permissiveness and pornography. It's a matter of satisfaction to me that I can produce bestsellers without resorting to those things.'

Just before I left him I tried to discuss other men's work but he would not be drawn.

'I don't know any writers,' he said. 'I know nothing about litera- ture. I'm not even interested in it. You'll never find me reading a book but you'll always find me with a scientific magazine. I'm not a fiction person. My real interest is science – physics and astronomy.

'Oh, I've read all the "great" books – Tolstoy, nearly all the Russians, and I suppose I should admire them but I don't. They're too heavy and sombre, not real story-tellers at all. In any case, to my mind, no novel can ever be a work of art.' To this, however, he makes one exception: Raymond Chandler. 'Now he was a real artist. You can learn more about America from his books than from any of the so-called serious writers.'

Meanwhile he sits and works on his terrace, looking down at the pleasure steamers on Lake Geneva, and if he talks at all of his success and affluence it is mainly to say, 'They're not important. The only important thing is when your big son says, as mine did to me last night, "Dad, you're not such a bad old Dad." That means something. That's what life is all about.'

This is the kind of thing many rich and successful people are accustomed to saying. MacLean says it with total sincerity.

Well, that may or may not have been true. But while Barry Norman was interviewing Alistair MacLean at Villa Murat, the marriage was disintegrating at a pace which did not escape close friends and family, nor the lady who had just been engaged to work for him. Jacky Leiper was a top-class secretary, brought up in Greenock, trained in Glasgow and by then working for a publishing company in the United States. Between times, she had worked for the headmaster at the International School of Versoix, on the outskirts of Geneva, who was now writing to tell her of a parent who was looking for a private secretary. Was she interested? The parent turned out to be none other than her fellow Scot, Alistair MacLean, whose boys were now at the school.

Jacky took the job just as the family moved into Villa Murat and was allocated an office in the house, by no means an ideal arrangement at a time when things were not going well between Alistair and Gisela and the presence of a third-party outsider could only add to the strain.

'I had very little contact with Gisela but, from what I saw, she seemed fairly aggressive,' said Jacky. 'Perhaps she felt insecure and the arrival of someone like a secretary in the house was the last straw.'

On the other hand, she had no problems with Alistair, who was a good boss, reserved and unpretentious and very appreciative of what she did.

Meanwhile, he had indeed turned his talents to writing a book about cancer, spurred on by the death of Robert Pitman. Lewis Jenkins was also to come under treatment for the disease and at one stage MacLean began to fear that he himself had become a victim.

The project started out with the title *A Layman Looks at Cancer*
and with the cooperation of a famous Scots cancer specialist, Sir
Thomas Symington of the Institute of Cancer Research, who happened to be a neighbour and friend of MacLean's publishing friend,
Ian Chapman.

While always wary of laymen looking at anything medical, a
number of experts attended a dinner party and had their reservations
jolted when MacLean got up and used his scientific knowledge to
show he was working from a sound premise. Final judgement would
rest with the finished article, however, and copies were circulated
when he completed the 35,000-word manuscript. The scalpels were
soon at work. In a report to Sir Thomas, another eminent specialist,
Sir David Smithers, gave it a promising start but wished it could
have continued in that vein. Flaws abounded. While MacLean cast
everything into the cancerous pool and talked about '50-per-cent
survival', Sir David was pointing out, even in 1971, that there ought
to be 100 per cent cure for rodent ulcers (skin cancer of face and
neck) and for the testicle variety. And while Alistair had given scant
mention to the connection between alcohol and cancer, Sir David
was saying there was good evidence that drinking raw spirits was
responsible for the high incidence of cancer of the throat in parts
of Russia and Africa.

Instead of sticking to his title's intentions, MacLean had become
too scientific and much of what he had written had already been
done by people much better qualified to do so.

Another specialist thought the manuscript was vague and ram-
bling and that the lay reader would end up more confused than
informed. MacLean had obviously been influenced by the clinicians
at the expense of the research workers. 'Quotations from holders of
extremist views (i.e. Sir David Smithers) should be balanced by
those of others who have had some experience in bringing scientific
judgement and expertise to this incredibly complex problem,' said
one man. 'In short, I feel the author would be ill-advised to publish
this work and the Institute should be wary of being associated with
it (even though this might mean the loss of a profitable source of
income).'

Having, among other things, run into cross-currents in the profession, MacLean took the hints and the book never did see the
light of day.

20

Soon after Jacky Leiper arrived at Villa Murat, Alistair MacLean announced he was to be working on a book and suggested that Gisela and the boys should go up north. 'Up north' from Switzerland meant back to her native Germany, and Gisela didn't hesitate over the suggestion. Off she went with the two younger children, Michael and Ali, away from the quarrelling which still persisted even now that they had changed their environment.

Michael can still recall the arrival back at Geneva Airport at the end of their vacation, when there was no sign of his father to meet them. 'My mother knew instinctively that something was wrong.' Something was very far wrong indeed. In their absence, Alistair had become caught up in a whirlwind of activity which began when his London wine merchant friend, Lewis Jenkins, unwittingly introduced him to another woman.

It all sprang from a phone-call to Jenkins, in which an insurance broker friend said he had met a French lady called Marcelle Georgius, who was interested in films and desperately keen to meet Alistair MacLean. When he told her that his friend Lewis Jenkins was also a friend of MacLean, he had spoken the first words in an amazing chain of events. There was nothing for it but a lunch at the London Waldorf, over which she pressed Jenkins for an introduction.

He assured her that MacLean had a limited tolerance of women, especially where business was concerned. Under pressure, however, he agreed to let him know about her request and the response from

Geneva was: All right, let her come – as long as she pays her own fare. (The sentiment was prophetic.)

On his next visit to Geneva, Lewis Jenkins took Marcelle Georgius with him and they all met for lunch at the Hôtel du Lac at Coppet, not far from MacLean's house. Lewis had taken out smoked salmon, which Alistair liked to give to his close friend Jackie Stewart, fellow Scot and former world champion racing driver, who lived nearby.

Marcelle's story was that she was working as a film producer and her company had given her the task of persuading MacLean to sell them the film rights to one of his books. The lunch was a convivial affair, after which Lewis Jenkins and the vivacious Marcelle flew back to London. Ten days later, the wine merchant had occasion to be back in Geneva and was due to be met at the airport by Alistair. But there was a shock in store. He was met by Alistair *plus Marcelle*.

Where had she come from? The mystery remains to this day as to who took the initiative but there is evidence of follow-up conversations on the telephone in which Marcelle made her seductive pitch and Alistair responded with the sudden release of a Scottish Calvinist who has been keeping his lust under control for too long. The outcome was that the new lady in his life had flown back to Geneva and moved into Villa Murat, in the absence of Gisela – all within ten days of their first meeting. What's more, Alistair had news for Lewis. They were planning to get married.

The Welshman wobbled in a state of shock and disbelief. But there she was, sporting a huge ring which must have cost Alistair a fortune.

'But what about Gisela?' he pleaded. 'She's a friend of mine.' He urged MacLean to pull himself together, but all he got in return was a request to fly to Jersey to see Marcelle's husband. What for?

'See if you can buy him off,' said Alistair.

Still reeling, and now bereft of his customary confidence, Jenkins flew back to Britain and onwards to Jersey to see the husband, Marcelle's second, who expressed no surprise at all and indicated that Marcelle would go anywhere if there was money.

So who was Marcelle Georgius?

Born in Paris in 1935, she was the daughter of well-known French music-hall entertainers, Georgius Guibourg and his wife, Marcelle Irvun. Georgius had once been a name to rank with that of Chevalier in his own homeland, even if it didn't mean much beyond France. Marcelle, a small, dark-skinned bundle of energy and ambition, who claimed aristocratic blood, wanted to be a ballet dancer but when that failed she crossed to England in the mid-fifties, aged twenty. Among the few people she befriended was the Belgian actress Bettine le Beau (remembered from television as the lady much pursued in the *Benny Hill Show*). On one occasion, they both went after a television role. Bettine landed it and admired Marcelle for her generosity in defeat. Working through the Aida Foster agency in London, she did pick up small parts, once appearing as a French maid in a George Sanders film.

While still very young, however, Marcelle met and married Stewart Pulver, the London furrier, and gave birth to her only child, Curtis, in 1956. That marriage was short-lived and she then fell in love with an acquaintance of her husband, Anthony Arden, a Londoner who was making his way in fashion and property. He was sales manager for Cyril Kern of Digby Morton at Reldun, the couturier who made the break-through in ready-to-wear clothes in Britain.

Cyril and Doreen Kern arranged the Ardens' wedding day and Doreen and Marcelle became friends, though they saw less of each other when the couple went off to live in Jersey, where Tony went into the property business. The contact was resumed when Doreen received a phone-call from Marcelle, who said she had walked out on Tony but was penniless and needed help. The Kerns invited her to stay, which she did for a month. Then her father died and left her some money, which enabled her to take a flat of her own in Church Street, Kensington.

'Marcelle always seemed to be on the perimeter of the film and theatrical world,' said Doreen, 'looking out for that script which would give her a break. I never quite knew what her role was to be. Then, out of the blue, I had another call to say she was going off to Switzerland but would be in touch in a few days. She was alone in London, without many friends, and I always felt somehow responsible for her.'

The next call came from Geneva, to announce that Marcelle had fallen in love and was staying. She had gone out to interview Alistair MacLean, the novelist, and it was love at first sight.

Marcelle had never been short on self-advertisement. As part of her dream to be involved in the film-world, she had taken a full page in a trade journal to announce herself as a producer. While married to Tony Arden she did have a part to play in a motion picture company which he ran, but she was always pitching herself beyond reality.

Still in property in Jersey and now happily remarried, Tony remembers his ex-wife as vivacious and living on a permanent high. 'Her parents were famous and successful theatricals and she was always trying to live up to that image.'

By 1971, when Tony was having that visit from Lewis Jenkins to test his reaction to a divorce, his marriage was on the rocks and he had no wish to delay the process, even giving grounds to expedite it. This all happened around the time of the Cannes Film Festival and, after a phone-call from Alistair himself, he went down to have dinner with him at Cap d'Antibes. It was the only time they ever met and it turned out to be a convivial occasion, during which they both got drunk and parted on the good and understanding terms of one man giving up his wife to another. Tony Arden's lawyer thought he had made the divorce too easy.

Back at Villa Murat, Jacky Leiper had learned in her short time as Alistair's secretary that the marriage was splitting up anyway and that he was going through a miserable period of self-analysis. She had not, however, bargained for the new lady in his life, who had clearly arrived at the most opportune moment for her purpose. Marcelle and Alistair were suddenly living at Villa Murat together – son Lachlan, who had not gone off with his mother, was also living there as a witness to this extraordinary scene – and she was announcing openly that she was going to marry him.

All hell broke loose with that call to say Gisela and the two younger boys were at Geneva Airport, on their way home from Germany. The panic to remove one woman before the arrival of the other would have been worthy of an early Hollywood comedy, Alistair swiftly but imperfectly evacuating Marcelle to the Hôtel Richmond in Geneva and the two women missing each other by the neatest of slapstick timing.

Michael remembers arriving back at the villa and the discovery, by his mother, of another woman's nightdress in the bedroom. If

Alistair had not yet had a chance to explain, the moment of truth had definitely arrived.

Gisela remembers it clearly. 'He told me he had met someone else and when I asked if he wanted to live with her or marry her, he said he wanted marriage. I realized how serious it must be. I just felt that that was it. And because we had had the bad moments, I also felt that at least I would be able to bring up the children in peace.

'To me, Alistair had seemed a person who was not easily influenced by people. I decided it must have been the alcohol. So he went away to live with her and from time to time would phone to see how things were. Now when I remember the bad times, it is very painful. So I want to remember the few good things.'

The calm and poise with which Gisela received his news came as a mixture of surprise and relief to MacLean, whose twenty-year connection with the German girl who so stirred his heart at the Godalming hospital was being swept aside by a ten-day vortex, with consequences which only the distant gods would know.

As the vibrations from Villa Murat reached Britain, friends and relatives were thrown into confusion. The first hint of dramas ahead reached Ian and Marjory Chapman while holidaying on Lake Como. It came in a phone-call from Alistair to say he had made contact with a woman called Marcelle, a film producer who was extremely interested in his work and wanted to visit him. In fact she was arriving next day.

Chapman was cautious. 'Whatever you do, don't sign anything. Just listen. Remember, there are lots of sharks in the film industry. Tell her, if she wants to negotiate, to see me when I get back to London.'

After dinner on the following evening, Chapman's phone rang again. 'She has just left and I was most impressed,' Alistair enthused. 'I have never met anyone with such charisma. She's brilliant. You are going to be as impressed as I am.'

Chapman would reserve judgement on that. At least nothing had been signed but it was clear that the canny Scot, who could be slow to rouse, had been bowled over by the charms of this mysterious lady. Ian Chapman wanted to see her for himself and didn't have long to wait.

He was just back in London when there was another phone-call from his favourite author, who had by now settled snugly into a newfound love-nest at Hôtel du Lac in Coppet, just down the road from Villa Murat, and was cooing like a man transformed.

'I'm coming to London, Ian. Will you have dinner with me? I'll be staying at the Royal Garden in Kensington.'

Ian Chapman duly turned up at the Royal Garden, asked reception to tell Mr MacLean of his arrival and went into the cocktail bar. Soon the normally introverted Alistair came bounding in, beaming all over, in a manner quite unrecognizable.

'I have to tell you something,' he said. 'And you are not going to like it or approve of it.' He was bursting with his news. 'We are booked in as Mr and Mrs MacLean, you know.'

'You and Gisela?'

'No. Me and Marcelle.' He gave the shock-waves time to settle before adding, 'I know you won't approve, you being a son of the manse and all that.'

'Me a son of the manse? And what are you?' Chapman exploded.

Before the conversation could continue, her ladyship floated in, all frills and feathers and gushing with charm. 'I have heard all about you, Ian, and have been so looking forward to meeting you,' she purred.

Marcelle talked endlessly about what she allegedly owned. She had a scrap business, and Alistair, by now carried away with the situation, was augmenting her claims with enthusiasm. 'Yes, and she owns cargo boats,' he added proudly, like a man hopelessly infatuated.

Chapman was incredulous. Here was a man for whom he had the greatest liking and respect being carried like a lamb to the slaughter. The final piece of intelligence before his departure was that Marcelle's father had written the song 'Sur le Pont d'Avignon'. He drove home, replaying the whole bizarre experience in his mind: the films, the scrap business, the cargo boats, 'Sur le Pont' . . . ? Surely that couldn't be.

He checked. Her story was a lot of baloney. (Her father had been responsible for other songs but not that one.) Alistair MacLean was indeed hooked by his Latin lover, all the more extraordinary to those who had never seen him as a lady's man and thought he was more at home just messing about in boats.

Those closest to him, however, did suspect a deep-seated fear of sex, dating back to that Calvinistic background which acknowledged the necessity of God's plan but condemned the sinfulness of enjoying it. Women were kept at arm's length in his fiction; but such men are frequently vulnerable. Gisela was almost certainly the first real woman in his life, a lady of undoubted calibre whose Teutonic veneer may have concealed more subtle depths of passion, if only Alistair had known how to reach them. But there was a coolness in her nature. And now along had come this fiery little Frenchwoman, with her more obviously winning, seductive ways, who combed his hormones into a belief that sex had truly been invented in the Swinging Sixties. This was discovery time, when more than eight bells tolled, the moment of carnal truth which he had long heard condemned from the Scottish pulpit – that moment when the gates of hell fling wide and lustful men descend into the pits of depravity. And now it had all happened to Alistair, the quiet, reserved, well brought up son of the manse who told interviewers he didn't approve of permissiveness.

It was significant that his mother had just died, she who exercised such control over her son, even in his middle-age, and in front of whom he hardly dared touch a drop of alcohol. Now she was gone, the forces within him were liberated, responding to a woman whose *joie de vivre* was disarmingly attractive and whose blatant and unsubtle determination to land him had a certain charm of its own. In this cauldron of passion, he didn't really stand a chance. At the beginning of the affair, the emotions aroused within him would have challenged any influence in his life, including his mother's. Whatever the clandestine affairs of the past, this one was open for all to see.

Soon MacLean was announcing plans for his divorce from Gisela, and Ian Chapman was making a last-ditch appeal. 'Go ahead and have your fun if you must, Alistair. But for God's sake, don't marry her!'

It was all to no avail. Having settled into his suite at Hôtel du Lac, he proceeded with his plans for divorce and was soon back in London, asking Ian Chapman to be best man at the wedding. Chapman accepted. If that was MacLean's wish, he would certainly oblige, however much he might regret what was happening.

The wedding itself took place, ominously, on Friday 13 October

1972. For the writer's friends, it was at the best a day for amused
resignation. There was MacLean arriving at Caxton Hall register
office in central London, a place of white tiles looking more like a
courtroom than a setting for a wedding. And here came the bride,
in a white shortie dress with the inevitable feathers. After the register
had been signed, she was sitting on a bench with little, short but
shapely legs dangling well off the floor, grinning like a Cheshire cat,
clapping her hands together gleefully and saying quite audibly, 'I've
done it! I've done it!'

The knot tied, they all went back to a flat in Little Chester Street,
for a reception at which Ian and Bunty tried to unravel the mixed
collection of people. (Discreet enquiry revealed that they were
mostly odds and ends from the film-world.) Then, away the loving
couple went for a honeymoon in Amsterdam, the bestselling novelist
swept off his feet by an unknown actress with ambitions to be a film
director.

But if the comedy of Caxton Hall seemed to herald a newly
wedded bliss, the ill-omen of an unlucky Friday the 13th was to dog
the celebration in the land of tulips.

On the first morning of the honeymoon, Marcelle was still in high
spirits as Alistair took her to a diamond factory and bought her a
ring for £2,500. Before that day was over, however, she had a much
clearer view of the obverse side of his nature. Indeed, she would
later claim that her new husband came very close to drowning her
that night in a bizarre scene which started at a party in their honour,
when Alistair became drunk and was photographed grabbing at a
young girl.

Marcelle said she was so upset that she ran into the street and
went for a stroll by the canal – one of those waterways used in the
exciting motor-boat chase in MacLean's film *Puppet on a Chain*.
Furious at her sudden departure, he allegedly chased after her and,
in the ensuing row, pushed her into the canal. It took some other
party guests to appear on the scene before she was fished out. That
was no more than a token of things to come.

David Bishop's introduction to Marcelle was hardly less of a
surprise than Lewis Jenkins's, coming out of the blue as he arrived in
Geneva to accompany his client on a drive to the famous Baumanière
Hotel in the Camargue. This was a few days after Marcelle had
moved into the Hôtel du Lac with Alistair. He found himself acting

as a chauffeur, with the lovers sitting in the back of the Mercedes holding hands all the way. Three days in the beautiful Camargue were more than enough.

Alistair was so befuddled with love that he asked David Bishop to take Marcelle to lunch so that he could discuss her proposal for running his business affairs. Quite apart from wanting to make films of his books, she wanted to have her accountant involved in what Alistair was doing. Tactfully, Bishop explained there should be no need to become concerned in his business affairs. If she wished to try setting up a film production of one of his books, that would be up to him.

At that very early stage in their relationship, she was not only elated at finding herself attached to a famous author but was delighted at the thought of having his money at her disposal. Bishop, too, was instructed to see Marcelle's husband, Tony Arden, who met him at his London club and was quite reconciled to losing his wife.

Bishop was alarmed to find that Marcelle's accountant was now on his doorstep, with nothing to offer except a curiosity about Alistair's finances. Alistair eventually agreed with Bishop's view and nothing more was heard of that particular man. But Marcelle was not letting up. She now had a solicitor who was pursuing the same aim and the two legal men flew to Geneva to discuss the joint activities of their respective clients.

The warning signs were clear but the stubborn Scot, who still fancied himself as a hard-headed businessman, melted into marsh-mallow in the hands of his new lady, who so dazzled him with his own diamonds and a variety of sexual novelties that he seemed totally blinded to reality. She had pin-pointed his Achilles heel, and exploited it to the full.

As some indication of the inner turmoil engendered by his involvement with Marcelle, he kept coming back to the fact that, 'I could never have done this if my mother had still been alive.'

Indeed he couldn't.

21

In view of a marriage which had lasted the best part of twenty years, producing a family of three sons, one might have expected a more determined fight from Gisela. After all, she had come to Britain in the aftermath of her country's defeat in war and fallen in love with a Scottish student with whom she struggled through penniless days of early marriage before being catapulted to prominence with the fairy-tale of her husband's success. Was this how it was all going to end?

Friends believe that Gisela had had enough and was privately adopting an attitude of 'good riddance', sad though the circumstances had been. When the separation reached the point of divorce, which she was granted on grounds of desertion in 1972, the whole matter was completed amicably, with Gisela given outright ownership of Villa Murat (an extremely valuable property) plus an annual allowance to keep her in good style for the rest of Alistair's life. She had custody of the children, though Lachlan, by then eighteen, chose to go with his father; and she was within easy reach of her native Germany, where she naturally had more connections than in Switzerland.

Having narrowly missed each other on that day of crisis, she and Marcelle came face to face just once. In fact, they all sat down to dinner together – Alistair, the two women and the children – at an arranged meeting in Hôtel du Lac. 'Marcelle acted very funnily,' Gisela remembers. 'But I can't say I resented her.'

Caught in the middle of the break-up, David Bishop harboured mixed feelings. He certainly knew of the strain and lack of intimacy between Alistair and Gisela and what dangers that presented; he also tried to take a less harsh view of Marcelle than some others and acknowledged her as an attractive and sexy woman for whom Alistair had clearly fallen head over heels. It had been a courtship of red roses and melancholy partings, all of which surprised Bishop as much as others. He too would have been among the last to brand the writer a womanizer, having found no trace of it when Alistair came on those visits to his bachelor flat, the sort of occasion when such matters could surface.

Bishop felt Marcelle was due credit for reviving MacLean's emotional life, bringing him out of his shell and encouraging him to take more interest in his appearance. He dressed more suitably, had his teeth attended to; it was the age-old story of a man being taken in hand by a new woman and surprising all and sundry by his sudden willingness to do all the things he wouldn't have dreamed of doing before.

That did not allay the solicitor's alarm about the lady's designs on his client's money. It was not long before she had set up her own film production unit, operating from a converted flat which she sometimes occupied in Knightsbridge, London, and was employing one or two well-known people in the British film industry to pursue the ambition of making movies from Alistair's books.

An enormous amount of his money was being used in an attempt to get productions off the ground, but to no avail. And wherever she went in this newfound life-style she insisted on five-star hotels and chauffeur-driven cars, squandering money in all directions. Having just extricated MacLean from the financial doldrums of his experience in England, Bishop was now appalled to see what was already happening as Marcelle tightened her grip on his business affairs. If he spared her the label of 'gold-digger' it was only because that inferred a hoarding of gains for personal use. Marcelle didn't wait that long.

Now that she and Alistair were married, they embarked upon an extraordinary nomadic life, in which they never had a settled home of their own. They would flit from Geneva to Cap d'Antibes, on the fashionable Riviera across the bay from Nice, or to a flat in Little Chester Street, London, onward to California and back to Cannes, renting property which ranged from Lord Blakenham's villa in the

South of France to the former homes of cinema legends in Los Angeles.

In the manicured magnificence of those broad Beverly Hills avenues, many a sumptuous mansion changes hands on the strength of having once been the home of this or that departed star. The MacLeans were no exception. Their rented little palaces included Marilyn Monroe's old home on North Doheny Drive – not that the famous sex symbol ever owned that house or any other except the Brentwood bungalow, where she met her tragic end in 1962 – and others which were credited to Boris Karloff, who played Franken-stein's monster, and Bela Lugosi, the Transylvanian-born actor who was even more steeped in horror, gaining fame for his Dracula performances in films. In view of what transpired in their Californian experience of later years, the MacLeans would have done better to seek something in the mould of a Doris Day residence!

During the various travels, Graham Lord of the *Sunday Express* managed to track down MacLean in his luxurious penthouse flat overlooking the bay at Cannes and was surprised to be given such a generous welcome, particularly since he had just described his most recent novel, *Caravan to Vaccares*, as 'the worst written, feeblest and most boring novel I have read by an established author this year . . . an insult to his vast army of faithful fans'.

Lord's reward for that was a ten-hour interview, though it has to be said that Alistair dropped off to sleep for four of those hours. The *Sunday Express* man had plenty of time to assess him, through speech and slumbers, and was struck by the mass of contradictions:

He is a resident of Switzerland who speaks with a broad Scots accent and lives in France although he speaks the language very badly. He is the father, by a German mother, of young sons who talk with a transatlantic twang because they go to an American school in Geneva. He now shares his life with a French ex-actress turned film producer and is a fabulously paid film script-writer – selling stories as films even before they become novels – and yet he says, 'I detest the film world. Why? I think it is meretricious, cheap. Apart from authors, they're the biggest band of rogues in the world.'

He says he finds writing a chore and describes himself in his passport as 'hotelier' yet has probably made more out of joining words together than anyone except Harold Robbins who, when he's not in California, lives, as fate would have it, just down the road in a villa at Le Cannet.

Unlike Harold Robbins, however, Alistair MacLean did not believe he was the greatest writer alive, either in 'basic English' or in any other type of English. Nor did he think a great deal of Mr Robbins's writing.

'I think he's bloody awful,' was how he put it. 'He and Ian Fleming are two writers I cannot stand. Take Fleming – I couldn't stand his basis of sex, sadism and snobbery. If you require those things, you are not a writer.'

Such was the peripatetic nature of married-life for Alistair and Marcelle that Gillespie MacLean was found writing in bewilderment to Ian Chapman at one stage, asking if he knew where he could find his brother with a letter.

In the beginning, however, their base was mainly at Hôtel du Lac at Coppet, those few miles nearer Geneva than Villa Murat, the splendid residence which should have been the family home but where Gisela was now alone with young Michael and Ali.

The situation at the Hôtel du Lac was nothing short of bizarre. Alistair and Marcelle occupied Suite 22, while there were adjoining suites for the secretary, son Lachlan, who was now eighteen, and Marcelle's sixteen-year-old son Curtis, a bright-eyed French-looking boy who had shown early promise as a child actor in films and had also appeared in the television series *The Pretenders*.

Alistair's Scottish secretary, Jacky Leiper, lived nearby but found herself working discreetly in the hotel suite, knowing that Alistair was achieving very little in the way of literary output. He was next door, otherwise engaged with Marcelle. Jacky was involved with the family, took care of arrangements, made appointments and had much to do with Collins in London, checking royalty statements and so on.

When Alistair did resume work, it was to write *Bear Island*, which took him back to familiar Arctic waters, that wartime graveyard of men and ships, and *The Way to Dusty Death*, in which a world champion racing-driver pretends to be a lush to trap those who are arranging fatal accidents on the track and causing him to be blamed.

Alistair had formed a close friendship with Jackie Stewart, and wanted to see him out of racing, feeling sure he was going to kill himself in that hazardous sport. Stewart was approached with a view to assisting in the making of the film and it was even suggested he might consider taking the leading role himself. He spent a great deal of time trying to make the project a success, taking them around the Grand Prix circuits of Europe and helping to film the Monaco race.

If it had been in the hands of an experienced and reputable director, instead of Marcelle, the project might very well have succeeded. But Jackie Stewart was soon to find that the whole idea had been aborted. He had been badly let down by both Marcelle and Alistair, who were lucky to get away without litigation. Stewart's lawyer had correspondence with David Bishop in London and it could only have been Stewart's own wish to retain good relations which persuaded him to let the matter rest.

During those researches, they would all be down on the Riviera, at the Cannes Film Festival and the Monaco Grand Prix. MacLean's villa at the time was right on the Mediterranean, an idyllic spot if ever there was one, and Jacky Leiper felt if he were seeking inspiration for his best work, he should have found it there. On those visits he would hold business talks with Jackie Stewart while, in the absence of socializing, Marcelle was already becoming bored and heading off back to London.

As if the plot were not sufficiently complicated, another key figure in the story of Alistair and Marcelle MacLean was introduced in the early stages of residence at Hôtel du Lac.

Anyone familiar with MacLean story outlines such as *The Hostage Tower* which were later developed as novels by other writers will know the name of Sabrina Carver, intelligence agent, whose dossier described her as 'sophisticated, independent, very feminine. This brilliant patrician beauty possesses all the social graces but when necessary can trade in her silver spoon for an AK-47.'

If MacLean created this under-cover character, he certainly did not create her name. Sabrina Carver was by then his real-life secretary, finding herself destined for the pages of his fiction before she even knew it. It was not the first time he had played this trick. He had done the same with an Italian waiter he befriended in Geneva,

Nikki Tracchia, who turned up as the villain in the motor-racing dramas of *The Way to Dusty Death*.

In the case of Miss Carver, her social graces were indeed very real, coming as she did from the English aristocracy, with Field-Marshal Lord Carver, former Chief of the Defence Staff, as her uncle, and being herself the daughter of Antony Carver, the writer, who had also worked as a military attaché in Madrid, at the Pentagon in Washington and with Nato at Fontainebleau.

Born in Madrid and educated in France and England, the real-life Sabrina Carver had all the sophistication and feminine charm described by MacLean, so much so that she would certainly have been a target for his amorous advances had she not already been sharing her life with the English painter Tony Fry, a member of the confectionery family. Tony still gives a passable imitation of Alistair's Scottish burr as he would tell him, frankly and reassuringly, 'I love that girl but I have never touched a hair of her head.' Sabrina confirmed that MacLean was in many ways a puritan and a prude, with whom she admittedly shared a deep affection but for whom she felt no physical attraction. Tony knew that Alistair was 'potty about Sabrina'.

She had come to him by another of life's curious routes. Looking for a job, she was advised by the American film producer Michael Brown to contact a Frenchwoman, Marcelle Arden. At what she described as a funny little flat in Kensington, she was met by this voluble lady who was fussing around in preparation for going abroad and asking if she would mind the telephone while she was away. 'Start on Monday' seemed to be the only arrangement. Sabrina Carver did that. The significance of Marcelle's trip abroad did not come until later. She was, in fact, embarking on her association with Alistair MacLean.

Minding the Peel Street telephone, Sabrina took a call from Geneva which asked her to come over straight away. In the brief introduction, there had been little enough time to absorb her new employer, but she knew from the beautiful black, straight hair that she was definitely Mediterranean, more French than anything, a Jewess and an amazing life-force, if more than a little over the top. In that dingy flat in Peel Street she had seemed to be conducting a range of incredible projects, from the importing of shrimps to the production of films.

'I had a certain admiration for her,' she said on reflection, 'though I thought she was on the edge of lunacy. She said her father was a composer of songs and I, too, got the story about "Sur le Pont". Her projects always seemed to be within a hair's breadth of coming off but they never did. There were no films; no imported shrimps.'

Sabrina flew out to Geneva and was met at the airport by Marcelle and Alistair. She was moved into one of the suites at Hôtel du Lac, the attractive but modestly sized hostelry by Lake Geneva which now housed MacLean's ill-assorted entourage. It already included one secretary, but the two highly competent ladies from different backgrounds sized each other up and tacitly accepted the incongruous nature of their situation, while deciding to make the best of it.

Jacky was the down-to-earth Scots lass with whom Alistair felt a comfortable affinity of race. Sabrina's uppercrust background gave her a cachet which he also found appealing. She had the self-assurance of the London set, was good fun and was very much at ease in any environment. Though total opposites in many ways, the two girls got on well together.

Once they had settled into the rather unconventional arrangement at Hôtel du Lac, Alistair asked the secretaries to go down to the South of France to find some alternative accommodation. Having parted with Villa Murat in the divorce settlement with Gisela, he had no ambitions to own property again. A rented place would suit the purpose and the Riviera seemed the natural choice for several reasons. Like Marcelle, it was French and warm, not that he was a sun-worshipper but he did like to sit out in the comfort of shirt-sleeves. It also satisfied his own love of the sea.

Not least, he was beginning to weary of the blandness of Switzerland and the South of France was within easy reach. So Sabrina and Jacky went in search of rented property and came up with the Casa Estella at Cap d'Antibes, a very pleasant, good-quality Riviera villa with its own garden sloping all the way to the sea. You could open the sliding doors in the dining-room and hear the gentle swish of the water below.

Once Alistair had moved into a new place and found his writing quarters, he could settle to the typewriter without difficulty. Given peace and privacy, he was not at all temperamental about a fresh environment, which was just as well in view of the peripatetic nature of his existence from then on.

While he applied himself to his books, Marcelle was to be found on endless shopping expeditions or dining out. Sabrina and Jacky lived out and the domestic arrangements were looked after by a marvellous cook, Marie-Thérèse.

Jacky Leiper found Alistair warm-hearted and attractive, in the way that a woman will want to mother a vulnerable man, especially when he seemed miserable. 'He definitely had charisma but I was not sexually attracted to him,' she says frankly. 'You needed to get into conversation with Alistair to realize what he was. You would not instantly have noticed him in a roomful of people. To me he was just a straightforward Highlander, not at all devious, but I used to feel a lot of people took him for a ride.'

There was a sense that he was buying friendship, with which to give his life a protective shield. Alistair was also becoming frustrated by the fact that he had written a splendid book like *HMS Ulysses* and had not been able to repeat that kind of performance. He would say over and over again, especially after a drink, 'I'm no good. But one day I'll write a good book.'

He wanted to write a trilogy on the Black Prince, adventurous son of Edward III and one of the figures from history who fascinated him. While still a boy of sixteen, the Black Prince had fought for his father and helped to inflict a memorable defeat on the French at Crécy in 1346. He was just the kind of romantic character to stir the writing capabilities of Alistair MacLean. Whether this was the new direction which might have produced the literature to which he aspired we shall never know. All we know is that he went relentlessly in search of greater heights.

His basic pessimism about life and continuous search for something more than he could find was a subject he had discussed many times with Gisela. 'Where do we go from here?' he used to ask her – and he wasn't speaking about their marital problems. 'There must be something more. All is chaos. All is chaos.' It was a phrase and a theme to which he returned again and again.

As for his own career, he knew his writing was not of the quality it had been before that three-year spell when he gave it up altogether. It had become more and more of a chore and a commercial enterprise rather than a literary satisfaction.

Jacky Leiper observed him carefully. 'I don't know why he didn't have the courage to write what he wanted to. He certainly had an incredible imagination but I sometimes felt he was scared to try the book which would have satisfied him.'

From her close-up view, she was astounded by that gift of thinking up a novel from page one to the end and then sitting down to write it – and not having to rewrite it. He completed his research and came to that point where it all fitted into place in his mind. From the time he sat down with all the thoughts, facts and structure already marshalled, it would take him no more than five weeks to complete a book. He would then pass over the manuscript for proper typing.

He was not the man to discuss his ideas but there were rare glimpses into the way his mind was working out details of a story. Walking with Jacky Leiper in Geneva one day, he suddenly stopped to look up at a penthouse flat which had a tree growing there. Something clicked. It had given him the idea about how to provide protection for his hero in *Circus*, which he was writing at the time.

Jacky Leiper was also reaching conclusions about Marcelle, having now experienced her at close quarters. 'She was unpredictable and extremely difficult to get on with. She could be great fun or absolutely ruthless but not someone you could really trust. I found her uncouth, showing little sign of breeding, a survivor who must have had to fight somewhere along the line.'

Marcelle had been close to her mother, who died early of cancer, but she didn't have a stable childhood. She was compensating with selfishness and was never slow to exploit the name of MacLean when it came to getting service and attention. 'I wouldn't have liked her as an enemy,' said Jacky Leiper. 'There was a vicious streak in her. There was a vicious streak in Alistair too but she could provoke it.'

But there were brighter moments, like the visits of Marcelle's godmother, Madame Paulus-Habans, who lived near Toulouse and would come to stay at the villa at Cap d'Antibes. She was a bright spark who had been a dancer at the Folies Bergère and was friendly with Edith Piaf's accompanist.

The situation, however, became all too fraught for Jacky Leiper, who left the MacLeans in the spring of 1973 and went off to work in Greece, determined to get them out of her system. Then, to her surprise one day, Alistair and Marcelle turned up at her Greek

Above *HMS Royalist* – Alistair's ship on the Russian convoys

Below Alistair as school teacher, with his class at Gallowflat School, Rutherglen, 1955

Above Alistair with his first wife, Gisela, and son, Lachlan, at home in Switzerland

Right Alistair at work on *The Guns of Navarone*, in his home at Clarkston, Glasgow

Right Alistair in Jamaica with his secretary, Sabrina Carver, and her friend Tony Fry, 1984

Below Alistair's second wedding. He and Marcelle cut the cake, 1972

abode and asked her to go back. Marcelle was doing the pressing, for reasons of her own.

'I think she thought Alistair might have an eye for Sabrina and that having me back might split any affection for her,' was Jacky's conclusion. 'She didn't see me as a threat.'

So she went back to work for the MacLeans, this time in a block of flats in the Florissant district of Geneva, a campus-like setting with manicured lawns and pathways winding between buildings, with geraniums on every balcony. The neighbours tended to be doctors and dentists.

The domestic merry-go-round had continued to spin. They had retained the flat in Little Chester Street, London (the one from which they were married and to which they would return between leases of foreign property), though Alistair's choice of a taxation base in Switzerland meant he could visit the United Kingdom for no more than ninety days a year.

When the lease at Casa Estella ran out, they rented a well-appointed flat in Cannes, at Résidence de Luynes on avenue Jean de Noailles, a top-floor apartment in a modern block, in which the lift came right into the flat. There was also a marvellous terrace. The rented properties were always fully furnished and expensive, though Marcelle would sometimes buy some pieces of their own to create a feeling of belonging. In all truth, however, they were never anywhere long enough to call it home.

They would turn up with an Irish address at Violet Hill in Bray, County Wicklow, which became known as 'Violent Hill' because there were ructions in the marriage even at that early stage. Sometimes in Cannes, Marcelle would end a row by stalking out and booking in at the Carlton Hotel.

While Marcelle and Sabrina were now to be found more often in London, Jacky settled into her second stint with the MacLeans, feeling that part of her duty was supposed to be keeping an eye on Alistair while his wife was away. From her own point of view, working for Alistair introduced her to a milieu which fascinated her, bringing her into contact with the kind of people you wouldn't normally come across in the course of a secretarial job.

Much of her work had to do with the family. Michael and Ali were still with their mother on the outskirts of Geneva while the eldest son, Lachlan, who had chosen to go with Alistair at the time of the divorce, was now living alone in the same apartment block as his father. ('We retain our privacy,' Alistair said, 'but manage to keep an eye on each other.')

Lachlan's skin disorder had not improved with time and at one stage his nose had to be reconstructed with skin from his forehead. Whatever the root cause of the condition, it was known that Alistair, too, could bleed from the side of the nose, perhaps indicating a genetic weakness of the arteries.

Lachlan was an intelligent and sensitive boy, with a fine turn of humour, well liked and arousing much concern and sympathy over his illness, not least from his father, who said many times that he would willingly give away all his money if only they could find a cure.

That indicated a parental love which was not always bestowed wisely, as the boys grew up with standards and expectations far removed from the prudence of Daviot. His favouritism for young Ali was ill-concealed and Gisela was still trying to effect a balance for Michael, another sensitive boy who was clearly not the genetic product of the MacLeans and seemingly aware of being the odd one out.

Lachlan and Marcelle's son, Curtis, moved around the various homes in that unsettled period of the seventies but were now in their late teens, when some sort of career should have been shaping up. Instead, for all Alistair's money and serious views about education, they had really missed out on a proper schooling. Their childhood had been little short of a mess.

In the family cross-strands, Curtis gave the impression of disliking Alistair and was naturally protective of his mother. He remembers being sent to one school where a headmaster made homosexual advances to him; thereafter Alistair engaged a tutor. Curtis went off to Israel for five months then set out to be a racing-driver when he was seventeen. That gained no support from Alistair, who was anxious enough to see his friend, Jackie Stewart, out of the sport. But Curtis persevered on his own and ended up in a serious accident.

His mother, meanwhile, had her eye on a flat in Rutland Court, London, and was determined to have it. Alistair bought it in her name, a fairly spacious apartment which became her British base from then onwards.

But wherever they were staying, a fair measure of chaos persisted in the lives of Alistair and Marcelle. In many ways it was a love-story, based on a fiery passion he had not known with Gisela, yet those around were in little doubt that it contained the seeds of its own destruction.

There were times when it became too much for Sabrina Carver. She would go back to work for another famous Scot, Bill Gibb, the top dress designer, whose clients included everyone from Elizabeth Taylor to the Begum Aga Khan.

22

For the first few years after he moved out of Villa Murat, Alistair had limited contact with the two younger boys. Then, suddenly, he and Marcelle took Michael and Ali on holidays to the South of France, the Greek islands and California.

Before leaving for America, they spent a few days at the Dorchester Hotel in London, where Alistair was drunk every day and Marcelle provoked him non-stop. The more he drank, the angrier she became, until she would scream at him about being an alcoholic.

His retorts would be on the level of 'Ach, shut up!' or he would pick up a fruit bowl and threaten to throw it at her. She matched him by breaking a mirror, which was neither a good omen for the journey nor the kind of behaviour youngsters should have been witnessing. Finally they flew off to California, checking in at the Beverly Wilshire in Los Angeles and helping to erase unpleasant memories by visiting Disneyland, the *Queen Mary* at Long Beach, and San Francisco.

Back home, Michael was sent to the famous Millfield School in Britain before going on, with Ali, to Aiglon College at Villars in the Alps, returning to Britain to sit their A-levels. Michael gained an O-level in maths and A-levels in French and English. Ali managed the O-level in Maths and English and the A in French and English.

They had drifted from school to school without any proper structure in their education or clear purpose for the future. They were spoiled, with too much money too soon, by a father who, for all his belief in the traditional ethics of his homeland, was giving them everything and nothing.

'He would give us twenty thousand pounds to buy a car and we could buy expensive watches and go where we wanted,' said Michael when I visited him in Topanga Canyon, in the hills above Los Angeles.

'That was all very unhealthy. You become complacent and it anaesthetizes your desire to do something for yourself, much more than if you didn't have money in the first place.'

He claims to be the only one of the three boys to have got a business going and to have made anything of it. He started an interior designing company in Geneva, albeit with a helping hand from Alistair. There was nothing wrong in that. But he had sold out while still in his twenties, having opted for the softer climes of California, where he lives with the beautiful Marie Madeleine Mees from Paris. They were married and divorced but happily share a home in the hills, where Marie seeks to become a novelist and Michael translates her work into English.

He has little or no contact with his two brothers and limited sympathy for the elder one. 'Lachlan doesn't work and is happy to live quietly from the MacLean royalties,' is his verdict. 'Of course, he has had all those operations over the years but there are people with worse afflictions. As for my brother Ali, I don't even know what he is doing, except that he lives in Lugano.'

In fact, Ali hankered after a career in the film business and went to work during 1985–6 for Geoffrey Reeve, the man who directed his father's *Puppet on a Chain* and *Caravan to Vaccares*. Alistair wanted to assist in that career but nothing materialized.

He was also offering to establish Lachlan in the restaurant business, after a glimmer of interest had been shown in that direction, but the most serious attempt to give some purpose to his eldest son's life came through a journalist friend of Scottish background.

Iver Campbell was a translator, living in Switzerland, who was introduced to MacLean at a showing of one of his films in Lucerne. There arose the subject of producing a dictionary of international translators, a venture in which Lachlan showed interest and which Alistair was happy to back financially, as a means of employing his talents.

Mr Campbell put a lot of work into the project and Alistair was pleased to see that Lachlan was taking a genuine and intelligent interest, working fulltime on it. Progress, however, was limited, at a time when Alistair had already backed it to the tune of £70,000 and had run himself into a sizeable overdraft. David Bishop, who was in favour of the idea in the first place, lost his enthusiasm when he became aware of Campbell's unbusinesslike attitude, and advised him to withdraw support, which he did.

So little of substance materialized for any of them, contributing to a rather sad picture of a family at odds – Michael living in California, translating those novels; Ali in Lugano; Lachlan back in Britain, having bought a house in Blairgowrie, though not living there and more to be found in the London area; Gisela now alone in the large Villa Murat, a melancholy figure whose life should have been more richly fulfilled.

Looking back on the boys and their upbringing, a friend of the family said, 'There was none of the affection or exchanges you would expect to find in a normal family. The boys came out of it as ill-educated, uncultured, spoiled children. A kind of love-hate relationship seemed to develop between Michael and Ali.'

Given a choice of that childhood or a more conventional one, Michael left me in no doubt he would have preferred being in a small, loving family.

'My relationship with my father wasn't a relationship at all,' he said. 'He wasn't exactly a father figure. No one had a relationship with him. His only relationship was with alcohol.'

Damning stuff, even allowing for Michael's special position within the MacLean household. But as the family friend added, 'It was difficult for the boys growing up with a father who was famous and dogmatic, often drunk and very strict on the one hand, then giving too much before pulling in the reins. They didn't know where they stood.'

But Gisela's influence doesn't seem to have been much better, at least as far as helping towards any kind of constructive careers. So they ended up with an aimlessness, not uncommon among wealthy children but all the more galling when their position of privilege should have given them a head start in making a useful life for themselves.

What they had seen was a father who could stay off drink when he was writing and with deadlines to meet, limiting himself to a glass of wine but sometimes shaking as his body craved for alcohol until it seemed to be driving him crazy. When sober he could be tense and abrasive. Then he would stop writing and start drinking and wash himself in alcohol and come over all mellow, making no sense to his children, sometimes like a deranged patient babbling things like 'Do you know I'm the Chief of the CIA?'

'He would tell us stories of being in South-east Asia during the war,' Michael recalled. 'They were coming ashore and blowing up bridges but once they were intercepted, arrested and interrogated by the Japs. He said they pulled his teeth to make him talk. But he still had his teeth.' Michael grinned. 'And pretty awful teeth they were too. The Japs apparently wanted to know the whereabouts of their boat. There was a scene and my father allegedly shot a hundred and twenty-three people. My mother said to take his stories with a pinch of salt.

'I remember we could witness his shifting moods; he could be insulting or mild and effusive and full of goodwill. Those abrupt changes were all to do with the drink. He would suddenly become the humble Scot, saying things like "Och ay, ma boy," and be friendly, especially to strangers.'

Just as his father welcomed all and sundry to his study at Daviot, Alistair would take the gardener in to have a drink and treat him like a brother in arms. Similarly, he would listen to their stories and give them more than the minister's half-crown. At Haslemere, Alistair discovered that the plumber who was working at the house had an ambition to go to Australia and have his own business. So he paid for the plumber and his family to emigrate and establish himself Down Under. But they found they didn't like it. So he paid for them all to come back again!

Michael is tall, fairish and articulate, with the bearing of a guardsman and recognizably Germanic. Though highly critical of Alistair as a father, he seeks balance in his comments and claims to have had compassion for him, aware that he was unhappy and uncomfortable with himself and therefore in suffering. His view of Marcelle was of a woman exaggerated in movement, as if constantly on stage, loud, outspoken, a bit vulgar but likeable. Although she had taken his mother's place, he did not dislike her as a human being. It was later before he heard of the things she did.

Gisela felt Alistair needed people to have good opinions of him and his generosity; she knew his approach with his own sons was totally wrong and probably dated back to his schooldays. 'He always

remembered a teacher who read out one of his essays in front of
the class and was critical. He was determined to show that teacher
he could write and I think that became his motive for succeeding.

'He thought the same challenging methods would bring the same
kind of response from his own boys so he was hard and critical with
them. But it backfired on him. They didn't respond in the same way
and it had a detrimental effect on their lives.'

Again, with the unbalancing effect of drink, Alistair would make
outrageous offers. He wanted Lachlan and Curtis to go off to Australia for work experience on a sheep farm, with the promise that
he would give them £30,000 each when they came back. Curtis
jumped at the offer; Lachlan didn't and, since it was on a both-or-
nothing basis, it fell through. Alistair probably wanted to get rid of
them for a time.

Again with drink, he would make the grand gesture. Marcelle
tired of sewing on the buttons he kept pulling off and one day
refused to oblige. At first he begged but finally offered her £5,000
to sew on a button – and paid her the cheque which, being Marcelle,
she kept. Similarly, he disliked going to the barber and asked her
to cut his hair; again she refused. With the same ritual, he is alleged
to have produced the cheque-book and paid her £10,000 for a
haircut. She later boasted of being the best-paid hairdresser in the
world.

Whatever vanity and nonsense was built into his generosity, there
is no doubting his sincerity in giving away vast amounts, finding
obvious joy in making dreams come true for people who could not
have afforded them otherwise. For that much he deserved credit.

For example, he took a fatherly interest in Nikki Tracchia, the
Italian waiter who was working at the Intercontinental Hotel in
Geneva when they first met. During the Gisela days, the MacLeans
would dine at the beautiful Carnival Restaurant in the hotel, a
favourite place in Geneva, where you could eat and enjoy a magnificent view of the city by night. Nikki (the one who became the villain
in *The Way to Dusty Death*) later moved out of town, by coincidence
to be head waiter at the same Hôtel du Lac, near the MacLean
home at Celigny. Alistair was a regular patron when Gisela went
home to Germany and would sometimes move into a suite instead
of staying by himself, ending the evening in the company of his
favourite waiter. Nikki was an early witness to the arrival of Marcelle

and was appalled at the way she seemed to insinuate herself into Alistair's life and was so swiftly able to tell him, 'I'm going to marry that man.'

Nikki Tracchia then left the Hôtel du Lac and bought his own place, the Cerf at Cran-près-Celigny, which was even nearer the MacLeans' Villa Murat. When he broke the news, Alistair walked away in silence and didn't reappear for two months. Then one day he turned up at the Hôtel Cerf. 'You are still alive? Tell me, what have I done?' asked Nikki. Shamefaced, Alistair took him aside and told him of the money he had lost with people who were supposed to be his friends.

'And you – you who I consider to be like my son – go away and buy a hotel and don't ask me for a penny. I wanted to help you. I'm sorry I took it so badly but that's how I felt.'

When Nikki was just a waiter, Alistair had often challenged him on what hotel or restaurant he would like to be his own. Now he had taken offence, as he was prone to do. It was when Lachlan went to work in Nikki's kitchen and seemed to enjoy the experience that Alistair had thoughts of buying his son a restaurant, perhaps involving his favourite waiter once more. But nothing came of it.

Nikki, who has now graduated to the spacious Hôtel Beau Rivage at Nyon, on Lake Geneva, accused Marcelle of trying to break his friendship with Alistair. Again, he arrived rather sheepishly to ask, tactfully, if it was true that, last time they dined there, Nikki had offended Marcelle. Of course he hadn't. Then he remembered how Marcelle had baffled him that evening by breaking into French. It was unusual. But Alistair wouldn't understand what was being said and she was then able to make the accusation.

When Nikki went back to marry a girl from his native village of Guilmi, near Pescara, he thought there was some mistake when a Rolls-Royce arrived for his honeymoon, complete with chauffeur. It had been ordered by a gentleman in Switzerland. Because he kept it for only two days, Alistair then presented the young bride, Teresa, with a new Fiat car when they returned.

'We couldn't accept it,' said Nikki. 'But they say Scotsmen are tight with money? This was the most generous man you would ever find. He was such a brilliant, intelligent man, I just wanted to sit and listen to him.'

Marcelle was desperate to meet Alistair's relatives in Scotland
and Jacky Leiper found herself dispatched to her native land to
accompany her and Curtis on a visit to Gillespie and Margaret and
their children, who were then in the hotel at Balintore.

It was an incredibly beautiful June as they headed up the west
coast, though Jacky felt somewhat uncomfortable with this rather
ostentatious invasion from the South of France. Alistair had decided
to stay behind at Cap d'Antibes.

Gillespie and his family awaited their first sight of Alistair's wife,
whose arrival was finally announced by wee Marie, who came rushing in to announce to her mother, 'There's a Paki at the door!'
Marcelle, who was indeed dark-skinned, thoroughly enjoyed her
visit, and Jacky had never seen her more relaxed. George, the chauffeur, took Gillespie's children to school in the Rolls but little Shona
missed the run. When offered a later drive in the posh car as com-
pensation, she announced that her uncle had a coal lorry and she
preferred a run in that.

Next time Marcelle visited Gillespie and Margaret, Alistair went
too and they seemed on good terms. Gillespie had doubts about her
from the start but Margaret accepted her at face value and thought
she was good fun. It was during the World Cup of 1974 and Marcelle insisted on eating her dinner on her knee while watching the
football on television.

If Gillespie had reservations about Marcelle, his elder brother Ian
was more explicit. He and Bunty had thought Alistair and Gisela
were incompatible but there were stronger thoughts when they met
his second wife. Ian took to referring to her as 'Alistair's French-
Algerian hure' (Scots word for whore), perhaps a Highlander's
acknowledgement of the lady's more blatantly sexual attractions. It
was just another example of Alistair's poor judgement of people, he
concluded. But everything was either black or white to Ian.

Her Scottish sojourn over, Jacky Leiper decided it was time to
leave the MacLeans for the second time. She had gone back for the
wrong reasons and found herself looking after family affairs, often
sitting around doing very little. It wasn't a normal secretarial job at
all. With her different background, Sabrina seemed better at handling the situation but even she departed from time to time. For
Jacky, it was no longer tolerable.

Alistair and his entourage were still living in such a whirlwind of unsettled activity that one wonders how he achieved any continuity of creative work. His books kept coming out nevertheless – and there were occasions when he could even stand back and look at other, non-fictional, subjects as well.

23

No names, no pack-drill, but some of the bestselling authors I have met down the years, not least thriller writers, have turned out to be the dullest, most self-centred and humourless creatures you could wish to avoid – writing robots so wrapped up in their own particular genre that they seem to raise their heads for little else.

Thankfully, Alistair MacLean took time to cast his brilliant intellect around other subjects. One non-fiction book that did make it into print was his biography of Captain Cook, which appeared in 1972. MacLean was patently honest about possible shortcomings in his research, and it was not a long book, but given his interest in the sea, the choice of subject was hardly surprising. Captain Cook became the greatest combination of seaman, explorer, navigator and cartographer the world has ever known. He and Nelson rank as the two most revered names in the history of the Royal Navy. His father was a Scot and his mother from Yorkshire (which MacLean regarded as good as being Scottish!). Born in 1728, he undertook three historic voyages of world discovery which are classed among the most amazing achievements in all history. On the last, he landed in Hawaii, where the inhabitants had previously welcomed him with affection. This time he fell victim to a vicious outbreak of jealousy and superstition and was murdered.

It was in the vein of non-fiction that MacLean was often most relaxed and uninhibited, and it is interesting to speculate on whether this might have been a route which could have led him to the book which tore at his conscience, the one which eluded and tormented him and was surely within his scope of creation, if only he could have found it.

He was sometimes highly critical of Scotland and the Scots, for example, an expression which greatly annoyed his mother. Good manners prevented him from applying his cutting humour to those countries which gave him refuge, though he would occasionally permit himself a wry comment about the Swiss and say that, if one of their citizens fell off an alp, he would catch a franc on the way down. But his homeland was fair game, and some of his finest and most humorous observations were reserved for his introduction to the André Deutsch book on Scotland published in 1972.

To him, the most striking feature about Scotland was the vast droves of its loyal citizens who regularly departed their enchanted heath with an avowed determination never to return. Speculating on the reasons for this, he reckoned it had nothing to do with antipathy towards their fellow citizens, since the Scots ranked with the Austrians as the warmest, most friendly and hospitable of people. Nor could it be aesthetic revulsion since, leaving out the central belt, there was no more beautiful country in Europe. He could find no explanation in lack of space, poor climate or grinding poverty, nor in Dr Johnson's dictum about the fairest prospect in all Scotland being the highway to England, for the great majority were just as anxious to shake the English dust from their feet.

The true reason for the never-ending exodus was surely that the Scots were born adventurers, the greatest wanderers on earth, to whom not even the Jews could hold a candle – and they had an excuse.

Unlike the English, the Scots were Europeans, an interesting observation in view of contemporary demands for independence, based on that premise. The Scots were cosmopolitan while the English cleaved to the parish pump which was their England: even when building up the largest empire in history, which they couldn't have done without the more gifted colonizers from the north, the English remained invincibly insular and parochial, incapable of adapting to the ways of the people they colonized. New Delhi never had a chance; it was doomed from the outset to become the London of the sub-continent.

He made good sport of the Scots establishing strong links with Europe while the English were engaged virtually fulltime in pro-

viding the raw and bloody material for Shakespeare's historical tragedies.

But why did the Scots wander in the first place? He went on to
explain:

> We just have to accept that they kept on compulsively sticking
> their noses in other people's business, going either where they
> had no right to go or where no person in his right senses would
> have thought of going in the first place. They crop up everywhere.
> Find a man herding sheep in the furthest reaches of Patagonia
> and the chances are that he is a Scot. I know a village in the
> Italian Dolomites where the most commonly held surnames begin
> with 'Mac' – the remnants, I assume, of some defeated army
> although I am not sure. Scottish explorers, almost single-handed,
> opened up the Dark Continent, while the greatest explorer
> ever, Captain Cook, was half Scot. Take the Scots away from
> Toronto or Melbourne, from the City of London or, indeed,
> from the whole of New Zealand and the most dreadful confusion
> and dislocation would immediately overtake those unfortunate
> places . . .

Equally fascinating is the obverse side of this wandering coin
– the Scots' lachrymal obsession with nostalgia. They are even
worse than the Irish and heaven knows *their* broken-hearted
homesickness for the Emerald Isle, especially in song, is appalling
enough, although one would have to admit that 'I'll Take You
Home Again, Kathleen' could give 'Scotland the Brave' a pretty
close run for its money. One comparatively recent Scottish song
– Andy Stewart's 'The Scottish Soldier' – splendidly epitomizes
the mournful depths of nostalgia and self-pity in which the Scot
is tearfully prepared to wallow at the drop of a Glengarry.

In this particular song, a Scottish soldier is clobbered by the
enemy – a jarring note, this: in Caledonian song it is invariably the
Scot who clobbers the enemy – and is consequently condemned to
spend eternity in the green hills of Tyrol, although what he was
doing in Tyrol in the first place I have failed to discover. Anyway,
that is not the point. Here we have this poor lad, cruelly slain
while gallantly defending his beloved land – some Scots have
rather vague ideas as to the precise delimitations of their national
boundaries – condemned to sleep for ever in some foreign field,

a horrifying and totally unthinkable idea for everyone knows that
there is only one proper place for a Scot to sleep, be he alive or
be he dead, and that is Scotland. One would hope, incidentally,
that the idea does not take an irreversible hold on the twenty
million Scots overseas: to put it at its most delicate, the accommodation factor might pose a problem.

It does not require the facilities offered by a governmental or
university research team or, indeed, any particularly acute degree
of observation to arrive at the conclusion that there is an extraordinarily close affinity between this nostalgia for Scotland, where it
exists in its more excessive forms, and Scotland's most famous
product which the Scots have infelicitously named *uisquebae* or
the water of life – whisky.

In conjunction with the above it will equally have been observed
that wherever two or three Scots are gathered together, be it in
Surrey or Tierra del Fuego, they will immediately set about forming a St Andrew's Society and, inevitably, a Burns Society.

The ostensible purpose of the former is to sustain and
strengthen the cultural links with Scotia stern and wild by singing
a very limited selection of purely Lowland songs – not Highland,
for the odds are heavy that none of those present speaks Gaelic
– filling a confined space with the hideous banshee wailing of the
bagpipes, dancing the Highland Fling in calf-length kilts and
in general making themselves ridiculous. The Burns Societies'
dinners, allegedly dedicated to the preservation and honouring of
the memory of the immortal bard, should, on the face of it, be
even more cultural occasions were it not for the fact that for the
majority of people at the majority of such gatherings, Burns is
synonymous not with poetry but with haggis and an endless river
of Scotch: it is compulsory, nay, it is a sacred duty, to drink to
the poet's memory and hopeful health in the hereafter: no such
ludicrous degree of obligation attaches to the actual reading of
his poetry.

The Scot is a hopelessly sentimental creature at the best of
times and this is entirely forgivable: but when he employs his
declaration of deathless devotion to the homeland as a supposedly
legitimate and natural reason for getting plastered then the ami-
able nostalgia degenerates into a maudlin hypocrisy singularly
lacking in appeal.

This kind of hypocritically expressed longing for one's birth-
place is not confined to expatriates: it can be found in as splendidly
rich a form within the confines of Scotland itself, and the place
where it finds its highest and purest expression – if that's the
phrase I'm looking for – is unquestionably the city of Glasgow.

As my father was a redoubtable Gaelic scholar and my mother
a Mod gold medallist, as I had to go to school to learn English
and was forbidden to speak it at home until the age of fifteen, it
will be readily appreciated that I was brought up in an intensely
Gaelic atmosphere.

As a consequence of this, I was frequently called upon – the
permissive age being then not yet to hand refusal was unthinkable
– to attend a seemingly interminable series (I was about to use
the word 'variety' but they were all exactly the same) of concerts
given by the numerous West Highland and Island Associations
which were composed of the natives of those remote Utopias who
had come to Glasgow to make their fortunes (few failed to do so):
more often I had to attend ceilidhs, small, informal gatherings in
homes, hotels or rented halls, but no matter how large or small
or formal or informal those get-togethers were, the proceedings
of the evening formed an invariable pattern and no departure
from the norm was permitted: singer or speaker, he or she, each
mounted the platform in turn and broke their anguished hearts
aloud for their little grey home in the west, for that golden beloved
isle that had given them birth.

It was quite some time before I discovered that it was not only
bad form but absolutely forbidden to ask them why the hell they
didn't go back and live in their beloved isles if they meant all that
much to them for those, it became clear, were thoughtless and
crudely distressing questions which could cause a change in the
colour of the complexion, make a trembling hand reach out for
further sustenance and result in an embarrassingly rapid change
of the conversational topic.

This curious ambivalence that is to be found among a people
who will venture boldly to the uttermost ends of the earth while
loudly proclaiming that they wished they had never left home, is
to be found again in their reputation for being a magnificently
martial race, a reputation acknowledged and praised the world
over but nowhere with quite the fervour that it is in Scotland

itself. That the Scots are a warlike race is beyond dispute and nowhere was this more evident than in the internecine warfare that ravaged the country down the centuries when the clans pillaged and burned the homes and the crops of neighbouring clans, stole cattle and women with splendid indiscrimination and generally and, in retrospect, for no valid reason, hacked each other to pieces.

That those disagreements were, on occasion, economically motivated, which is nicer than saying they were based on sheer greed, is beyond question: but it seems, basically, to have been a form of national pastime, very likely because there wasn't much else to do in the Highlands in those days.

There couldn't have been much to do in the Lowlands either, for the Border reivers, advanced specialists in cattle rustling before anyone had ever heard of the Wild West, acquired a fearsome reputation to match that of the bloodiest of the Highland clans. Feuds were the great thing then and no clan worth its salt could afford to be without one, although there seemed to be general agreement that a feud that didn't last two or three hundred years wasn't really worth the having. My own clan, the MacLeans, who appear to have made a comfortable enough living from waylaying seafarers so incredibly foolish as to venture within eyeshot of their island fortress of Mull, had a permanent and permanently gory disagreement with the Campbells which both sides cherished down the centuries. It is demonstrative of how long memories can be in Scotland and how hard enmities die that when the Chief of the Clan Campbell, the Duke of Argyll, hired – only twenty years ago! – a MacLean as piper for his seat at Inveraray Castle, the consternation, near apoplectic shock and black burning shame of the MacLeans to whom such things were of near paramount importance – and it would seem there were considerable numbers of them – would not have been out of place three hundred years ago. In the good old days the claymores would have been out; today, the preference is for Biro pens and some pretty stiff letters to the *Glasgow Herald* and the *Scotsman*. We have fallen upon effete and anaemic days.

In more recent times the battlefields have moved from the glens to the cities.

MacLean was recalling the pitched battles between the pre-war Glasgow gangs, mainly from the Gorbals and Townhead, for which staff at the Victoria and Western Infirmaries stood by resignedly on a Saturday night. The young heroes of those clashes, their martial spirits deflated since the police relieved them of their knives, razors, bicycle chains, nail-studded clubs and other offensive impedimenta, rarely kept the doctors waiting long.

Regular confrontations between supporters of Rangers and Celtic football teams added to the length of the doctors' day.

Alistair MacLean's delicious analysis of the Scottish psyche not only gave him a welcome alternation to the normal writing style but showed clearly what depths of humour lay within him. It may even have allowed for a sublimation of the unhappiness which was gathering around him.

24

From time to time in their nomadic life, the MacLeans would turn up in London, separately or together, at their flat in Little Chester Street, or at the Connaught Hotel, or, later, at the house in Rutland Court which Alistair had bought for Marcelle. Bizarre happenings were not uncommon.

On one occasion, Ian Chapman received a phone-call in the middle of the night from a hysterical Marcelle, who said she was locked in a cupboard and that Alistair was outside with a carving knife, threatening all kind of things sexual. He asked if she had called the police but, anyway, he would be straight over. He dressed quickly and drove into London from his home in Cheam, only then beginning to wonder how Marcelle could have been phoning from a cupboard!

Arriving breathless at the flat, wondering what mayhem could be expected on the inside, he was received by a more composed Marcelle. 'Where's Alistair?' he asked, dashing past her. 'Upstairs?' He took the steps two at a time to find his bestselling author comfortably established in bed, no doubt after a few drams, and sleeping like a baby as if he had been there for hours. Marcelle was waiting at the bottom of the stairs.

'I'm so glad you have come, darling,' she said. 'Come and have a drink with me.'

'What's going on here?' asked Chapman, suddenly realizing that the lady was in a diaphanous négligé.

'I was just lonely and you are the only person I can talk to,' she said. Her husband's publisher disappeared speedily out through the door.

Lewis Jenkins was another who arrived at the London flat to see Alistair one day, only to find Marcelle alone and in seductive mood. It was evidently not unknown for her to disappear from the room and reappear naked.

Though Jenkins, like many more of Alistair's friends, had distanced himself from the Marcelle connection, he and his wife did go to dinner with them both at the Savoy in London. It turned out to be a night to remember – or, better, to forget.

Perhaps it was the quiet charm of Caroline Jenkins, but Marcelle seemed to take a dislike to her, and before the evening was out she had aimed a bottle of wine across the table, spilling it all over her. With that, she stalked out of the dining-room leaving a highly embarrassing situation and a distraught MacLean, crying on Caroline's shoulder and beginning to want Gisela back.

Ever a man of action, Lewis Jenkins took the situation in hand and tried to arrange a private plane to take Alistair straight back to Geneva. But by now Marcelle was back at the Connaught, complete with Alistair's passport. There would be no escape that night.

Until then, the Jenkins had been deeply concerned that Alistair had yet to realize his marital mistake. Having seen some tell-tale signs, they were also convinced that, under Marcelle's influence, he was no longer a stranger to drugs.

When Lewis managed to get Alistair on his own, he felt free to tell him that his own role in introducing him to Marcelle in the first place would haunt him as the worst day's work of his life. Lewis and Caroline were always happy to welcome Alistair, as long as he came without his wife.

On her visits to London, Marcelle would hold fabulous parties at the Rutland Court flat. There you would find guests like Liberace and Danny La Rue vying with each other, on one occasion, for the grandeur of their full-length mink coats, and Liberace entertaining on a piano which Marcelle had hired from Harrods for a mere £2,000. It was just one of her lesser extravagances. Alistair wasn't there that evening and what pleased Marcelle was the fact that she had sent out the invitations in the name of 'Mrs Alistair MacLean' and that so many guests had come in response to her and not Alistair. The signs were that her confidence was waning and she was needing the reassurance of her own position.

For another big social splash, Marcelle agreed to share the cost of the reopening party at the famous Walton Restaurant in London, after a terrorist bomb had been thrown into the premises. The Walton had been a favourite haunt of Alistair and Marcelle, a place where they had their own recognized table and were fussed over in the way that celebrities tend to be. There was a tragic story behind that night of terror, which might have rendered any subsequent celebration as rather inappropriate. Marcelle's son Curtis had a girlfriend whose parents became friendly with the MacLeans. For an anniversary celebration, they were welcomed to the Walton with the kind of reception accorded the MacLeans and were enjoying their meal when the terrorists struck. An explosive landed in their ice-bucket, and the girlfriend's mother was one of two diners killed.

Marcelle was nevertheless to go halves with the owner on reopening night but there were problems over her contribution; what friends were beginning to realize was that she was running out of money. For example, she borrowed £250 from Doreen Kern, her sculptress friend, to pay her maid – she still had a maid – and that was the last Doreen saw of her money.

Having originally gone to California to write a screenplay of *Circus* for Irwin Allen, Alistair MacLean was spending more and more time there. So it was to the West Coast that David Bishop was summoned in January 1976, to sort out the latest financial position. Among other things, MacLean had engaged an excellent American lawyer, Jerry Mehlman, who reckoned Collins were not paying enough for the writer's books. Mehlman was looking for more money in advance guarantees whereas Collins, in accordance with MacLean's own wishes it must be said, had tended to pay on the basis of royalties earned, thus spreading it more evenly. The American lawyer did eventually visit London, where the publishers agreed to a small percentage increase.

During the first six years of the seventies, MacLean's income had averaged around £550,000 per year, which should have been enough to keep him and his various dependants in reasonable style. Despite the high earnings, however, there was a large-scale draining of

finances which led to a highly embarrassing situation. Having earned
his first flush of money in the fifties and sixties, he had set up a
trust fund not only for his own children but for his eight nephews
and nieces, from which they would all eventually benefit to the tune
of around £25,000 each.

The Marcelle years had so depleted his funds that he confronted
his lawyer with the proposition that he would like a loan from the
family trust. Representatives of the beneficiaries came back with a
sharp and unequivocal reply, showing they didn't have faith in the
security of any loan. No money was going to be returned.

If it was to be squandered in the same way as the rest, their
intransigence was understandable; the other view would be that it
was Alistair's money in the first place and for his generosity he now
deserved some compassion. His pride would surely have compelled
him to pay it back.

Apart from the financial mess, it was now becoming clearer that
the marriage itself was running into ever deeper trouble, with strong
evidence that Marcelle was taking lovers, particularly in America.

In London, her sculptress friend Doreen Kern was in shock from
her own marital separation and the MacLeans invited her to come
over and stay with them for as long as she wished. Taking up the
offer in the early part of 1976, Doreen joined them at an address
in Alanda Place, Beverly Hills, one of two homes they were occupy-
ing in the film-stars' paradise, where she was introduced to a third
party in the life of Alistair and Marcelle.

Marcelle had already indicated that her sex life with Alistair was
less than satisfactory, and she told Doreen that he had asked this
other man to 'take care of her', presumably in both the physical and
emotional sense, at a time when he himself was going through a bad
drinking bout and had just discharged himself from a drying-out
clinic, the one frequented by Richard Burton.

Alistair was in the middle of a swirl of people and panic, created
by the fact that his absence for drying-out had left him far behind
with the next book, which the publishers were eagerly awaiting.
Someone was there to uplift each chapter as it rolled off his typewriter. Amid the chaos, Doreen suggested the others might care to
move down to the house in Doheny (the Marilyn Monroe connection) and to leave her to look after Alistair in her own quieter way.
This was agreed.

Given a small room near the kitchen, she locked her door at night as a precaution but felt sure he would not be violent with her. On the first morning she woke at four-thirty and heard cupboards being banged. Gingerly, she peered out and saw Alistair making breakfast, so she joined him for coffee as he cooked his sausages.

Then he went to his room, sat down at the typewriter and started work. For weeks and months he had evidently done nothing but now he was typing furiously. All he had needed was the peace and calm which Doreen was providing.

Marcelle phoned in the morning and was astounded to hear of the transformation. She said she would leave him to the care of Doreen, who sat happily by the poolside of what had been Bela Lugosi's old house. There were worse places to be than Beverly Hills, she thought, nursing the hurt of her own marital upset. From time to time she would take Alistair cups of coffee as he worked. Finally, after five or six days, he emerged from his room and said, 'Let's celebrate. I've finished the book.' Marcelle had overlooked a decanter of port and he took out two glasses and poured them a drink. Then he dropped his glass, which broke, and went for a brush, saying he would need to clear it up before Marcelle saw it.

Elliott Kastner had picked up an early warning that the MacLean marriage was heading for the rocks, financially and emotionally. Since *Where Eagles Dare*, he had always been looking for a chance to do more with Alistair but felt his books were losing their quality.

'I had heard he was in bad shape and was becoming a drunken, stupid bore,' said Kastner. 'I used to say to him, "Alistair, why are you poisoning your body this way? You should stop f—— moaning and get your f—— act together.' He seemed to be drowning emotionally, unable to produce.

'I had also met Marcelle and decided she was a dunce, a self-proclaiming, foolish woman without ability, who had no grace, dignity or class.'

Claiming a desire to put some meaning back into Alistair's life, he got him to an office at Twentieth Century Fox, gave him an idea for a film and told him, in his own inimitable way, to get on with it.

Set in Nevada in 1873, the idea took shape as the story of a relief train rolling across the frozen west of America to Fort Humboldt. Matching villains and heroes in the best tradition of the American

Old West, Alistair introduced mysterious passengers with smuggling and murder in mind. What started out as Kastner's therapeutic exercise for his alcoholic friend came on screen in 1976 as *Breakheart Pass*, directed by Tom Gries and starring Charles Bronson and Jill Ireland, whose real-life marriage gained worldwide attention in later years with Miss Ireland's courageous but losing battle against cancer. MacLean's health problems were self-inflicted.

After his close relationship with Alistair, Elliott Kastner was beginning to resent the encroachment of other film people on the writer's life. Having introduced him to the idea of scripting his own films with *Where Eagles Dare*, and feeling that he had brought him back on the rails with *Breakheart Pass*, he realized he no longer had his exclusive attention where films were concerned.

'He was a dead man when I picked him off the floor, breathed life back into him – and made him write,' he was to claim. 'He was looking to destroy himself and his books had become rubbish.'

Kastner certainly deserved credit for changing Alistair's fortunes with *Eagles*, though as far as the declining standard of his books was concerned it could well be said that that dated back to exactly the same point, when he transposed his habits and began to think in terms of film scripts first.

Though they remained in touch and mainly on good terms, *Breakheart Pass* was to be the last of their four films together, Kastner having become the most significant figure in MacLean's flirtation with the cinema.

Meanwhile, Sabrina Carver, who had been back working with Bill Gibb in London, received a call from the MacLeans to say they were now living in California and why didn't she come out and work for them.

To assess the situation, Sabrina set out with her friend Tony Fry and his three children, Lucy, Mark and Wilde. On arrival in Los Angeles, they were taken to the Doheny house.

Like Doreen Kern, Sabrina was surprised to find another man staying with the MacLeans.

But if the new arrivals from England thought they were to be staying at the Doheny house, there was another surprise in store. They were to be driven across Beverly Hills to another rented villa, the former home of Boris Karloff in Bowmont Drive, near Rodeo Drive, where they would be staying with Alistair, while Marcelle and her boyfriend remained at Doheny.

Like the Doheny house, the Bowmont Drive residence was modest by Beverly Hills standards, white-walled and red-roofed, with a pool – and a den for writing, for which the Doheny house had no provision.

As she settled uneasily to this curious domestic split, Sabrina encountered scenes so bizarre as to persuade her that Marcelle had gone mad and was really quite dangerous. For a start, it became clear that she was scheming for divorce while at the same time trying to establish Alistair's residential status in California, where she knew she would secure a better settlement.

Marcelle's lawyer was asking Sabrina for some of Alistair's headed notepaper, a strange request, she thought, until she remembered that Marcelle had been good at forging her husband's signature. Sabrina now suspected that the plan was to write letters in his name, saying how happy he was in the sunshine state.

Strange things had already begun to happen. Even before Sabrina's arrival, a letter bearing Alistair's name had been sent to Ian Chapman in London, saying:

I am in California to stay. I'm tired of being a wandering gypsy, living out of suitcases in hotels or rented flats. I have this place [the Doheny house] on rental for some months but hope and intend to buy a home here. Both Mary [his name for Marcelle] and I love this part of the world – to the staggering extent that she has put her much beloved flat in Rutland Court on the market.

Establishing domicile in California? Sabrina is convinced that Alistair had no intention of staying there. The signature also makes an interesting study. But that was not all.

Alistair and Sabrina, accompanied by an out-of-work American actor friend, set out for Mexico, where he could write his next book, *Seawitch*, outwith the taxation territory of the United States.

They found a condominium base at Puerto Vallarta, hired a couple of typewriters and became immersed in work, Alistair battering away on his IBM golf-ball to great effect and passing over the pages to Sabrina, who checked continuity and retyped them for final submission.

During their absence, however, Ian Chapman received another letter, this time signed by Marcelle, which included this further emphasis on residential intentions:

We are both extremely happy in California and it is hard to believe that we have been here for more than six months. At long last we have found a place where we can always live.

Always live? At that very moment, she was living it up in unconcealed adultery with her latest lover.

Down in Mexico, when the day's work was over, there was dinner and drinks and some discussion about the situation back in Los Angeles. Sabrina felt it was untenable.

'I know Alistair could be difficult, dogmatic and complicated and, like many rich people, he got spoiled. When he wanted something, he wanted it there and then. But at least he was a proper human being.

'When we went to Mexico, Marcelle mounted a campaign to say Tony's daughter, Lucy, had stolen money. I realized she had gone quite unbalanced and said I couldn't work there any longer.'

Back from Mexico, they were met at Los Angeles airport by Marcelle, complete with stretch limousine and sparing no expense. The marriage had obviously now gone wrong in a big way but, despite her cynicism, Sabrina still takes the view that Alistair believed in the marriage. 'He was no fool and would not have married her if he had not considered himself to be in love. Even at that late stage in Los Angeles, he still loved her and thought it could work.'

Following the return from Mexico, there were sinister happenings which would not have been out of place in the fictitious context of those MacLean stories in which 'Sabrina Carver' appeared as an undercover agent.

Young Lucy was called to the telephone one day when a voice told her, 'You had better get out of town. And don't try to see MacLean.' It is the kind of menacing incident which can happen in Los Angeles.

Tony Fry had returned to England but he was now back in California and he and Sabrina and the children quickly moved out to a base in Santa Barbara, intending to let the air clear at Doheny and Bowmont Drive. Anxious about Alistair, they tried to make contact but were unable to find him. Within that mystery, deep and potentially sinister, there were hints that he may have been virtually kidnapped by Marcelle and her strong-armed aides, force-fed with drink somewhere in Beverly Hills and held in some kind of crude attempt to establish his residence for the purposes of divorce.

Somewhere in that period, David Bishop received a letter from Alistair, asking for copies of all his contracts with a view to changing his American paperback publisher. They were to be sent to the Alanda Place address, where Doreen Kern had seen him. It was a strange letter in which he said: 'Always being hounded from pillar to post. The above is our latest address but we're only here on a very short lease.' That was dated April 1976, just a month after Marcelle's anticipation of living in California for ever.

Though the mystery was still unsolved and she was still deeply worried about Alistair, Sabrina was relieved to get back to her flat in Notting Hill Gate, London. Then one day her door-bell rang and who should be standing there but the man himself. 'I've got out!' he exclaimed. While anxious to know what had happened, Sabrina also knew him well enough to know what a secret and private and proud man he was. Unless he raised the subject, it was not for her to mention it; he didn't enlighten her.

He looked much the worse for wear but at least he had escaped any plot to keep him in California until his wealth was cornered – not that there was all that much left after those few calamitous years.

'He was a strong character to get out of that situation,' said Sabrina.

Alistair now wanted her to work for him once more but she refused. He pleaded and promised a new basis for their working relationship, in which she could stay in London and merely fly whenever required to wherever he happened to be living.

She moved from Notting Hill Gate to West Halkin Street, not far from Harrods, and entered a new phase as Alistair MacLean's secretary, which would cover the last ten years of his life.

The Californian experience was over. It had lasted for less than a year. Whatever expectations of it he had harboured when he went there, it had ended in misery and disaster. The fact that there was no sign of friends or glittering parties or even the most tenuous flirtation with the Hollywood set was of no consequence to Alistair, who was never one for the superficialities of life anyway. The deficiencies were of a more deeply personal nature.

Having now caused offence by not turning up at the wedding of Ian's daughter, Margaret, he met with a cool reception when next he phoned her parents to say he was planning a visit.

'Actually, Alistair, I don't care if you come or not,' was Bunty's response.

'Do you really mean that, Bunty?' he asked, taken aback.

'Yes I do.'

He duly turned up, anxious to make amends but also wanting to have a heart-to-heart talk about the state of his marriage. 'Do you think I should divorce her?' he asked.

Ian was straight to the point as always. 'Divorce her? You bloody fool, you should never have married her!'

It was time for action.

25

Crisis time in the marriage arrived in June 1976, when Alistair MacLean instructed David Bishop to consider divorce proceedings.

The two men met in London, along with Ian Chapman, and Alistair explained that he had no intention of remaining married to Marcelle, who had spent all his money and was widely denigrating his name. He was staying temporarily in London before returning to Geneva but was still talking about a return to California. Once again, Bishop had to point out the dangers of playing into the hands of Marcelle, who might bring a petition resulting in a very expensive divorce.

When Marcelle herself later came on the phone to Bishop, she was furious to discover that Alistair was planning to divorce *her* instead of the other way round. The lawyer told her there was plenty of evidence of her adultery, which she could hardly deny, and advised her to see her own lawyer. As a result, she gave instructions in both London and Geneva, the Swiss gentleman mentioning £500,000 as Marcelle's requirement for a settlement.

In subsequent talks with the London lawyer, it was suggested that Alistair would have to put up about £350,000, in addition to making a substantial annual payment. A figure of £25,000 was suggested.

Meanwhile, Marcelle was making phone-calls to Alistair, employing tactics which could only be described as blackmail, and her lawyers were advised to restrain her. While the legal people argued out a possible settlement, she managed to get herself into the Nigel Dempster column of the *Daily Mail* to explain why *she* wanted to divorce Alistair. That antagonized him considerably, especially when she was claiming in print that he was worth £5 million.

As Bishop explained to her lawyer, that was what he might have been worth if he had never set eyes on Marcelle; in fact, he was now down to no capital at all, having lived above his income for many years and well above it during his second marriage.

Before the crisis had reached that point, however, Marcelle made one last attempt at what she had so far failed abysmally to achieve – the actual making of a film.

Unwittingly, by approaching a young Canadian producer, Peter Snell, she was introducing yet another new character to the saga of Alistair MacLean, one who would play a significant part in his fortunes. Just as Elliott Kastner had arrived in Britain from the United States and decided to settle there, Peter Snell came fresh from the University of British Columbia with a degree in economics, reaching London in time for the Swinging Sixties. It seemed the place to be in that vibrating decade, with its Carnaby Street and King's Road, Chelsea, and the surge of Beatlemania. With all his life in front of him, Peter Snell was just happy to be young in Britain.

Anyone with thoughts of the film industry in those days had the choice of Rome, London or Hollywood, and Snell had not only fallen in love with the English capital but with one of its young ladies as well. Entry to the mysterious realms of film was a different matter, however, and it was a chance meeting with a guest at a social function which provided the catalyst.

That guest was none other than Rudolf Nureyev, the famous ballet dancer, whose defection to the West and subsequent rise to fresh prominence as the partner of Dame Margot Fonteyn had made him the target of many a documentary film-maker. But Nureyev was wary of approaches and that attitude didn't change until his trust and confidence had been gained by the quietly persuasive Peter Snell. This was different. Nureyev struck an agreement with Snell, who raised the money, put a crew together and, with no experience of the medium, watched them pursue their various tasks. With a title of *Behind the Scenes at the Royal Ballet*, he sold his documentary to television.

Now bitten by the bug, he was determined to remain in the industry and found his way into the production of Shakespeare films, including *The Winter's Tale*, starring Laurence Harvey, *Julius Caesar*,

with Charlton Heston, Jason Robards and Sir John Gielgud, and
Antony and Cleopatra, adapted for the screen and directed by Heston.

By 1972 Snell had become head of production at British Lion
Films, one of Britain's three major film companies, responsible for
the widely acclaimed *Don't Look Now*, with Donald Sutherland and
Julie Christie, and the award-winning *The Wicker Man*. British Lion
was sold to EMI in 1974 and Snell had become an independent
producer, with a base at Pinewood Studios, when he was called one
day by a lady who introduced herself as Mary Marcelle MacLean,
wife of Alistair MacLean, the author. Her purpose was to enlist
Snell's help in raising the money which would turn one of her
husband's books into a film.

The book was *The Way to Dusty Death*, she explained, about a
champion racing-driver who turned private detective in a bid to
uncover the activities of a European drugs ring. That was how Peter
Snell came to be introduced to Alistair MacLean, who regarded
him with the same distrust he felt for most film people, adding a
few jaundiced refinements in the case of the young Canadian since
he had come to him through the offices of Marcelle. Snell was not
to know that he had landed upon the run-up towards MacLean's
second divorce. He merely forged ahead with preliminary plans for
The Way to Dusty Death, only to find they couldn't sell the idea to
the film world. As often with motor-racing stories, there was a
difficulty in maintaining a character who had to spend so much time
behind the disguise of goggles. From Snell's point of view, it had
given him a year of contact with Alistair MacLean and he had also
discovered a splendid associate producer in Ted Lloyd, who worked
with Marcelle from the London flat.

While the MacLean marriage headed towards its end, Snell managed to retain his connection with Alistair, who helped with his
living expenses for a whole year while he pursued the idea of turning
another of his books into a film. This was *Bear Island*, set in the
Arctic Ocean, where a unit was to shoot a top-secret film.

Snell was now operating independently of Marcelle, who was
disappearing from the scene, and on this occasion he did indeed
produce a film, backed by Columbia and starring Vanessa Redgrave,
Donald Sutherland, Richard Widmark, Christopher Lee, Barbara
Parkins and Lloyd Bridges.

It was in the setting up of *Bear Island* that the long arm of coincidence stretched out to prove again that fact is stranger than fiction. With thoughts of finding a suitable screenwriter, Peter Snell had phoned the talented actor-turned-writer David Butler to ask if he had read the book. Though he had not read *Bear Island*, Butler could say very honestly that he was well acquainted not only with MacLean's other work but – would he believe it? – with MacLean himself. His father had been headmaster at Gallowflat School, Rutherglen, when the future novelist was teaching there, and they had met in the family home when David was back from St Andrews University, before going on to the Royal Academy of Dramatic Art in London. Butler had both appeared in *Emergency Ward Ten* and written some of the episodes, on the way to writing plays and other television material.

David Butler settled to reading *Bear Island*, coming to the conclusion that, while the idea and setting were very good, the story itself left much to be desired. Snell gave him his head to amend it for film purposes and Butler ended up as screenwriter for the film.

It took a little time before MacLean realized that the man who had reshaped one of his books for the cinema was none other than the son of his old boss, James Butler, but when he did, there were cordial messages to say they must get together some time. In his more alcoholic moments, however, he would confuse David Butler with his brother Denis, who had taught for a time at the same school where his father was headmaster and MacLean was a teacher. With such a lot to discuss from more innocent times in Glasgow, it seems a pity that the meeting never did take place. Butler went on to a whole range of other writing, the most recent of which has been a television series on the life of Ivor Novello.

Under pressure to deliver a regular book for Collins, MacLean was always glad to have the kernel of an idea. Elliott Kastner had given him the thought for *Where Eagles Dare*; Geoffrey Reeve had pointed him towards *Puppet on a Chain* and *Caravan to Vaccares*. Now Peter Snell was planting another thought, springing from his youth in Alberta, where one of the dreams of the fifties was to find a way of extracting the oil which lay near Lake Athabasca. Within the soil, sand and clay of that area there were oil reserves said to be as great as those of the Middle East – if only someone could find a means of extracting it.

Snell and MacLean left for northern Alberta, where they were given the complete guided tour of the Athabasca region, essential background for the book he was later to write. But Snell was about to play an even bigger role in the writer's career.

Having reached Alistair through Marcelle – and made a film of *Bear Island* in spite of it all – he challenged him one day on the fact that he had done nothing in television. With shows like *Kojak* and *Columbo* so popular, why didn't he take a look at the medium? Alistair's response was predictable. 'Ach, I don't know anything about television. I don't even watch it.'

On his next visit to Britain, however, Snell persuaded him to sit down in his Mayfair hotel and watch those popular shows, although having run through episodes of *Miami Vice*, as well as *Kojak* and *Columbo*, he concluded that the impact had been minimal.

Next time he was in Los Angeles – and by then not unaware of MacLean's perverse nature – Snell mentioned his name to Jerry Leider, an important TV producer, whose company had a special relationship with CBS, one of America's three national television networks.

Tempted by the idea that Peter Snell could perhaps 'deliver Alistair MacLean for television', Leider responded immediately and the two men worked out a suggestion to put to him. He would be asked to write no more than the outlines of some television stories and, to assist the process, Leider would offer the talented American writer-producer Burt Nodella to collaborate with him.

Having poured cold water on Snell's original suggestion, Alistair called Pinewood Studios one day to say, 'About that television idea . . . I've written something.'

What he had written was an eighty-seven-page novella with the promising title of *Air Force One is Down*, the story of an American president's Boeing which is hi-jacked on a flight from Geneva to Washington with important people on board. At least they had something to work on.

A man of some charm as well as energy, Jerry Leider arrived in London from Los Angeles and a deal was thrashed out at a meeting in Claridge's, attended by MacLean and David Bishop. It meant that the author would be paid $25,000 for each television film made from one of his stories and a further $25,000 for any which went into cinema release. He would also reserve all copyrights so that they could be developed into novels as well.

With instructions to cast an eye over it, Burt Nodella, who was already well versed in MacLean's novels, was handed the *Air Force One is Down* story. He had reached the last few pages when he was struck by a throw-away line, to the effect that 'McCafferty, in his own inimitable fashion, averted World War III.' Leider had tumbled upon the same poignant line and called Nodella to say, 'What the hell does he mean by that?'

With the experienced eye of the screenwriter, Burt Nodella was given the task of developing that story. 'I picked up Alistair's style, wrote about thirty more pages and sent it off to him,' he said. 'Alistair then called Peter Snell to say he wanted to meet me. So I was dispatched to Cannes to meet this Scottish writer for the very first time and to collaborate with him.' It was 1978.

MacLean knew nothing of the stranger who was coming to work with him. Hollywood has a habit of turning out the most diverse range of talented writers, each one likely to have a fascinating background.

Burt Nodella was a New Yorker who started on the *Steve Allen Show*, booking singers like Peggy Lee before heading for Los Angeles in 1952 to write for daytime television and become an actors' agent for people like Lee Marvin, Jeff Chandler and Charles Bronson. Through his agency contacts, Nodella went to ABC Television as head of programme development, bringing us such memorable series as *The Fugitive*, in that period when the motion picture companies were realizing they would have to get themselves more clearly identified with the small screen. By the late sixties, he had moved on to Universal and Columbia and was winning Emmy awards for his television work.

It was when he went to MGM as executive producer for television that he met and worked with Jerry Leider, a successful name in Hollywood, who was about to make the third screen version of *The Jazz Singer*. Nodella was diverted from that project, however, and was winging his way across the Atlantic for a first encounter with Alistair MacLean, whose reputation for disliking film people who meddled with his work had not diminished.

Since Nodella had undertaken a major conversion of *Air Force One is Down*, it was all the more of a compliment when he was greeted with the words, 'I couldn't tell where I ended and you began.' The two men hit it off immediately.

A tall, impressive man of style and flair – his trendy appearance belied the fact that he was only slightly the junior of the two – Nodella seemed more acceptable to MacLean than most film people he had encountered. Both had been through the Second World War and both, as it emerged, were wrestling with private emotional problems.

Having just rid himself of a disastrous second marriage, Alistair was now longing for a return to his first wife, Gisela, who was still living in Villa Murat with Michael and Ali, now in their mid-teens. They had never lost contact and were on civilized terms, but whether or not she would have him back was a very different matter.

Burt Nodella had another kind of problem. After a failed marriage, he had just seen the end of another twelve-year association with a woman who meant a great deal to him. Alistair was much more interested in talking over their respective problems than discussing their joint future in television.

Burt simply wanted to get on with the mission which had brought him to the South of France. Broadly speaking, they had agreed on a basic outline for their television stories, which was presented in the form of a memorandum, signed by Alistair. Much of the detail was worked out by Nodella and another talented man, Joe Morwood, an executive producer back in Hollywood.

While honouring his contract, MacLean was lacking enthusiasm for the project and Nodella had to admit, to himself at least, that this kind of television was beneath the man.

After the nightmare of California, Alistair had once more gravitated to the Riviera, taking a one-year lease of the Villa Cassandra, belonging to Lord and Lady Blakenham. It was a modern villa on high ground just west of Cannes, with a magnificent view of the sea and the hills of Esterel; although not up to the standard of the Casa Estella, his earlier home on the Riviera, it was still a house of great charm, with a pleasant English garden, which appealed to Alistair.

When that lease expired, he was on the move to an apartment in an attractive block called Semiramis. Wherever he lived in the Cannes area – indeed wherever he went in the world – there was someone to keep an eye on him. That task fell to Madame Madeleine Dol, the housekeeper who came every day and could be depended upon to check on his drinking habits. The other indispensable servant in Cannes was a local taxi-driver, Constant Allemandi, who would appear whenever required and would set aside his taxi service to act as chauffeur in the Mercedes.

Alistair and Constant took Burt Nodella and Peter Snell, who had flown the last lap from London with Burt, to the famous Carlton Hotel. After checking in, they continued to the Villa Cassandra to begin their discussions.

Over the next week there were idle moments, which became all too frequent. To fill in the time, Nodella applied his writer's mind to jotting down diary notes. They build up an interesting picture of Alistair MacLean at that mid-fifties period in his life when the future had never seemed more uncertain. These are a few extracts:

4 April 1978. He is a delightful host. Drinks. Talks. Very fond of Peter [Snell]. Denigrates himself verbally. But has healthy ego. Concerned about his fifteen- and sixteen-year-old sons. Recently divorced. Lonely. Acerbic. But gentle man overall.

After countless drinks he hosted Peter and I to dinner at Carlton. He's greeted like royalty there. They fawn over him. He fell asleep at the bar (passed out might be a better phrase) so Peter and I took a forty-five-minute walk along the Croisette. No one seemed surprised at his little 'nap'. Great dinner. Peter left us alone to talk. Went to the small bar and topped off our alcohol consumption with brandies. Alistair didn't want the evening to end.

5 April. Ten a.m. Alistair, who usually gets up at five a.m., not yet awake. Madame Dol, his housekeeper, fixes coffee. He finally appears, fit and chipper. 'Too much hospitality last night.' We talked around our film project. He avoided it, saying he's not qualified for television. Difficult getting him to stay on the subject. Wants to philosophize and questions me about myself. He insists I move out of hotel and into villa. I figure it's a way to get more done. Check out of hotel and we drive Peter to airport. Me driving Mercedes. Had lunch at Nice terminal. Alistair managed to put away double Scotch, a double brandy and a couple of glasses of wine. He's sloshed again. Peter warned me. Obviously just a few good hours in the morning. He slept all the way back to Cannes. His sons, Michael and Ali, at the villa. Their dad questions them incessantly about what they're doing. Where they're going. And why. Both nice boys but, as Alistair says, 'wealthy'. He feels poor. He dresses 'poor'. Denim workshirt, wrinkled chinos and when he knots a tie it's always askew. He fell asleep sitting up, as he did yesterday evening at the Carlton bar.

Typical of Alistair's generosity that I sleep in the master suite upstairs while he has a nondescript little servant's room down-stairs and sleeps in a single bed. Or is that all he thinks he deserves? He's very critical of himself.

It may have been a mistake moving in here but I can't very well leave now without hurting his feelings. He's obviously very lonely. Wants company, conversation. He's charming, articulate and bright when he's sober. But difficult otherwise. Mumbles a lot. And his Scots burr gets thicker and slurred.

He's finally awake. Fixed himself another Scotch. I don't know how he does it. We work a little but it's like pulling teeth when he's in this condition. As we start to leave for dinner, the boys arrive. The contrast between them and their father is really marked. Both dress in the latest fashion. Elegant watches. Gold cigarette cases and lighters. And dowdy old Alistair. We drop them off at *the* discothèque in Cannes, midst admonitions by Alistair to be back early. Sure they will! They know how to manipulate their father by immediately agreeing to everything he says. Then doing exactly as they please.

We head for usual dinner at Carlton but he's really too far gone. I convince him it's better to return to the villa. All he wants to talk about is my broken relationship and why I allowed it to happen. Obviously he's talking about his own failed relationship. Left him sitting in living-room 'waiting up for the boys'.

6 April. As soon as he heard me stirring, he came up with glass of chilled orange and is now making me bangers and eggs. Very touching man. So eager to please. As I eat, he peppers me with questions. Am I a layabout? What do I want to do with my life? (What did he want to do with his?) 'I'm the world's greatest living writer,' he says. 'But I write rubbish. I am a clown. You are a clown. Why did you walk away from her? What is she like? You love her. Tell me honestly. Why did you walk away? Where are you going with your life? Where do you want to be ten years from now? I want to write a really good book. Not rubbish. There's no greater writer than me. I know that. But it doesn't mean anything being the greatest. It's rubbish. It's empty. I'm daffy about my boys. But if I had a girl I'd ruin her. After all, you can't sit a boy on your lap . . .'

He reaches for the tall water glass full of gin. It's now eleven a.m. He drinks half in great gulps. The clear liquid overflows his mouth and dribbles down the corners of his lips. Then to his chin and neck. He seems unaware and doesn't bother to wipe his face.

Reaches for a cigarette. Falls asleep immediately with cigarette half out of pack. He sleeps for half an hour this way, still holding pack of cigarettes in one hand and his gold lighter dangling from the other. He wakens suddenly and resumes the conversation. His speech and Scotch burr slurred. He looks down and away. Then at me with that endearing little smile of his. Elfin charm. All of his questions are really aimed at himself. He sleeps till six.

I write – and read *Puppet on a Chain*. The boys wake at four after heavy night at discothèque. Alistair finally rises too. The gin, Scotch and Campari bottles are all empty. We dine at Carlton then talk and drink till midnight. Aware that people like him because of his fame. I tell him I couldn't give a shit who he is. He's nice man who brought me orange juice this morning, with a little-boy grin on his face. At dinner, revealed he was member of Interpol for thirty years. Also showed remorse and chagrin for having killed 223 people, mostly Asians. Almost cried at memory. [His telling of the killing-field story is obviously expanding with time and drink!]

7 April. I notice last night's bottle of Scotch is half gone. Don't know how he does it. Trying to get to work before his total collapse. He says about our work, 'It's dishonest. I feel guilty.

'Why did you walk away, you clown? Why don't you go back? Is it pride? I asked my first wife to marry me again. She said yes. [In fact she said no.] Should I? My secretary, Sabrina Carver, is my lassie. Been with me for six years. Been all over the world with her. People can't believe I've never touched her. She loves her man. An artist. A very good one. Fifty-two years old. He doesn't mind her travelling with me. People trust me. Don't know whether they should.'

Went to Carlton for lunch. Alistair fading fast with double

Scotch and brandy. At the small bar I noticed a very beautiful blonde at nearby table with a man and child. She avoided looking at our table. It turned out to be Alistair's second wife. Or so he said. [A blonde doesn't sound like Marcelle.] They are not on speaking terms.

8 April. Guess my mission with him is over now. Not much more I can get. He's just too out of it all evening and all day long. Amazing how his mind stays sharp but he just won't stay on the subject.

Despite all the frustrations of the drinking, Nodella was able to fly back to California next day and, together with Joe Morwood, complete the planned outlines of the UNACO series as explained in the memorandum. It gave the background to the proposed television idea like this:

Several years ago, an undisclosed number of special envoys met in a little-used conference room at the United Nations building. The meeting was held under conditions of extraordinary secrecy because these envoys carried extraordinary instructions. Representing virtually every race, nationality, religion and political ideology on earth, they had been ordered by their respective governments to render each other the utmost assistance in solving the problem at hand. Obviously only a crisis of world-shattering proportions could have prompted such a gathering.

What was the crisis they faced? A tide of international crime swelling so fast it threatened to swamp the very foundations of world stability. The perpetrators were a new breed of criminals. Armed with all the latest devices science and technology could provide, they chose their targets accordingly. Why knock off a mere bank when you can purloin a national treasury? Why hi-jack an airliner when you can hold an entire city hostage? Why kidnap a millionaire's son when you can nab a chief of state?

And they were pulling it off. Unrestricted in their movements, they could strike in one country then hop to safety in another as easily as a fox jumps a fence. National and local police forces, saddled with jurisdictional boundaries and procedural disputes, were hopelessly hamstrung in their efforts to stop these jet-set

crooks. Something had to be done and done fast. The answer was
UNACO (United Nations Anti Crime Organization), a top-secret
force operating under the aegis of the UN Security Council.
Its mission: 'to avert, neutralize and/or apprehend individuals or
groups engaged in international criminal activities'.

UNACO is composed of key agents siphoned off from police
forces and intelligence organizations around the world. Un-
fettered by red tape and protocol, these agents are highly mobile
and can cross international boundaries with impunity. However,
to avoid possible political embarrassment, the Security Council
has insisted on a policy of 'plausible denial'. It will never admit
that such a strike force exists.

But it does. At least in my mind it does. And so does the tiny
office on the 22nd floor of the United Nations building in New
York. There is no indication that this otherwise thoroughly
innocuous room is an ante-chamber to the world's most sophisticated intelligence headquarters . . .

Thus the series was given the UNACO formula, which could be
applied to a whole range of stories. Considering Alistair's lukewarm
interest in the project it is surprising that he and Nodella managed
to lay any kind of foundation.

In the event, they came up with eight stories but, despite the
efforts already exerted over *Air Force One is Down*, which would be
one of them, it was promptly set aside in favour of another, *The
Hostage Tower*, which the American television network preferred as
an opening to the series.

This was to start with two burly men chasing a lithe teenage girl
through the early-morning streets of Paris. She eludes them by
ducking into the Eiffel Tower and boarding the first elevator of the
day. What goes up must come down. All they have to do is wait.

When the elevator reaches the uppermost platform, one of the
passengers suddenly produces a pistol. His two confederates remove
their topcoats to reveal sub-machine guns, explosives and wire
strapped to their bodies. Paul Jaubert, their leader, informs the
shocked group that they are all hostages and privileged witnesses to
the hi-jacking of the Eiffel Tower.

Back in New York, the UNACO team are hastily briefed. They
are told the hostages will be killed and the Eiffel Tower blown up

unless 10 million francs' worth of uncut diamonds are delivered within forty-eight hours. There is one other factor which, if revealed, could lead to grave international complications. One of the hostages is Maria Kreznikov, seventeen-year-old daughter of a first deputy of the Soviet Politburo. Accompanying her father on a state visit, the precocious young lady slipped away from her KGB bodyguards to see Paris on her own. The priorities of the mission are clear: rescue Maria Kreznikov and, if possible, save the Eiffel Tower.

A screenplay was commissioned from Robert Carrington while Jerry Leider, who had once been head of Warner film production in Europe, secured permission to shoot on the tower itself.

So Burt Nodella set out for Paris, with the sensitive Claudio Guzman as director of the picture and a cast which was not lacking in names. Peter Fonda, Douglas Fairbanks Junior, Celia Johnson and Rachel Roberts were just some of those who were to take part in what was Alistair MacLean's first projection on American television. He had already been paid $80,000 for his novella of *Air Force One is Down* but the stories were to have far greater significance for the future of his estate.

Considering the location, *The Hostage Tower* was made on a reasonable budget of $4.2 million, backed two-thirds by the American network and the rest through first sales around the world. It was released as a feature film in the cinemas of Europe but was confined to television in the United States.

It did well enough but didn't 'take the night', as the Americans say, and with the TV ratings no more than average the bad news was that CBS decided not to proceed with the rest of the series. Tastes in television can change swiftly. All of a sudden, the action-adventure which seemed like the current flavour goes inexplicably out of fashion. Hollywood men don't hang around.

Moving on to other things, Jerry Leider sold out his interest to his partner in the venture, Peter Snell, who thus acquired the rights of the series for his own company, Feature Films Transac. But that was by no means the end of the UNACO story.

Though of course he owned the rights to those outlines, Alistair MacLean decided he personally did not want to develop them into novels. Instead, after consultation with Collins, a writer called John Denis was engaged to write the novel of *The Hostage Tower*, which appeared under the same title and was reasonably successful.

Though *Air Force One is Down* did not materialize as a film, John Denis was engaged once again to write the novel.

The name of Alistair MacLean dominated the front cover, since the 'stories' were technically his; but he began to receive embarrassing correspondence from unhappy followers, saying he would soon lose his readers if he allowed other people to write his books. Some were accusing him of misleading his loyal public and MacLean accepted the point very quickly.

He issued a strict instruction that no more of those novels from the UNACO outlines were to be published in his lifetime. David Bishop approved of the decision, pointing out nevertheless that, in the event of his death, they could continue to generate money for his estate, in much the same way as John Gardner had been writing the James Bond books in the years after Fleming. MacLean's dour response was, 'What happens after I'm gone doesn't concern me. In any case, it's time I retired, dammit. Everybody gets to retire.'

Though he had placed a ban on further books, he was looking forward to a succession of those films, which were an entirely different matter, and in that respect he felt more could have been done to bring those stories to the screen. In view of the CBS decision, however, it is difficult to see what more Snell and Leider could possibly have done.

In the cyclical habits of fashion, he would have been delighted to know that, more than a decade later, Peter Snell was finalizing his plans to film another of the UNACO series and was setting out from Pinewood Studios *en route* to locations in Yugoslavia, with a $4.4 million budget. This time the story was *Death Train*, a joint production for television with the backing of Viacom, a major New York TV distribution company, Jadran Films of Yugoslavia and, at the British end, Yorkshire Television.

The catalyst for this activity was MacLean's lawyer, David Bishop, by then his literary executor and keen to perpetuate the author's name in the years after his death. It was he who raised the question: Whatever became of the other six outlines?

William Collins accepted the challenge and became interested in engaging a writer to develop the left-over outlines into full-scale novels, now that MacLean was gone, perhaps bringing them out on an annual basis. Just as John Denis had written *The Hostage Tower* and *Air Force One is Down*, so did Collins then engage another writer, Alastair MacNeill, to continue the process.

MacNeill, a Scot born in Greenock but brought up in South Africa, had studied hotel management and worked for the Holiday Inns chain before returning to Britain in 1985 and submitting a manuscript of his own to Collins. Marjory Chapman saw it and identified the writer as someone who could tackle MacLean's outlines.

It was a heaven-sent opportunity for a man still in his twenties. Starting with *Death Train* in 1989, he followed up with *Night Watch* and *Red Alert*, with *Time of the Assassin* to come.

The task of those two writers differed to the extent that Denis was working fairly heavily from the screenplays which had been written for the first two books. MacNeill had a much more limited story line from which to develop the subsequent books.

When *The Hostage Tower* was published in 1979, Bishop complained to Collins about the size of lettering used for Alistair's name at the top of the page, compared to Denis's credit at the bottom. The format was retained but an explanation was given at the beginning to indicate the division of authorship. Similar steps were taken when MacNeill took over, but it was not until 1991 – twelve years after *The Hostage Tower* – that anyone cared to challenge the practice in court. As a result of 'a complaint by two Warwickshire readers', trading standards officials took HarperCollins (the new name for Collins) to court on a charge of applying a false trade description. The matter was adjourned until September 1991.

Certainly the revived series of MacLean's story lines proved successful enough to account for more than half the income of the copyright settlement in the year 1990–91. That was on the basis of receiving 70 per cent of the royalties from the UNACO books.

Understandably, Alastair MacNeill was negotiating for more than his original 30 per cent share. But, when you consider that the MacLean copyright settlements' total royalty income for 1990–91, four years after his death, amounted to over £500,000, you begin to grasp the importance of the UNACO idea, which had all begun so innocently.

Peter Snell had not suffered for his association with Alistair's name. Having guided Alistair towards the UNACO idea in the first place, he was now reaping the benefit of revived interest in turning the stories into television films, starting with that *Death Train* story which told of a German vagrant heading south for the winter, hopping on a freight train and discovering it was loaded with beer kegs. Happy vagrant.

He smashed one open, but instead of beer it contained a luminous white powder. A few days later he collapsed with mysterious burns and loss of hair. The diagnosis: radiation poisoning. The prognosis: a few hours to live.

The train had to be found. The UNACO team moved into action, discovering that a German scientist had been blackmailed into stealing plutonium for a consortium of illegal arms merchants. The implications of atomic weapons becoming available on the international black market are self-evident. Thus another MacLean-type gripping drama began to unfold.

As a tail-piece to the real-life story of the young Canadian who came to Britain and found himself making films for British Lion, Peter Snell completed another cycle when, in 1988, he bought out that company from Thorn EMI and set about revitalizing the name of British Lion, which had been a major part of the country's film industry since the twenties.

As for Burt Nodella, who had been more deeply involved with the UNACO series than MacLean himself, I caught up with him in Los Angeles, by the poolside of the Beverly Hills Hotel, where we raked over the whole episode.

Burt, by then adding to his youthful look with a pony-tail haircut, though well through his sixties, had gone back to visit Alistair in Cannes the year after their original collaboration but found that little had changed. There were still dinners at the Carlton, with Alistair arriving three sheets to the wind. He was still worried about his venture into television and brought up the name of Leslie Charteris, creator of *The Saint*, and the effect TV had had on his career. He was still feeling worthless and ashamed that he hadn't written a great novel. And he was still deluding himself that he and Gisela were getting back together.

Nodella returned to the Hollywood life-style, living on a boat at Marina del Rey, writing for the theatre and cinema, to be found perhaps at a Frank Sinatra party or visiting, as we did, the fabulous Hollywood home of Claudio Guzman, director of *The Hostage Tower*, where the name of Alistair MacLean was discussed with great warmth.

They had exchanged birthday and Christmas cards in the ensuing years but there the contact ended. A genuine man of some elegance, Nodella appealed to MacLean as much as most film people repulsed him.

In that Californian land of swaying palms and sunbaked brains, he probably summed it up himself when he said, 'I think he knew I was not part of the Hollywood bullshit.'

26

By the time the divorce petition was issued by Alistair MacLean in Geneva on 20 January 1977, he had taken to seeing his first wife, Gisela, again, now realizing what a fool he had been in breaking up the first marriage for such a worthless second one.

Though Marcelle had by now sacked both her London and Swiss lawyers, the settlement figures being bandied about were not getting any less. Finally, David Bishop made it clear that the most he could recommend was a payment of £250,000, plus a further £150,000 for buying back the film rights of *Bear Island* and *The Way to Dusty Death*, both of which Marcelle had managed to have legally vested in her name.

In the end, what she walked away with amounted, in effect, to £400,000 spread over three years. At that stage, the man then acting as her agent (he was not a qualified lawyer) came up with the suggestion that, if a further £150,000 was paid, Marcelle would not proceed with her plan to publish an autobiography. That kind of overture may have several definitions but the general public knows it by a simple word: blackmail.

David Bishop sent the man away with a flea in his ear, inviting him to go ahead with the autobiography if that was Marcelle's inclination. They would meet again in the defamation court. (The manuscript never reached the stage of a book, but some of its allegations did turn up in a Scottish Sunday newspaper in the week of MacLean's death. But more of that later.)

The divorce settlement was a highly satisfactory one from MacLean's point of view, secured largely because Marcelle's advisers had failed to obtain full particulars of his income. They were negotiating on the assumption that his annual income was £300,000, whereas if they had properly sought out the details they would have been dealing with a sum more in the region of twice that. His income for that divorcing year of 1977 was actually more than £800,000.

On the other hand, for someone who had brought more froth than substance to the union, having insinuated herself into the life of one of the world's most popular authors and squandered vast amounts of his money on her variety of fruitless schemes, Marcelle could be said to have done not too badly for herself.

The divorce went through smoothly, Alistair gaining it on grounds of desertion, the actual deed in relation to the financial arrangements being signed on 19 December 1977. As a final gesture, he agreed that Marcelle could have the rights to a full length screenplay he had completed, called *The Golden Girl*. It was the basis of what could have been a film or television series, but once again it came to nothing in her hands and David Bishop bought it back into the MacLean estate in 1989 for the purpose of having it developed as a novel. That was achieved by the author Simon Gandolfi. The novel is to be published by Chapmans in 1992.

So Alistair was now reflecting upon two failed marriages within six years, the Scotsman who had found love first with the more reserved Gisela, reflecting fairly accurately the popular image of her German race, and then with Marcelle from France, once more embodying the joie de vivre and seductive allure of the Parisienne. A mixture of the two might have produced the kind of woman necessary to bring fulfilment to his life, a combination which might have been more readily found in his own homeland. The potential of a second marriage is generally higher than the first, if only for the advantages of experience, but this one was doomed from the start, given Marcelle's proclivity for harebrained schemes and high-spending, on top of Alistair's wayward habits.

All that was now in the past. The hard facts were that Marcelle had gone with £400,000 in her pocket, not a vastly different settlement from Gisela, who gained Villa Murat and could have sold it for a comparable amount; except that she had an on-going payment which would enable her to remain in the villa if she wished. She had, after all, been the innocent party.

Gisela retained not only the house but Alistair's goodwill, which secured her future beyond his own death. Twenty years after the divorce, she lives alone and quietly at Villa Murat.

During that year of dissolving his second marriage, Alistair was still on his rootless wanderings, renting a flat in Geneva, the houses in Cannes, and inviting his two lawyers, Bishop and Brechbuhl, to accompany him on a trip to the Camargue, where he was always particularly happy and relaxed.

He was in great form again when he appeared at the Author of the Year party in London, and during that same spring he managed to meet one of his literary heroes, Dennis Wheatley, when David Bishop arranged a luncheon party at Justerini and Brooks in St James's Street, where Wheatley had worked before the war. It emerged that he was just as keen to meet Alistair and the lunch became a huge success, with the latter on his best behaviour, even deciding to address Dennis Wheatley as 'Sir'.

With Alistair *en route* to divorce, his bachelor lawyer was heading in the other direction, having married and settled in Hartley Wintney. It was during a visit to the Bishop home that Alistair was taken down to Slimbridge for lunch with Peter Scott, the famous ornithologist and son of Scott of the Antarctic.

Alistair had previously been drawn into the World Wildlife Appeal, launched by Prince Bernhard of the Netherlands, and had subscribed $10,000 as a founder member. It was by this route that he came in contact with Sir Peter and embarked on a paper on the World Wildlife Fund. It was also his intention at that time to write a biography of Sir Peter's father and he had been promised full access to the archives for this purpose. This was the project being discussed over lunch at Sir Peter's home that day, when Alistair was once more at his impeccable best, even walking round Slimbridge and taking an inordinate interest in the wildlife. The book never did materialize.

Alistair was not exactly known for his presence on the film-sets, but in November, with the divorce nearing completion, he and Bishop embarked on a journey to Opatija in Yugoslavia to watch some of the shooting of *Force Ten from Navarone*, taken up after all those years by Columbia Pictures and produced by Oliver Unger (no relation to Kurt Unger of *Puppet on a Chain*). It was a horrendous rail journey from Zurich to Ljubljana, starting with expectations of an Orient Express adventure but ending up in a train which had neither bar nor refreshments and took twelve hours to reach its destination. They survived thanks only to a kindly ticket collector who sold them a loaf and some rough red Yugoslav wine.

Once in Opatija, however, they spent a couple of interesting days, largely in the company of Robert Shaw, the actor who was playing the lead in *Force Ten* and with whom Alistair had become friendly many years earlier. Bishop had also met Shaw through their common enthusiasm for squash.

The film-star was housed in a beautiful villa, formerly owned by an Austro-Hungarian count, and was living in some style during the filming of *Force Ten*. Needless to say, he and MacLean did some hefty drinking together during that visit. But if he got on well with Shaw, he did not hit it off with Guy Hamilton, the director. Still, it was a fascinating experience, in which they got to know other stars like Franco Nero and Ringo Starr's wife, Barbara Bach. MacLean met another male actor, hovering in the background, who had not yet gained fame for his roles in *Raiders of the Lost Ark* and *Indiana Jones*.

Apparently Harrison Ford did not particularly enjoy his involvement in *Force Ten from Navarone*, and told me that he had succeeded fairly well in blacking it out of his mind!

Journalists seeking interviews with MacLean were finding it as hard as ever to reach him, but one Scottish scribe succeeded with a novel trade-off which appealed to him – an interview in exchange for a box of the finest Mallaig kippers.

Terry Houston, then of the *Daily Record*, sat anxiously on the Geneva-bound aeroplane, sniffing at the triple-wrapped parcel on his knee and praying that the heat of the cabin wouldn't produce tell-tale signs of his cargo. His imaginative gift broke the ice and gave him the chance of another encounter, this time in Cannes, to which Alistair liked to escape from the more severe northerly winters.

Houston was even invited to stay at Villa Cassandra while pursuing his own attempts at writing a novel and it was then that he could observe the master at work, noting a routine which took him to the typewriter by six-thirty a.m. and continued till three o'clock, broken by occasional cups of tea and a ham sandwich at lunchtime. He would stop earlier if too many typing errors were telling him to.

With his dislike of the vapid, empty life-style of the aimless rich, Alistair might have seemed an unlikely resident of Cannes; Houston had no such qualms in sharing the villa with its vast, scenic view and sheer slopes ablaze with mimosa in February. The owner had installed bullet-proof glass in the windows but Alistair said he didn't fear kidnapping. If it ever did happen, he had given instructions that no ransom should be paid. As for his three sons – well, that was a different matter.

What he didn't tell Houston was that there had indeed been kidnapping threats. After a visit to Israel with Kurt Unger, producer of *Puppet on a Chain*, he had considered writing a book about the Israeli War of 1967. His intentions became known and he confided in close friends that there had been letters threatening the kidnap of his children if he went ahead with the book.

Terry Houston was driving Alistair to Monaco one day when he burned out the brakes of the Mercedes and found himself careering downhill towards a comic-opera policeman in white pith helmet, holding out his white glove but finally leaping to safety, like something from the Keystone Cops. The vehicle charged on, out of control and through a crash-chain which snapped its moorings.

After a lucky escape, they were detained for questioning and went home by train, a strap-hanging, stifling journey which ended with the discovery that the house keys were in the abandoned car. Alistair was fairly stoical in misfortune, Terry Houston remembers.

Even more clearly, he recalled one of Alistair's black periods, sitting in a Cannes restaurant with tears running down his cheeks and whispering a question which had echoed down the years: 'Do no birds cry?'

'The significance was that birds are incapable of crying for they have no tear ducts. And here was a lonely albatross of a man who drifted across country after country, fêted for work which he personally considered inferior, without ever finding personal ease. He could be forgiving of others but never of himself.'

In a rare reference to his war, he stared into space, as if some untold horror was being re-enacted before his eyes, and talked about an allied ship in his group which had been torpedoed. The survivors were bobbing around in the icy wastes in their life-jackets, all but dead from cold.

Eyes brimming with tears, he had whispered, 'We machine-gunned them in the water.' His head was cocked to one side, as if listening to their silent screams. Fact or fiction? For Alistair it was real, though shipmates say he must have been believing his own fiction.

While he would encourage a young Scot towards writing, he had no interest in the established scribes who lived nearby. Apart from the odd comment about Fleming or Robbins, he would hardly even talk about them. He thought Hemingway was a coward for committing suicide.

Much as he was still prepared to talk about his dislike of the film-world, Alistair acknowledged a love-hate relationship with it, leaving him with the biggest regret of his professional career. It concerned the book which he felt, above all, should have been made into a film – and wasn't.

27

Even allowing for literary preference, there is a consensus of opinion that the first book Alistair MacLean ever wrote, *HMS Ulysses*, remained his best. His powers of description were fully tested in that gripping drama of the Arctic Ocean as the wartime convoys sought to reach Murmansk with supplies to keep alive the Soviet effort against the Germans.

HMS Ulysses seemed as natural for conversion to the silver screen as *The Cruel Sea* by Nicholas Monsarrat. Yet, for a variety of reasons, it didn't happen in Alistair MacLean's lifetime, and that was a major regret which he carried to the grave. Surely, of all the books which had found favour with the film people (oddballs though they might be!), ranging from *The Guns of Navarone* and *Where Eagles Dare* to *Puppet on a Chain* and *Bear Island*, this was the one which should have made its mark in the cinemas of the world as well as the bestselling lists, where its phenomenal success was beyond dispute.

With the spectacular arrival of a first-time author, his fellow Scot Robert Clark, head of Associated British Picture Corporation, bought the film rights for £30,000, a great deal of money in the fifties, and it seemed only a matter of time before the film was made.

So what happened? Why has it not yet been made? The history of popular fiction is littered with tales of paid-up film options which kept the authors in reasonable comfort but left them disillusioned and disappointed that no film was ever made.

For one reason or another, Robert Clark made no progress with his intentions for *HMS Ulysses* and finally, after more than a decade, sold on the rights to an Italian aristocrat, Count Giovanni Volpi, who has held them for a further twenty years or more, and still nothing has happened.

Volpi's name first appeared in a letter from Alistair MacLean to Ian Chapman in 1969, when he wrote:

About this Italian approach for the film of *Ulysses*, Geoff [Reeve] phoned and asked me to contact this Count Volpi in Lausanne. This I duly did the same evening and he asked me to meet him in an hour's time in Geneva. I had to decline because – I know this must sound incredible – Lachlan's headmaster (and his is the most exclusive school in Switzerland; Eton and Millfield are comparatively poor relations) had asked me out for a night's gambling in a French casino! (He won and I neither won nor lost for gambling is anathema to me but the free champagne was most acceptable.)

I met Count Volpi on Thursday night. He took me to dinner in Geneva's best restaurant. I've never heard of him but he is a comparatively young chap. His qualifications as a film-maker would appear to be less than impeccable. His old man started the Venice Film Festival back in the thirties but, as far as I could discover, that is his only direct connection with the trade. He himself owns a firm that builds racing cars and he is very much a power-boat racing boy – he won the first Cowes–Torquay race in the *Tramanatona*. This sounds disparaging and is not meant to be. He is no rich playboy. He is quite brilliant and has a mind like a knife. He is convinced he can make a go of *Ulysses* and, judging by the number of vessels he has already lined up, I do think he will be as good as his word. He asked me to do the screenplay. I said I wouldn't . . . he asked if I would pass judgement on any screenplay he commissioned and I said I would . . .

More than twenty years beyond that letter – and with no further progress towards a film of *Ulysses* – I found myself seeking out this remote Italian aristocrat to see if I could elicit an explanation. That was what took me speeding down the broad vista of Venice towards the Grand Canal, in a water-taxi which offered some hint of what it must have been like for Paul Sherman, the Interpol agent, in the exciting pursuit of the drug baron through the Amsterdam canals in *Puppet on a Chain*.

The speedboat delivered me safely at the door of the Volpi Palace
in the centre of Casanova's home town and there I met Count
Giovanni Volpi, whose family name may be little known outside his
native land but has significance for students of twentieth-century
Italian history.

Coming from an old Venetian background, the present Count's
father made his fortune from hotels, insurance and property in the
early part of the century and played an even more important part in
Italian affairs as a diplomat, deeply involved, in 1911, when his
country gained Libya from the Turks, who had had the territory
since the sixteenth century. The Turks returned during the First
World War and the first Count Volpi had to take Libya for the
second time, now becoming its Governor-General. He was a well-
known Fascist in the days of Mussolini, when Il Duce had the
support of his nation.

A man of many talents, he spread himself to the world of the
arts and had indeed created the idea of international film festivals,
founding the Venice one in 1932, not long after the arrival of the
talkies. That remained the world's only film festival until after the
Second World War, when Cannes and others came into being.

He was into his sixties and a second marriage before gaining a
son and heir, the present Count Volpi, who grew up in the family
palaces of Rome and Venice and the home in Switzerland.

Involved in his business empire, Giovanni Volpi was browsing at
an airport bookstall one day, *en route* to Libya, when he picked up
a paperback by an author whose name meant nothing to him. It was
HMS Ulysses, which so intrigued him that he read it through the
night and felt a compulsion to make it into a film. Though totally
outwith that business himself, he sought contacts which led him to
that remarkable lady of the British film industry, Robin Dalton,
renowned as a film and literary agent before turning, late in life, to
the actual production of movies herself. It was Robin Dalton who
acquired the rights of *HMS Ulysses* for Count Volpi and introduced
him to one of her own clients, David Osborn, who was willing to
write the screenplay.

Osborn, tall and lean in the American liberal mould, was another
of those talented writers who fell victim to the McCarthy witch-hunt.
His pedigree was impressive. A descendant of Benjamin Franklin,
famous American statesman and scientist, he was sent from New

York as a boy with health problems to live in Santa Fé with his uncle, Oliver La Farge, the famous writer and Pulitzer prize-winner for his novel *Laughing Boy*.

A fighter pilot with the American Marines in the Second World War, David Osborn eventually found his metier as a writer, catching the eye with his screenplay for the 1957 film *Chase a Crooked Shadow*, starring Richard Todd and Anne Baxter, in which an heiress finds her home invaded by a stranger posing as her dead brother.

Hounded from his native land, he found refuge in the British film industry, writing *The Trap* for George H. Brown in 1966 and *Some Girls Do* for Betty Box in 1969.

It was while living in Panex, near the Swiss resort of Montreux, that he received word of Count Volpi's commission and the request to make his own contact with Alistair MacLean in Geneva. Having read the book before he knew of any assignment, Osborn wasted no time in meeting him and discussing the possible shape of a screenplay. Then he went home to Panex and settled down to the task. He told me, 'I cut out half the book, including all the business about the aircraft. I didn't see how it was possible to tell the whole story in one film. My technique was to show the action through the radar screen. With all my cuts, however, I didn't change the story and remained faithful to the human element. When it was finished, I took it to Alistair in Geneva. He said he would take the screenplay into the next room and read it alone. Meanwhile, I sat in his living-room for more than an hour, reading magazines and feeling distinctly uncomfortable. What would he be thinking?

'Well, the door opened and out came Alistair, walking up to me, throwing his arms around me and bursting into tears. "It's a fabulous script," he said. "You are the only person who has been able to do it the right way. This calls for a drink."'

Osborn was a confident screenwriter but MacLean's reaction, which was more emotional than he would have believed, brought him close to embarrassment. MacLean felt that, on this occasion, his work had not been messed about by another writer. Given his own lack of experience and know-how about the cinema, he recognized that this was how he himself would have liked to do it. So now, with a story by one of the world's bestselling authors and a screenplay by a well-known film-writer, backed up by the power and enthusiasm of Count Volpi, the prospects for a film coming to fruition must have seemed exceptionally good, even allowing for the historical trail of screen casualties.

The distinguished British film producer, George Brown, was brought into discussions, coming up with a projected budget of £12 million, which was a big sum in 1969.

Osborn didn't agree that the film would have to cost so much and differences of opinion developed between himself, Brown and Volpi. He didn't agree with the suggestion that they needed to use the cruiser *Belfast* and said the purpose could be perfectly well served by a destroyer. This was, after all, the age of low-budget films like *The Graduate*.

On top of all that, however, Count Volpi did not share Alistair MacLean's enthusiasm for Osborn's screenplay. There was no one to pull the project together and Volpi is very frank about the failure. 'It was in the wrong hands, including mine,' he confessed, as we tried to analyse why nothing positive had happened. 'I wasn't a professional. So why did I go out of my way to buy this property? I suppose I did it like I might have bought a painting. If you are an Orson Welles you can make a film anywhere. Otherwise, you must be in Hollywood. George Brown was in England but this had to be American.'

There were further talks, lunches and meetings about *HMS Ulysses*, with Osborn being paid his expenses by Volpi, but finally the two men fell out and parted company.

It was a setback for MacLean's deeply felt ambition but it didn't affect his connection with Osborn. He would drive round Lake Geneva for lunch at Panex, arriving in his dark blue Mercedes with its sliding roof. Despite his reputation for informal dress, he could achieve sartorial correctness when he felt like it, turning up in tailored slacks, shirt, collar and tie.

Osborn remembered the small things, like the array of eight or nine pairs of spectacles, or Alistair's delight in challenging you at Indian wrestling, that test of arm strength where men place their elbows on a table and try to bend the opponent's forearm backwards. His skill in this art astonished his friends. Osborn, who seemed much the stronger, recalled, 'Alistair took no physical exercise and was a frail-looking man, with small hands and thin wrists. When you shook his hand you were afraid you would crush his bones. But at Indian wrestling, he had my arm bent back before I knew what had happened. There is an art in it and he would tell you how he had taken on farmers, dock workers, anybody with strong arms, and beaten them all.'

Like Ian Chapman, David Osborn had an emergency call from MacLean early one morning, to say he had been beaten up by the Palestine Liberation Organization. One man had a revolver and they said they were coming back. Osborn said he would be right over and, grabbing his mason's hammer, he was on his way when his wife restrained him. Instead, they called the gendarmerie to seek advice and found that their Special Branch was already aware of the situation. He never did get to the bottom of the incident but it seemed to have been another of Alistair's delusions.

Osborn liked MacLean for the fact that he didn't swear or tell dirty stories. 'As for his talent, his early work showed a great sense of adventure but he suffered a long downward slide. He was a lovable oddball with all the hallmarks of a real British eccentric.'

David Osborn turned to writing novels, like *The Glass Tower* and *Open Season*, which became a film, and after a spell back home in America, he returned to London, where he continues to earn his living from novels.

But if Count Volpi was getting nowhere with his plans for *HMS Ulysses*, why did he hold on to the rights? Couldn't he have sold them to someone who might have more success?

'I had no need to sell them,' he told me bluntly. 'I didn't want to give *Ulysses* away so that it might be badly made by someone else.'

Meanwhile, he had been diverted by his interest in motor-racing and, in this connection, he did manage to make a film, a definitive documentary on the sport, based on the life of world champion driver Juan Fangio of Argentina. Though meeting with only moderate commercial success, it had been well brought together under the direction of Hugh Hudson, who would go on to enhance his reputation with the Oscar-winning British film *Chariots of Fire*, produced by David Puttnam.

Curiously, in his search for a successor to *Chariots*, Puttnam gave Volpi his very best chance of guiding *HMS Ulysses* into film production.

'David Puttnam wanted very much to do it for Rank,' the Count told me. 'He thought it should be in black-and-white and went the length of having two screenplays written. But I made a major mistake. I knew if I took a share of the profits, I would never see a penny. Only if you have a *Gone with the Wind* or a *Batman* do you see a return from profits. Instead, I wanted a share of the gross takings and David Puttnam couldn't promise me that. I now realize it was more important to make the film than to make money. I should just have taken the risk of not seeing a penny. I suppose David Puttnam was a guarantee of the quality I had been looking for. I don't expect he will come back. Instead, he went off to do other things. Then he made *Memphis Belle*. That could have been *HMS Ulysses*.'

(David Puttnam has confirmed to me that that was exactly the position. He had felt the need to produce a picture of the Second World War and had earmarked *Ulysses* as his choice. When negotiations with Count Volpi broke down, he turned elsewhere and ended up with *Memphis Belle*. Now he feels that that particular need is out of his system. But he also believed that the commercial fortunes of *Memphis Belle* would be a guide to the viability of *HMS Ulysses*.)

Taking full responsibility for the fact that MacLean's greatest film ambition had not been realized, Count Volpi was decidedly pessimistic about its prospects as we mulled over it in Venice. There had been other offers but none that would tempt him to release the story. Gloomily, he did not believe it would now be made.

He then announced that we were going for supper at the home of friends along the Grand Canal. His speedboat whisked us there and soon we were being shown into a gaunt stone hallway of cathedral proportions and up a broad carpeted staircase towards an upper hall of crystal chandeliers, priceless paintings and exquisite stucco-work. Within this grandeur, in which those merchants of Venice had lived, a cosmopolitan gathering of guests moved elegantly from room to room to admire the riches, sample the buffet and drool over vintage wines.

By far the most interesting piece of society gossip that evening came from the American lady who assured me that the old Duchess of Windsor, to whom the Count's parents had played host in Venice, was really a man! She had it, second-hand, on the authority of a nurse who so tired of bottling up her secret that she let loose one night and revealed that, from her experience of bathing the former Wallis Simpson, she could tell she wasn't a woman.

The journalistic instincts had to be prised away from this titillating morsel and returned to the task on hand. As the evening glowed more warmly, the Count became less laconic and threatened to cast off his pessimistic tones. Signalling me to a chair in one of the grand rooms of our host's residence, he said, 'I shall make one last attempt at turning *HMS Ulysses* into a film. If we could get a certain person to say he is interested in it, everything else would fall into place – screenplay, directing and so on.'

Count Volpi named the film-star who would guarantee a response from the money men of America, and before that evening was out we had generated a fresh enthusiasm for the project. In his newfound interest, he was reminding me that no modern naval warship film had lost money, whether it was *The Cruel Sea* or *Sink the Bismarck*.

'Why are naval warship films successful? Because there is a special charm about warships; you cannot be bored by them. For *HMS Ulysses* I had ships lined up. You could use the *Belfast*. And the *Belgrano* would have been ideal!'

Count Volpi met Alistair MacLean only a few times but remembered his Scottish hospitality, not least his mischievous habit of serving you with a large goblet brimful of whisky, before enquiring if you would like it topped up with water!

That night was for Italian wine, however, inducing a sense of levitation which rendered immaterial the prospect that Venice might be sinking beneath us. Even in the cold light of morning, as Count Volpi's speedboat hastened me back to the airport, I retained the feeling that new steps had been taken towards the fulfilment of Alistair MacLean's dearest wish.

28

Having already become acquainted with Yugoslavia, not least from his visit to the set of *Force Ten from Navarone* and his riotous drinking sprees with Robert Shaw, Alistair MacLean went back in the summer of 1978 to look into the background of a book he had in mind.

It concerned the operations of a female double-agent during the Second World War, a story he had heard while visiting Tito's country with Geoffrey Reeve in 1967. He went to Mostar, where the lady had operated, and also met Kruno Simon, who translated his work into Serbo-Croat. The outline of *Partisans* was taking shape but it was when Alistair later went down to Dubrovnik that another idea began to formulate. Looking round that picturesque old town, with its ancient walls and sense of timelessness, he told his secretary, Sabrina Carver, that he would like to spend more time there.

That was her cue to seek out yet another rented property, a more complicated task in Yugoslavia since there were no estate agents in the communist country. Knowing that hotel porters are often good sources of information, Sabrina made enquiries and found herself directed to a man called Avdo, who worked at the reception desk of Hotel Argentina.

She tracked him down and found that Avdo Cimic came out of that mould of enterprising characters who, even in a communist country, will always beat the system and improve their conditions. Avdo was a smallish, dark, square-cut figure who, with commendable industry, had built a house of his own, twelve miles north of the city, on a rocky shelf which gave him a magnificent view across the Adriatic Sea. There was more than enough room for him, his wife Inge and their daughter Sandra, so the lower flat was let to holidaymakers.

Alistair was driven out to Villa Sandra and shown over the four-roomed apartment, with its spacious lounge-cum-kitchen opening out to a garden patio, bedrooms off to either side and another room which could serve as a working den for a writer. Declaring himself pleased with the accommodation, he left some money and instructions for alterations but didn't reappear until the following year. Then he came back and settled into his bachelor flat, gazing out through white arched windows to the Adriatic below and arranging the tools of his trade. He typed on a cross-legged table, not unlike the old card-table with the green cover he had used at Hillend Road, Clarkston, when he was writing *The Guns of Navarone*. He would sit on a brown leather swivel-chair and pick out his words on the IBM golf-ball machine, the *Times* world atlas to his right, with its magnifying glass resting on top for quick reference to locations.

Leather-bound copies of all his books were stacked on a shelf to his right, alongside the same portrait of himself which graces the cover of this book. And there, at the age of fifty-seven, he settled to a more regular pattern of living which meant he would spend eight months of each twelve in his Dubrovnik retreat for the years that remained to him.

It took a little time for Avdo Cimic to confirm the identity of his new tenant. He had seen *The Guns of Navarone* in the cinema but knew little about its author. Sabrina occupied the spare bedroom until Alistair settled in, and when she returned to London Alistair and the Cimics established a fairly formal relationship of landlord and tenant, Avdo bringing him food and messages from the town.

Having come ashore from a spell as a merchant seaman, plying between Dubrovnik and Odessa, Avdo had developed an interest in art and ran a little gallery near Hotel Argentina, where he still earned his bread-and-butter at the reception desk. Apart from his exchanges with Avdo, who spoke English, there was very little conversation for MacLean; he never did learn the local language.

As the familiarity grew, however, he gained confidence in his new landlord and began to ask him about his job, how much he earned at the hotel and how long he had until his retirement. (Avdo was still in his early forties.)

With the hotel closed for the winter, Alistair invited Avdo to

accompany him on a trip to Geneva, where Gisela still lived, though
he was now resigned to the fact that she was not going to have him
back. She still wanted to keep an eye on him but made it clear to
David Bishop that she had been through hell once and had no wish
for a return excursion.

During their stay at Hôtel Angleterre in Geneva, Alistair had an
appointment with his banker, which tied in with a proposition he
was now putting to Avdo Cimic. He wanted him to give up his job
at Hotel Argentina and make himself available as his chauffeur,
boatman, general handyman and companion for as long as required.
For this task as glorified minder, there would be no contract to sign,
no guarantees to give, only a gentlemen's agreement, in return for
which M. Cimic would receive the envelope now being held behind
the bank counter.

Streetwise and enterprising, Avdo had always lived well by Yugoslavian standards, but what was on offer knocked him speechless.
When he opened the envelope, he found the equivalent of his hotel
salary, not for the rest of the winter but for the next twenty years!
How many are ever privileged to collect a lump sum which covers
the rest of our working lives? Whatever qualms he may have had
about giving up his regular living, he was facing the classic case of
an offer beyond refusal.

While he would in theory be on constant call, the practicalities
would be different. With MacLean at his typewriter, there would
be plenty of time to devote to the art gallery; and now there would
be scope for a much better one. Avdo accepted the deal without
question, sold his little gallery to Savo Rudolovic, an old Bohemian
character returning to Dubrovnik from a lifetime's exile in the
United States, and opened more spacious premises on the central
thoroughfare of Prijeka, within the walled city.

His interest in art had been enhanced by his marriage to Inge, a
charming, softly spoken introvert who balanced the outgoing nature
of her husband and immersed herself in a considerable talent as a
painter. Though she had some reservations about the new arrangement, their future was more secure than they could ever have imagined and Avdo proceeded to fill the role of Alistair MacLean's
right-hand man for the rest of the author's life.

Alistair came to value the quiet, background presence of Inge, as
well as to appreciate her skill as an artist. He bought several of her

originals and you will find them today hanging in places like Gillespie's lounge at Muir of Ord. In fragile times, she would be there with a bowl of soup and quietly washing his shirts, a calm and reassuring presence.

Alistair had carried into his adult life the habit of early rising, a virtue of rural Scotland which dated back to his days at Daviot, when the boys helped out with the cows and morning chores. Even now he was awake by four a.m., rising to make himself a full breakfast of bacon, sausage, eggs and fried bread and, whenever possible, adding the Scottish dimension of a kipper, to which he remained partial. After breakfast he typed until ten, when he broke off to relax on the sofa and read the newspapers, usually *The Times* and the *Daily Express*.

What a pleasurable place to live when you could saunter out through french windows to breathe in the fresh sea air of the Adriatic and pick yourself an orange from Avdo's trees. With the house built into the rockface, the main entrance from the road above reached the Cimics' own quarters first. You then went downstairs to Alistair's apartment, which was on the level of the front garden.

After his break, it was back to typing until one o'clock, when he might cook himself a steak. (He was a strong believer in the protein diet.) At other times, he and Avdo would drive round the Bay of Zaton, several miles away, park the car and walk the last stretch along the water's edge to the Restaurant Mali Raj, where Marko the host would serve up his specialities. Alistair seemed to enjoy the company of locals, even though they could speak his language no more than he could speak theirs. After a leisurely lunch, they walked back along the waterside to the car and drove home to Villa Sandra. There he typed some more on the golf-ball machine and Avdo would be available around eight o'clock in case he wanted to eat out. Then it was bed by eleven-thirty for that early start. He loved to see the sun rise.

Meanwhile, Sabrina had resumed her role of secretary under the new agreement of living in London and flying to wherever he might be. She looked after his mail, helped with research, acted as the link with Collins in London and flew out to Dubrovnik every so often to collect manuscripts and take them back for proper typing in Britain. In those years, the titles which were spilling from the typewriter were *Athabasca*, *River of Death*, *Partisans* and *Floodgate*.

Avdo stood by as required. There would be trips to Geneva or Cannes, where Alistair had retained the rented property of Semiramis, with its inspiring view, until he saw how things worked out in Dubrovnik. In Cannes, he would walk or visit galleries but did very little writing. It was his meeting place for family and visitors from Scotland; there was always someone coming to see him in Cannes.

Beyond Europe, Alistair would set out on exotic trips to places like India, Peru and Brazil, accompanied invariably by Avdo, Sabrina and Tony Fry. India inspired him to thoughts of a novel but it reached only to the extent of a title – *The Rose of Kashmir* – and was never written. The South American safaris were to do with research for *River of Death*, and in Peru Sabrina wondered if she ought to be taking notes because Alistair didn't appear to be bothering.

'It was later, when I came to typing his manuscript, that I realized what an extraordinary memory he had,' she recalled. 'For there, without a note, he had worked in the most amazing detail of what we had seen and heard.'

Alistair's fondness for the sea drew him much to the terrace of the Dubrovnik villa but nothing would be quite so gratifying as having his own boat again. From the days of his adventures on the *Silver Craig*, down the Clyde and up the west coast of Scotland, he had rented the odd craft in the South of France but had owned nothing but the *Ebhora*, during those years back in England.

Sabrina went in search of something suitable and came up with a Chris Craft called *Insan*, which cost Alistair £25,000. It had a Volvo turbo-engine, an extra propeller, an electric anchor windlass, six life-jackets as well as tape-decks and radio, and it was berthed in Dubrovnik Harbour, from which they would sail up the Adriatic on gloriously relaxed adventures, Avdo's experience as a merchant seaman coming in useful.

Sabrina, Tony and his son Wilde would join them, and there was always the valued hand of Mario Milutin, a Yugoslav sea captain, whose presence was appreciated and enjoyed by Alistair.

Young Ali, the most regular family visitor to Dubrovnik, made much use of *Insan*. His father loved taking it round to the island of Sipan, which was close enough for a lunchtime visit. The family of the house prepared wonderful food and Alistair would simply ring up to say they were coming. He would also sail his visitors to a little harbour called Cavtat, south of Dubrovnik.

While he welcomed visitors from the homeland, Alistair preferred them in small doses and would instruct Avdo to take them on car trips round Yugoslavia or on Adriatic cruises while he kept up the momentum of a book, slouching deep in his sofa until it was all worked out in his head, then springing to the typewriter to rid himself of the final chore of writing it.

Alone in his bachelor flat of an evening, he would watch a video of old movies like *Casablanca* or *Ben Hur*, or watch football on television, particularly during the World Cup. He listened eagerly for the Scottish football results on a Saturday night, rekindling memories of his regular treks to Ibrox Park to watch Rangers with his pal Alastair Cameron.

The Mercedes brought from Cannes was soon overtaken by a new Rolls-Royce, which Alistair bought at the Motor Show in Geneva. The circumstances of parting with the Rolls give some hint of the sensitive nature of Alistair MacLean.

When dining out of an evening, he preferred to do so in groups, more to relieve the concentration of one-to-one company than through any wish for hordes of people around him. (Even the charms of Avdo by himself would wear thin after a time.) It was while leaving Hotel Argentina after a dinner party one night that they passed a group of English tourists at the doorway.

As they stepped into the waiting Rolls, Alistair overheard one of the Englishmen say, 'These people must be filthy rich.' He went quiet and didn't speak all the way home. Then he told Avdo, 'We're sending the Rolls back. I'll get a Mercedes instead.' Having always frowned on the decadence of the idle rich, he didn't like what he heard. Unwittingly, a glib Englishman had brought home the truth of Robert Burns when he wrote: 'Tae see oorsels as ithers see us . . .'

The Rolls-Royce was duly dispatched and replaced by a Mercedes, which had all the appearance of an ordinary model though, in all truth, it was a rather specialized version, complete with velvet seats and a highly computerized system well before its time. At least the ostentation was out of sight.

So he was torn between the comforts of wealth and the simpler life which had been his lot in those far-off, uncomplicated days.

Avdo Cimic tells another story which illustrates Alistair's peculiar, quirky nature. Among his vast legion of followers was Sir John Sainsbury (now Lord Sainsbury), chairman of Britain's biggest grocery chain and member of one of the country's wealthiest families. Sabrina Carver was a family friend of the Sainsburys and gifts of bacon and sausages would arrive from his wealthy admirer, a particular treat since Alistair dearly loved his big British breakfast and sorely missed the quality products he had known back home.

One day there was a phone-call to say the Sainsburys would like to meet Alistair, who returned the message that they would, of course, be welcome in Dubrovnik. That didn't necessarily mean they would meet him. On the appointed day, he dispatched Avdo to pick up Sir John and Lady Sainsbury from their private jet as they flew into Dubrovnik Airport from their house on the Greek island of Corfu.

The instructions were to take them in the Rolls-Royce to the yacht and thereafter on a cruise to one of the Adriatic islands, while making some excuse about Alistair being too busy to see them. (The Sainsburys heard another version – that he was too drunk to see them!) Avdo entertained them to a delightful picnic on the island and then prepared for the final part of his instructions. He was to sail past Villa Sandra on the way back to the harbour, keeping a safe distance, from which the visitors would see the famous author on his balcony.

At the appointed hour, Avdo curved the yacht in towards his own house where, sure enough, the bold lad was poised for his distant admirers.

'He was even dressed up in his best suit and tie,' Avdo remembers with astonishment, 'and there he was, waving to the Sainsburys like God from his balcony. It was like something from a surrealist painting by Dali. I was amazed.'

Avdo berthed the boat at the harbour, drove his visitors back to the airport, and the Sainsburys were gone. For some reason best known to himself, Alistair MacLean, who could sometimes turn modesty into a boast, had decided to keep his wealthy admirers at bay with a curious exhibition. Was he perhaps wary of a man so much wealthier than himself? Were the aristocracy being put in their place? Or was it just mischief, with him lording it from high, above his lordship? In a situation where he had little enough real company, living and dining among rustic people, where his own superiority was beyond dispute, it is hard to believe he couldn't occasionally have enjoyed some stimulating conversation. The Sainsburys would have provided it.

Other visitors had more access, even film producers. Elliott Kastner or Peter Snell would arrive at the sparkling Adriatic resort to discuss their various projects – separately, of course, since film people keep much the same distance from each other as famous authors. (It is fairly typical that Kastner and Snell had occupied offices on the same floor of Pinewood Studios for many years yet scarcely knew each other, never pausing to exchange a word about their mutual acquaintance, even friend.)

In a Dubrovnik hotel, there was a particularly stormy meeting between Alistair and Elliott Kastner over money which Alistair claimed was due him from the film agreement on *Where Eagles Dare*, which was still pulling in large sums all those years after its production in 1968.

As Alistair's lawyer, David Bishop had been investigating why certain royalties had not materialized when the contract purported to entitle his client to 50 per cent of producer's share of profits.

As the producer of the film, Kastner argued that there was a side deal whereby MacLean was not entitled to anything like 50 per cent. It had to do with the interpretation of a contract which had complications. Alistair faced him across the table like an adversary, in a situation of hostility far removed from their adventure together in creating one of the most successful films ever made.

Though well accustomed to the tough dealings of Hollywood moguls, Kastner still recoils in some horror at the memory of the meeting. At one stage, he walked out. But the turning point came when Bishop was able to produce a letter written to MacLean by Kastner in 1968, leaving little doubt about MacLean's rights in the matter. Kastner had totally forgotten that letter and conceded that Bishop had established the legal position.

It was not the first time Bishop and Kastner had crossed swords. The producer had wanted to cross-collateralize *Where Eagles Dare* with another of his productions, *The Walking Stick*, an arrangement not uncommon but one to which the lawyer took exception. If MacLean had accepted the proposal made by Kastner, it would have cost him over half a million dollars, the sum so far received from the *Where Eagles Dare* interest. There had also been differences over another of MacLean's films, *When Eight Bells Toll*.

Kastner's defence was that they were mainly due to those side deals into which Alistair had entered as part of his attempt to get round the financial schemes of Stanley Gorrie in the sixties.

That stormy meeting ended cordially, with a dinner at the hotel that evening. But the rugged Kastner felt humiliated and harbours some resentment about it to this day. Outwith the MacLean connection, he had been through some bad financial times and didn't have the money. In view of what he had done for the author, he felt he might have been due more understanding. Into the nineties, he was still recovering financially from the experience.

In a world where business is business, however, David Bishop had to look after his client's interests – and the evidence was on his side.

29

In 1983, Alistair MacLean was invited to return to his old University of Glasgow to accept an honorary Doctor of Letters degree. There was some faculty disagreement about his choice as a recipient but such happenings are not uncommon in the ivory towers of ancient institutions.

He was joined on that auspicious occasion by an entourage which included his first wife, Gisela, his two brothers and their wives, the Chapmans, Sabrina Carver and Tony Fry and the indispensable Avdo from Dubrovnik.

They all met up in a fine sense of fellowship as they booked in at the Stakis Grosvenor Hotel in Glasgow and prepared for the big day. But here again, the Jekyll and Hyde personality of MacLean was to surface, spurred on as ever by drink. On the one hand, Sabrina and Avdo, who were closer to him than most, assured me that Alistair was quietly delighted about his degree, filled with a sense of pleasure and pride that such an honour had come his way, from the alma mater of both himself and his father. At the same time, he was struggling with a conviction that he didn't deserve the honour and had made it known that he never wanted to be addressed as 'Dr MacLean'.

At the eve-of-graduation dinner, given by the Principal of the University, one of his fellow graduands, the Reverend James Martin from Carntyne, Glasgow, took the chance to tell him how much he had enjoyed his books down the years.

'Ach, it's a lot of bloody rubbish,' was MacLean's retort, covering his embarrassment in self-deprecation. So they settled to dinner and, as the evening wore on and the drink flowed, his behaviour became no less erratic. Finally he told James Martin, 'I'm fed up with this bloody boring affair,' and got up to leave. (Others remember that he had to be carried from the dinner, which was attended, among others, by Thomas Winning, the Roman Catholic Archbishop of Glasgow.) This, naturally enough, caused a stir, and James Martin was among those who were disappointed that their image of the great MacLean had been tarnished. Yet the author himself would have been appalled by any thought of ingratitude or discourtesy. It was the obligatory response of his quirky nature to situations of that sort, not unlike his critical mutterings at the première of *The Guns of Navarone*.

One of the Reverend James Martin's roles happened to be that of chaplain to Collins in Glasgow, and two days later there was an engagement at the company headquarters in Bishopbriggs, which both men were due to attend. The contrast was unbelievable. 'As we toured the printing works, Alistair was absolutely marvellous,' said the minister. 'There were lots of women employed and he was so good at talking to them. I had seen the two faces of Alistair MacLean and could hardly believe it.'

The graduation ceremony passed without incident, MacLean being presented for his degree by Andrew Skinner, Professor of Political Economy, who not only happened to be well versed in MacLean's work but had the added connection that his elder brother had also been a sailor on the Russian Convoys which inspired *HMS Ulysses*. In front of a distinguished gathering, Professor Skinner said wryly that there was at least one academic authority who had expressed doubts about MacLean's chances of success in this world, to the extent of believing that 'if he intends to make a living from writing, he'll have a damned hard job of it'. He added, 'Fallibility, it is to be hoped, may be one of our more endearing academic qualities.'

He recalled that Alistair had graduated with honours from Glasgow University in 1950, in a class which had produced a novelist (it produced two, MacLean and Alexander Trocchi), an Edinburgh professor (John MacQueen) and a man who gained a first-class degree and a Commonwealth Games gold medal in the same year. He traced his career from Highland childhood to his adventures as a sailor on the Russian Convoys.

'Written in three months [*HMS Ulysses*] became the first British novel to sell 250,000 hardback copies in the first six months after publication. Fulltime writing brought a rapid flow of novels, some twenty-five since 1957, many of which were made into films, a medium which has opened up another area of creative activity. The books are, in the main, stories of adventure and suspense, with the notable exception of his historical, non-fictional study of the voyages of Captain Cook.

'In accepting this honour, Mr MacLean reminded us of the fact that, in the Royal Navy, a ranker can be awarded a good-conduct medal for twenty-one years of undiscovered crime. Mr MacLean knows well that the honorary doctorate is not simply a reward for good conduct, although it should not be inconsistent with it. It is rather offered in recognition of the accelerating discovery of a formidable talent to amuse – in the best sense of that term.'

Harking back to the embarrassment of the dinner table, Avdo Cimic says in mitigation that Alistair was very tired that night. Already a mild diabetic (his mother was, too) and regularly failing to take his insulin, he was developing nose-bleeds and showing signs of running into a poor state of health. Avdo would fly him for medical attention to Geneva or Cannes, where he had one particular doctor friend who looked after him. Latterly he reached a stage of incontinence, while still in his early sixties, and no one was allowed to touch his body except Avdo, who had the task of washing him.

Brother Ian and his wife, Bunty, went to visit him in Dubrovnik and realized he was still drinking heavily. He also had an unnerving habit of walking in the middle of the road, even on the dangerous Adriatic Highway, and they were heading back to Avdo's villa one day, after a jolly lunch at a nearby restaurant, when they turned round in time to see his heels disappearing over an escarpment.

He fell twenty-five feet down a steep slope and landed on a pile of rubble. Since the gods protect drunk men and children, Alistair survived a dangerous fall (presumably having leapt to safety from a passing vehicle), but was lying unconscious while Ian and Bunty hailed some workmen in a car.

They clambered down and brought him back to the roadway before he was rushed to hospital, where he was found to have cracked his cervical vertebrae. With no private care in the communist state, MacLean landed in a small room for six patients, a situation from which he wanted to escape as soon as possible. Eventually he was allowed home, only because Bunty was a State-registered nurse and persuaded the authorities that she could look after him just as well in his own flat.

Astonished as ever by the Jekyll and Hyde behaviour of his brother, Ian recalled, 'When he had been drinking, Alistair became big-headed and started lauding his own genius. "I'm the best," he would brag, even though he was so modest in his sober state. His bragging was out of character. He used to think he was the cat's pyjamas when it came to navigation. In fact he would have sailed his boat into a brick wall!'

But if MacLean had suffered mishap on that Adriatic Highway, there was more distress in store for him along that ribbon of roadway passing close by the villa which had become his home in a distant land.

30

If Villa Sandra was a retreat of contentment for the solitary MacLean – and youngest son Ali was the apple of his eye – those two elements came together to produce one of the most distressing experiences of his life.

While Gisela continued to take an interest in his welfare from the distance of Geneva, she never did visit him in Dubrovnik, and that connection was left to Ali, who would fly down from time to time to see his father. He arrived on one such visit in 1984 and was warmly welcomed as ever, preparing to book in at Hotel Argentina. Sabrina had been staying at Alistair's apartment, on one of her periodic visits to collect manuscripts, but was due to leave that day. Avdo drove her to Dubrovnik Airport, *en route* to London, and it was when she rang back that night to say she was safely home that she heard the news.

No sooner had she left Yugoslavia that day than disaster had struck. Avdo's house has an awkward driveway, which slopes and turns sharply towards the Adriatic Highway above, calling for the most careful negotiating of a vehicle. Dusk was approaching as Ali reversed the Mercedes up to the main road, before heading for his hotel in the city. Alas, he reversed into the path of an on-coming service bus from the town of Cibenik. As the vehicle hurtled towards Ali's car, the driver instinctively swung his steering-wheel to the left, avoiding the Mercedes but heading his bus towards a solid face of rock on the other side of the road. That caused a lorry driver, coming from the opposite direction, to take similarly evasive action, which landed him on Avdo's garage below.

Hearing the commotion, Alistair and Avdo dashed from the villa to the road above to find a scene of utter chaos by their own gateway. When the dust had settled and they sorted out the confusion, the bus driver and three of his passengers were found to be dead. The only consolation was that Ali had escaped unhurt.

The police arrived and took possession of Ali's passport so that he would be unable to leave the country until his trial, which took months to arrange. When they finally completed their investigation, they faced him with a charge that his negligence had been responsible for the deaths of four people.

In the general devastation, Alistair was stunned and wouldn't accept that it was Ali's fault. In defending his favourite son, he was convinced that the bus driver must have been in the wrong. Ali didn't accept the burden of guilt either, though it didn't seem to help his prospects when word got around that one of the dead was secretary to a local judge.

When the trial finally opened, Alistair, still feeling his son had been unfairly accused, was in court with Avdo to follow every word of the proceedings. It had been a worrying time, and his increasing despair was not lessened when young Alistair MacLean was sent to prison for a year. In view of the non-criminal nature of the offence, it wasn't a case for handcuffs. He was ordered to report to an open prison near Belgrade at an appointed hour and Avdo flew with him to the capital and drove in a hired car to the prison door, trying to explain to the governor the background of the young man.

No stone was left unturned to see what could be done about easing Ali's plight. A key figure was to be Sir Fitzroy MacLean, another famous Scotsman from the same clan, whose wartime position as commander of the British military mission to help the Yugo-slavs gave him a very special relationship with President Tito and his people. Such was their regard for this distinguished soldier that he became the first foreigner permitted to have full ownership of a house within the communist state. Tito took a personal interest in the matter and the legislation which permitted this privilege for those who fought there during the war became known, appropriately, as MacLean's Law!

As well as his home at Strachur in Scotland, the same district where the author had his roots, Sir Fitzroy bought a house on the island of Korcula, sixty miles north of Dubrovnik. It was there that

Alistair MacLean made his discreet approach, desperately seeking some help for his young son.

'My wife and I had dinner with him a couple of times in Dubrovnik,' Sir Fitzroy told me. 'We wanted him to come to Korcula but he was not in good health. My wife came from Inverness originally so she and Alistair had that in common. He had quite a remarkable war and talked to me about his experiences in the Russian Convoys. By coincidence, my wife's first husband was also in the convoys and was killed later in the war.'

While MacLean sought the help of his fellow clansman, Avdo pursued an influential contact of his own, Bato Tomasevic, a Belgrade publisher, who had the ear of ministers. By further coincidence, Bato's older sister, the beautiful Stana, had been a famous sniper with Sir Fitzroy during the days of Partisan fighting, after which she became an ambassador and Speaker of the Parliament. But she died young.

'Bato Tomasevic was most helpful and I was very glad that, together, we managed to do something for Alistair's son,' said Sir Fitzroy, whose Scottish homeland of Argyll and Bute now has a twinning arrangement with his beloved Adriatic island.

With the approach of Yugoslavia's annual freedom celebrations in November, there was always a pardon for prisoners. The efforts on Ali's behalf all came together to reduce his prison sentence from a year to just a few weeks. The news that he was being released came at short notice.

His father was visiting Gisela in Geneva at the time but, as soon as he heard, he chartered a private jet, stocked it with champagne and caviar and two beautiful stewardesses and set out for Belgrade. Ali had not suffered too much in prison. Avdo visited him with food, books and newspapers. But now he was free and, within three hours of hearing the news, was winging his way home to Geneva, travelling in comfort and celebrating in style.

Alistair was a generous benefactor of charity in Yugoslavia – he gave much support to the country's mongol children – and there is little doubt that a combination of influences worked to the advantage of young Mr MacLean who, nevertheless, would carry the memory of four dead people.

His nightmarish link with Dubrovnik was counterbalanced by the consoling fact that it was also the place where he met Nevena, the

ALISTAIR MACLEAN: A LIFE

Belgrade girl who was to become his wife. They married and settled in Lugano, the Swiss town where they are to be found today.

Though it had not been evident with his own family, Alistair MacLean could be good with children (a throwback to his natural talent as a teacher?) and was splendidly relaxed when giving a birthday party for the Bishops' daughter, Camilla, at Hotel Argentina.

The effect of a famous uncle on the younger generation is well expressed by Shona, one of the five children of Gillespie and Margaret at Muir of Ord. While a pupil at Dingwall Academy, her progress was followed with much interest by Uncle Alistair, who encouraged her own thoughts of becoming a writer. While often chauvinistic, the Scots are equally quick to assume their own inadequacies when pursuing their potential. If Shona had any such doubts, the example of her famous uncle at least gave proof that the family background was no handicap to her ambitions. He encouraged her to write something for his inspection and was keen that she should follow his own route and study English at Glasgow University. Instead, she read history at Aberdeen and triumphed with a first-class honours degree.

Shona made some telling observations on the way Alistair would try to fire the imagination of the young with thoughts about their future. Perhaps speaking from personal experience of wrong turns, he was anxious that the young were making the right choice in their lives – and that it would lead to happiness. He was not so concerned about what they wanted to *do* as what they wanted to *be*. There was a subtle difference, which did not escape his talented niece. Her suggestion of becoming an English teacher left him uneasy, as if she would only be heading for the cul-de-sac from which he was fortunate to escape.

'It was as if he was looking for something more,' she recalls. 'Sometimes he would say I should be a writer and at others he was more concerned that I should be happily married and have children, as if there was a choice of making your mark in the world and being happy.'

While at university, Shona had a spell of study in France, and Alistair's letter before she left Aberdeen shows the depth of his family interest and generosity, as well as the wit with which he genuinely sought to make little of it:

I don't know how you intend to maintain yourself there, but whatever you have in mind is probably wrong. Traditionally, of course, you wash dishes or serve up vin rouge to the sozzled French citizenry until the early hours of the morning. This is supposed to be romantic and glamorous. It's neither. Both the kitchen's and the bar patrons tend to be sleazy and undesirable. Don't tell me it's none of my business because it is; because you're my niece and I'd rather you passed up that particular form of romantic glamour.

I have a better idea, which is to open up an account in your name in a bank in Rennes and deposit £3,000 which you can draw either in cash or by cheque. If you run out of that, I'll look after it. You can pay me back when I'm old and decrepit and bankrupt.

Furthermore, I don't think any young lady should be abroad in Europe without her own transport. It is a simple matter for me – if it makes you feel better, I've done it for several young people in the past – to buy a car of your choice anywhere in Europe and have it transported to Rennes ... When I say 'a car of your choice', I don't refer to Rolls-Royces. These are reserved for destitute writers.

Please don't quibble, Shona. Argy-bargy upsets the aged. In any event, young nieces, no matter how academically gifted, are not permitted to argue with elderly uncles.

From this particularly elderly uncle, much love ...

Shona found that Alistair enjoyed portraying himself as the long-suffering ageing uncle. 'It was a way of getting round, or cutting through, his vast generosity to us, so that he was Uncle Alistair rather than a rich and famous writer.'

He could be deviously playful in planning and camouflaging his generosity. After meeting Shona and her sister Mairi at Dubrovnik Airport, he drove them to Hotel Argentina and arranged a rendez-vous after they had freshened up. When he arrived, he feigned consternation at their being there before him. He asked to see their watches. Shona wasn't wearing one. Mairi's must be fast, he concluded, because he was never late. Two days later, Cartier watches from Paris were delivered by Avdo. His wife, Inge, took the girls to the boutique, and Lachlan accompanied them to the jeweller's with the wherewithal to set them loose like kids in a sweet shop; the travel arrangements were made by Sabrina.

Uncle Alistair, who had already left envelopes of spending money to make sure the holiday cost them nothing, stood back from direct involvement. 'It was the only time I ever came back from a holiday with more money than I went away with!' said Shona, who also defends him from any notion of vulgarity in giving.

Caring was very much at the root of his kindness. He had been concerned that she might be lonely in a strange land when arriving to study in France. A few days after she reached Rennes, her cousin Lachlan turned up on her doorstep, 'just passing through from London to Geneva'.

'I enjoyed his visit and I may be doing Lachlan a disservice,' she said, 'but I had a feeling "the old man" might have dispatched him to Rennes to make sure I was settling in.'

She has warm memories of Uncle Alistair, from early childhood days, when she would hold his hand on walks along the harbour, to those student years, when she was more conscious of his position.

'I was pleased and proud to be Alistair MacLean's niece though I didn't like to tell people. Yet, if someone mentioned it, I was glad that they knew,' was how she put it, with a natural Highland modesty and charm.

'He certainly made a big impression on me and I think of him still as a very kind and generous man, also astute but very lonely. He was interested in people for their own sake and liked to have around him those, like Sabrina, who were genuine and not just interested in his name.'

Shona was among those to benefit from Uncle Alistair's trust fund, money which came in handy when she married and became Mrs Fisher in the small town of Ellon in Aberdeenshire. Her husband, Martin, works in the offshore oil industry from Aberdeen. There was a mortgage to meet and a house to furnish and Shona stays at home to look after the baby.

She had indeed prepared a sample of her writing but it never did reach Alistair. Displeased with her effort, she felt it was too naïve to warrant his scrutiny. As a stay-at-home mother, however, she has turned her mind to writing once more and, with the benefit of maturity, is concentrating on the genre of murder and mystery. Who knows what those MacLean genes might produce in the future?

Meanwhile, back in Dubrovnik in the mid-eighties, David Bishop was relieved that Alistair's money problems had been largely resolved. He advised him to resign as a member at Lloyd's, to which he had been introduced by Lewis Jenkins, since the insurance risks to which he was exposed by far outweighed the financial return.

The Bishops joined Alistair at the opening of the 1984 Winter Olympics in Sarajevo and had an uneasy feeling that his life was going downhill. He turned up on a bitterly cold day, wearing an open-necked shirt, a leather jacket and thin trousers. Attempts to make him wear thicker clothing were met with bursts of bravado. 'Ach, I'm tough,' he assured them. He was so tough he had to retire to bed with such a bout of flu that he saw no more of the Winter Olympics except on television.

He was harbouring a dream of owning an island in the Adriatic, but even though the famous MacLean's Law was extended to include other foreigners as well as the MacLeans, it was something which never did materialize.

31

Despite mixed reports about his health, the books were still flowing from the prolific pen of Alistair MacLean. But for a man who had reached the heights of international fame and popularity, it does seem extraordinary that, even in the latter stages of his career, he was still having to fight battles with publishing people who thought they knew better.

When the manuscript of *River of Death* landed in the hands of Sam Vaughan, editor-in-chief of his New York publisher, Doubleday, it was returned with so many scores, changes and suggestions as to send him into one of his more bristling bouts of caustic fury. In a letter to his main publishers, he lashed out at Vaughan's criticism, which had ripped his work to shreds with adjectives like 'confusing, depressing, draggy, tiresome, unrealistic and lacking credibility'.

Alistair's response, in putting Sam through his own slicer, gives us the opportunity to sample the MacLean variety of mocking wit at its biting best. This is what he had to say about Mr Vaughan, shortened to S.V.:

> The comments are well matched by the actual editing, where we have countless pages scored and scarred in a fashion characteristic of a peculiarly witless and retarded schoolmaster taking a sadistic pleasure in destroying a virtually illiterate eleven-year-old's pathetic attempt to write his first school essay.
>
> How can S.V. possibly compromise Doubleday's high standards of pride, integrity and regard for the truth by publishing such patently unpublishable rubbish? I would much rather he followed

an ethical code and came straight out and said 'This is trash and I won't publish it.' He knows he doesn't have to.

S.V. says I have the unfortunate habit of overusing the word 'clearly' and, to a lesser extent, 'obviously', 'dark', 'very', 'quite' and 'indeed'. He is quite right in this and I shall watch it. But this does not entail a blanket elimination of all such words.

There are cases where 'clearly' and 'obviously' are, clearly and obviously, the only suitable words in the context. And that's all I've learned from the hundreds of corrections.

The rest boils down to what may laughingly be called style. The style-changes for change's sake are particularly infuriating. I am actually being told, for the first time, how to write English and that any amended version that S.V. and his editors choose to light on simply must be better than mine.

I tire of this. So many of S.V.'s comments are so silly that I won't waste my time refuting them. It might, I think, be a good suggestion and advisable if he stuck to his publishing and I to my writing. I do not care for – and, if pushed into a corner, will refuse to have, whatever the consequences – trans-Atlantic editing.

If that was the atmosphere in which one of the world's most popular authors had to ply his trade, one wonders what could be left for lesser mortals. In view of that extraordinary exchange, it is interesting to come across the opinion of another of the world's top-selling thriller writers, Jack Higgins, who has given us books like *The Eagle Has Landed* and *Storm Warning*. On the publication day of that same book, *River of Death*, Higgins put down his views for the benefit of the *Sunday Standard* newspaper. Marvelling at what he described as a unique career, in which MacLean had become the most successful British novelist of his time, he went on:

What is the secret of that incredible success? If we knew, we would all be doing it, for there is no doubt that he is one of the greatest page-turners in the business. I don't think one can analyse the exact gift he possesses which enables him to accomplish the trick, because gift it is, and as impossible to explain as the flair which makes one actor competent and the other a great performer.

One can make an attempt at some kind of assessment, of

course, and his latest book, *River of Death*, is as good a starting point as any. MacLean, more than anyone else in the thriller genre, has always varied his backgrounds. The war story as displayed in the brilliant *The Guns of Navarone* or the classic *Where Eagles Dare*, the pure thriller of *Puppet on a Chain*, the Secret Service exploits of *The Last Frontier* or *When Eight Bells Toll*.

In *River of Death* we start in a classic MacLean situation. The last few weeks of the Second World War, the death throes of the Third Reich and two extremely unpleasant SS officers plundering Greek gold before shipping out by submarine to the safety of South America, one betraying the other and leaving him behind to apparent certain death at the last moment.

From that situation, we jump to present-day Brazil, with its startling contrast in life-style . . . MacLean gives us the heat and the smell of the place, with his unerring eye for time and place and along with the story of the mysterious adventurer, Hamilton, and his search for vengeance for the murder of his wife and father-in-law, weaves in an exact description of the plight of the wretched forest Indians of Amazonia today, facing a planned extinction at the hands of the white man . . .

A word of warning. Don't start reading *River of Death* unless you have time to finish it at a sitting, for the old master is in top form with this one.

You wonder what Sam Vaughan made of that paean of praise. Meanwhile, the same Scottish newspaper which carried the Jack Higgins review, the *Sunday Standard*, was curious about the doings of one of the country's most famous sons.

As *River of Death* appeared on the bookstands, the newspaper's diarist was tracking the author to his Dubrovnik retreat and finding him strolling through the garden of the villa, pausing to pluck a fresh lemon for his morning tea while extolling the virtues of the simple life behind what was still then regarded as the Iron Curtain.

The secret was to live off the land, he was saying as he returned to the house to fry the breakfast of bacon and egg. Sure enough, a jar of dark mountain honey from the hills above the villa stood on the kitchen dresser beside a bowl of fresh eggs, a newly baked loaf, home-made cheese and oranges from the garden.

He continued to eschew the trappings of wealth and said they meant nothing to him now. He didn't need toys. In twenty-five years of fame and fortune, he had had them all – mansions, sleek limousines, luxury yachts. He no longer drove because of poor vision and was thirled to that dictum about being able to wear only one suit at a time.

'I keep telling my boys that flashy cars and bright lights are all meaningless,' he said. 'And they reply, "But Dad, you've had all that."'

Even so, he practised what he preached. Despite a cleaning woman coming in regularly, he washed up after every meal and did his household chores, like making the beds. Usually she would find him hunched in his favourite corner of the sofa, a rumpled, frail figure of a man, staring quizzically over his reading glasses into space.

'She's firmly convinced I do absolutely nothing, you know,' he confided. 'I've heard her say "That Mr Alistair, he just sits there." It's true, of course. But I'm usually thinking something out.'

Alistair confirmed that he seldom returned to Scotland and, when he did, it was for a sailing holiday with his brother. 'He's a hard taskmaster – works me like a dog,' he said cheerfully.

Finally he gave some clue of his attitude to the Yugoslavian land which had become his main base. 'I like the country and I like the people. They are tough, independent and friendly. A bit like Scots people, I suppose. I don't ever see myself living in Scotland again, though. I've been away too long. I'm a European now.'

32

Into the eighties, Alistair MacLean wrote to the editor of the *Glasgow Herald*, Arnold Kemp, to ask if he could have the copyright of 'The Dileas', the short story which had sparked off his career when it appeared as the winner of the paper's competition in 1954.

It was, he said, the only piece of his literature which remained outside his personal ownership. The request was willingly granted, with a suggestion that he might care to write an exclusive article for the *Herald*. MacLean responded immediately and gave us one of the rare insights into his thinking.

Recalling the competition and the fact that the £100 prize-money had been a considerable lure for a person who had no money at all, he went on to review his career since that day, in the fifties, when he became a Collins author *en route* to fame and fortune:

During those twenty-seven years I have written twenty-seven books, fourteen screenplays and numerous magazine and newspaper articles. It has been and remains a fair enough way to make a living. I have been called a success but 'success' in its most common usage is a relative term which has to be applied with great caution, especially in writing.

Quantification is far from being all. Some of the most successful books, magazines and newspapers in publishing history have beggared description when one tries to describe the depths to which they have descended. Enlightenment may not be my forte but, then, neither is depravity.

It is difficult to say what effect one's books have had, what degree of success or failure they have achieved. Consider, for instance, the reactions of those who had the debatable privilege of being on the *Glasgow Herald*'s editorial board at the time when those short stories of long ago were under consideration.

Some may feel, or have felt, a mild degree of satisfaction that they had the foresight or acumen to pick on someone who was not to prove a total dud; all too many writers produce one story and then are heard of no more. Others on the board may have felt a profound indifference. Still others, gnashing their figurative teeth, may have rued the day they launched on his way a writer whose style, they felt or feel, in no way matched the high standards set itself by Scotland's premier newspaper. I shall never know.

The effect on the reading public is equally hard to gauge. I did write a couple of books which I thought might be judged as being meaningful or significant but, from readers' reactions, I was left in no doubt that the only person who shared this opinion was myself. I should have listened to Sam Goldwyn's dictum that messages are for Western Union. I have since then concentrated on what I regarded as pure entertainment although I have discovered a considerable gulf may lie between what I regard as entertainment and others' ideas on the subject.

I receive a fairly large mail and most of it is more than kindly in tone. I am aware that this does not necessarily reflect an overall consensus of approval. I am essentially a non-controversial writer and people who habitually sign themselves 'Indignant' or 'Disgusted' of Walthamstow or wherever don't read my books in the first place or, if they do, don't find the contents worthy of disparaging comment.

The effect of writing on myself, of course, I know fairly well although I am aware that, even here, there may be room for blind misappraisal. The main benefits of being a fulltime writer are that they confer on one a marked degree of independence and freedom, but that freedom must never be misinterpreted as irresponsibility. I don't have to start work at nine a.m., and I don't; I usually start between six and seven in the morning. But then, though I often work a seven-day week, I don't work a fifty-two-week year. Being in a position where there is not one person anywhere who can tell you what to do – and that's the position I'm in – is quite splendid. But no one is wholly independent. I have a responsibility towards my publishers.

Publishing houses are not, as has been claimed, a refuge for rogues, thieves and intellectual criminals who depend for their existence on their expertise in battening on the skills and talents of the miserably rewarded few who can do what the publishers are totally incapable of – stringing together a few words in a meaningful fashion. Some publishing houses are run by people who are recognizably human. Mine is notably one of them.

I feel some responsibility, though not much, to book editors. Collins New English Dictionary defines an editor as one who revises, cuts, alters and omits in preparation for publication. I feel moderately competent to attend to the revising, cutting etc. before it reaches the editor. But they can be of help, to some more than others.

I feel no responsibility whatsoever towards book critics. The first criticism I ever read was of my first book, HMS Ulysses. It got two whole pages to itself in a Scottish newspaper, with a drawing of the dust-jacket wreathed in flames and the headline 'BURN THIS BOOK!' I had paid the Royal Navy the greatest compliment of which I could conceive; this dolt thought it was an act of denigration.

That was the first so-called literary review I ever read; it was also the last. I'm afraid I class fiction book reviewers along with the pundits who run what it pleases them to term 'writing schools'. One must admire their courage in feeling free to advise, lecture, preach and criticize something which they themselves are quite incapable of doing.

My greatest responsibility and debt are to those who buy my books, making it possible for me to lead the life I do. Moreover, while deriving a perfectly justifiable satisfaction in pointing out my frequent errors of fact, they never tell me how to write. I am grateful.

One great benefit arising from this freedom is the freedom of travel. I do not travel to broaden the mind or for the purposes of research. True, I have been to and written about the Arctic, the Aegean, Indonesia, Alaska, California, Yugoslavia, Holland, Brazil and diverse other places, but I never thought of writing about these locales until I had been there: on the obverse side of the coin, I have been to such disparate countries as Mexico and China, Peru and Kashmir, and very much doubt whether I shall write about them.

About future writing, I really don't know. From time to time Mr Chapman has suggested, a trifle wistfully I always think, that some day I might get around to writing a good book. Well, it's not impossible for, no doubt to the despair of all those book reviewers I never read, I wouldn't like to retire quite yet.

To celebrate his thirty years of authorship, Collins decided to publish a collection of MacLean's short stories, including 'The Dileas', which had started the whole process. Unfortunately, everything other than 'The Dileas' had been stored away and lost, but Lachlan undertook a search which landed him in the cellars of Villa Murat. There he came across the bundle and only then could the book go ahead, under the title of The Lonely Sea. It included fourteen stories. (One which was not used, 'The Cruise of the Golden Girl', appears as an appendix to this book.)

On publication day of 1985, Alistair was due in Cannes but, before setting out from Dubrovnik, had a visit from Caroline Moorehead of The Times. Once more he was strong on self-deprecation, speaking of his latest book in mocking tones and pointing out, in his low, guttural, Scots voice, that he himself kept none of his own books, giving away any copies that came his way immediately he received them. He expressed himself pleased enough if, at the end of the day, he produced a saleable product. 'And that I do,' he conceded.

As Caroline Moorehead pointed out, what distinguished Mac-Lean from other writers was not that he ranked among the top ten bestsellers in the world, earning around a million pounds the previous year, but that he had been at the top for so long.

With the James Bond books, there had been a spell when Ian Fleming had beaten him in that league of people with books which sold over a million copies. Fleming had reached thirteen books in that category but MacLean finally drew ahead of him with eighteen.

Do we really have so far to search for the secret of his success? It all boils down to his exquisite gift as a story-teller, that ancient art which survives all trend and fashion. From as early as The Guns of Navarone, he had struck on a formula which proved such a winner

that he seldom deviated from its course. Those tales would move at
such a breathtaking pace there was little time to plumb the depths
or subtleties of his characters' emotions. They were simply a varied
collection, cast into one hostile environment or another, trapped in
seemingly impossible situations, compelling the reader towards page
after page to find out how there could conceivably be a solution.

The formula became irresistible. The further secret was to vary
the locations, whether it was beneath the polar cap of *Ice Station
Zebra*, the Grand Prix setting of *The Way to Dusty Death*, the high-
wire intrigue of *Circus*, the San Francisco threat to the American
President in *The Golden Gate* or the sinister mood of Amsterdam in
Puppet on a Chain. And always the unveiling of an unlikely Judas
figure.

Caroline Moorehead touched on that point when she concluded
her visit to Dubrovnik with an observation about Alistair's own lonely
existence:

> To the visitor, his days seem sparse. He lives what appears to be
> an inner existence unaltered over the years, inventing his in-
> variably treacherous villains, his irreproachable heroes and intri-
> cate but bloodless plots according to a formula once proved
> unbeatable and ever since adhered to.

He was repeating to her that he knew nothing about writing or
writers, a piece of facetiousness to which he was partial.

But his regard for people like Graham and Chandler was real
enough, and although he wouldn't comment in public about fellow
writers, except the occasional swipe at Fleming or Robbins, he did
of course hold opinions about who was who.

In 1967, for example, he let slip in a letter to his publishers that
he regarded Winston Graham as the best writer in Britain at the
time. The Le Carrés, Deightons, even MacLeans, weren't in his
class and 'in a few short years – without descending into our murky
market-place – he will be the best-selling author in Britain'.

33

The mercurial Marcelle might be out of Alistair's sight but she would never have allowed herself to be totally out of mind. Since the divorce, she had been living between the Rutland Court flat and a number of addresses in Los Angeles, mixing the dramas of a drug overdose with the effrontery of seeking a loan from her former husband – and trying to get back with him on a permanent basis!

MacLean had had such an overdose of Marcelle that even the attempts of Avdo Cimic to introduce him to other women were met with resistance. 'He had had more than enough,' said Avdo. The only woman who could now have stirred his enthusiasm was Gisela, but the reconciliation he dreamed about remained a forlorn hope.

With her financial settlement from the divorce, which many would have regarded as more than adequate, Marcelle had no reason to be short of money. But she went on such a spending spree, splashing out tens of thousands on everything from luxury cars and holidays to expensive paintings and a Cartier bracelet worth £40,000, that the funds were running out at an alarming rate. Worst of all, having already been suspected of dabbling in drugs in London, she was now hopelessly drawn into that scene in California where, by her own admission, she squandered £100,000 on cocaine for herself and a bunch of so-called friends in Beverly Hills.

It was the tragedy of this strangely mixed-up woman, sometimes warmly generous and likeable, sometimes unbelievably foolish and vindictive, that she ended up in such loneliness as to buy friendship at any price.

In London, she was selling and pawning her valuables and telling her sculptress friend Doreen Kern that she was planning to dispose of the London flat. Doreen kept asking what she was doing with all the money and urging her to retain the flat as some kind of security for the future. It was worth upwards of £250,000 even then.

It was not so many years ago, on that first visit to the MacLeans in Los Angeles, that Doreen had been asked to bring out Marcelle's furs and jewellery and was petrified by the responsibility when she realized what a fabulous collection there really was. Now, incredibly, it had all but disappeared, and in a final interview with the journalist Robin McGibbon, Marcelle claimed she had even been visited by Mafia-type people saying they had come to collect money which was due for drugs. There were threats of cutting off her fingers at the rate of one finger for every £5,000 owed, though she maintained she had always paid for the cocaine on the spot.

The degradation to which she had sunk was fully confirmed by those who still saw her in Los Angeles. Doreen Kern was as much a witness as most. 'The last time I visited her she was absolutely broke and living in a state of abject poverty. She had no home and nowhere to go. She had been living at the house of a woman who worked for Elizabeth Arden in Beverly Hills but, from the time she left there, it was downhill all the way.

'I saw her in a dreadful place in Burbank, where she was sleeping on the floor. I took her in food bags. There were young men hanging around and I couldn't figure out the situation. Grossly bloated, with her body now misshapen, she did say she had not been too well and there was a mention of leukaemia. By then I had learned not to take what she said too seriously. I thought it was just another of Marcelle's dramas.

'She was still optimistically calling herself a film producer and talking about flying off to Texas and selling scripts.'

But now, even more than usual, there was nothing in her plans for films or anything else.

Much later, MacLean's son Michael met a lady who told him of visiting a woman who foretold the future with tarot cards. She found her in a trailer-type home, sleeping on a mattress on the floor in considerable poverty and reading the cards fairly unconvincingly. She chatted for a while and said she had been married to a famous author. It was indeed Marcelle. She had for long claimed startling predictions from her sixth sense. She knew the girlfriend of pop-star Marc Bolan and was said to have predicted his death. As to her own likely fate, she had always said she would die 'under the bridges of Paris', which was a French saying for dying in poverty. Had she substituted the bridges of Los Angeles, her crystal ball could not have been clearer.

Her only son, Curtis, arrived to see her at the County Hospital in Los Angeles, one of the last refuges of the poor and down-and-out in California. He was appalled at her surroundings. 'Here was my mother, a woman who had had breeding and class and good taste – a woman with a fabulous talent for driving men crazy, like gelignite heating up – and here she was, ending up in a place which was like something out of Dickens.'

She sat on the edge of a bed, a pathetic shadow of her former self, yet still bursting into reflexive pursuits of the unattainable dream; making ambitious plans; still nursing her pride. The infectious flame was flickering; the power itself was gone.

A plea for financial help was relayed through David Bishop to Alistair MacLean, who was researching a book in Greece, accompanied by Sabrina Carver. The message said Marcelle was dying of cancer but it might have been just another of her ploys for all they knew.

Sabrina tried to handle the situation delicately but MacLean, who could react sharply, was adamant that no money was to be sent. This time, however, it was for real.

Marcelle sat down and wrote a beautiful letter to Doreen Kern, whose mother had just died, not even mentioning how ill she herself had now become. Her illness had developed into cancer of the pancreas and she died on 16 May 1985, just four weeks after her fiftieth birthday, though her age at the time was given as forty-five.

Alistair paid for the funeral. Doreen Kern was anxious to find out what happened to her ashes because she had always wanted them scattered at sea. Curtis brought them back to this country and called on Doreen, saying he had thought of burying them under a rose-bush at Elstree, near the film studios which were such a part of his mother's ambitions.

Curtis was already married to Shirley, a Borehamwood girl who had been working in Los Angeles. 'My mother was a good Jewish momma, though not an orthodox one,' said Curtis, 'and she did so want grandchildren. Sadly, she just narrowly missed seeing our first child.

'I knew she was fond of the sea so I took her ashes down to Lynmouth in Devon and scattered them on a waterfall.'

So Marcelle put out to sea, a free spirit, gone but not forgotten – and destined to rise again, in characteristic fashion, to haunt the name and reputation of Alistair MacLean in a way he could hardly have imagined.

34

In the summer of 1986, Alistair MacLean set out with Avdo Cimic from the picturesque villa near Dubrovnik to make one of his rare visits to the homeland of Scotland. It was to be his last.

They met up with two of his sons, Lachlan and Ali, and drove north through England, across the border, to arrive at Muir of Ord, near Dingwall, in the Scottish Highlands, not far from where the MacLean boys had grown up in the inter-war years.

It is a Scottish tradition to go forth in the wider world to seek a living, maybe even a fortune, but his family and friends knew that, for all his escaping, Alistair was always in his element back home in the Highlands, not least on that July visit of 1986, when they had never seen him more relaxed or contented. He was back where he belonged, pleased to have the company of Lachlan and Ali, who was paying his first visit, and delighted to see Gillespie and Margaret and their children again. After his years in the hotel trade, his brother was enjoying semi-retirement as deputy clubmaster at the local golf club.

Alistair had no sooner breezed into the house at Muir of Ord than he was calling to Margaret, 'Have you phoned Tom yet?' Yes, of course Margaret had phoned Tom – his bosom pal, Tom Fraser; she always did when Alistair was coming and Tom and his wife, Rena, would be over shortly from the nearby town of Beauly, where Tom ran his ironmonger's business.

If Alistair was more at peace with himself and the world than they had seen for a long time, there was just one blight on the visit. His friend Tom, with whom he had shared that undying bond from innocent boyhood days, was said to be suffering from cancer. Alistair made the most of the reunion, taking up with Tom and Rena where they had left off last time but brooding privately and confiding to the family that he feared he would never see Tom again. There was irony in that thought.

With a sense that life was boiling up to some kind of crisis, the reunion became a matter of concentrated fellowship, in which they recalled their childhood and the good times which belonged to far-off days of the late twenties and the thirties.

Well aware of the situation, Rena Fraser looked on with her distant thoughts and remembered her anxiety when she married Tom and prepared for the first visit from his famous friend, Alistair MacLean. 'Don't worry,' Tom had assured her, and soon she came to realize the sense of that.

'He was quite obviously a brilliant man, on a different intellectual level from us, yet he was always on your level, never making you feel that you didn't know as much as he did,' said Rena.

With Alistair insisting on paying the fares, Tom and Rena had soon become accustomed to flying off on visits to Switzerland, the South of France or Yugoslavia.

'Alistair always wanted to do for you the things you normally couldn't have afforded yourself,' said Rena. 'When we went on a tour of Yugoslavia, I just took a few casual items from Marks and Spencer. Then we discovered he had booked us into the most marvellous places and I told him, "You might have warned us where we were going!" But he had wanted to surprise us. That was Alistair.'

Though Tom and Rena, forever respectful of his privacy, were always cautious about introducing him to friends, Alistair did occasionally enjoy his identity being revealed. On that last visit to Muir of Ord, he spent part of the time at the Priory Hotel in Beauly, where they were choosing the local gala queen one night. He was invited downstairs to present the prize and join in the fun, and was delighted to do so, seeming to be quite relaxed that people knew who he was.

During the Scottish visit there was one more mission to be accomplished. With that love of the sea, he had retained a connection with boats all the way from the *Silver Craig*, the one he shared with Dougie Seggie, to the more luxurious *Ebhora*, the fishing boat converted in Dublin, which he would sail up the west coast of Scotland, to be joined once more by Dougie and his family.

Alistair's latest boat, *Insan*, lay in Dubrovnik harbour, but he had dreams of a better one and he and Avdo had been discussing it throughout the previous winter. This was to be the big one. And where better to look than his own Moray Firth coast of Scotland, where they were accustomed to building fishing boats which would withstand the hazards of the great North Sea?

So Alistair set out with Avdo and the boys to visit the small town of Buckie, the home of Herd and Mackenzie, one of the best boat-builders in the country. The boss of the firm, Iain Sinclair, remembers it well.

He had recently led a management buy-out of the company and was planning the future when he received a phone-call to say a Mr MacLean was on holiday in the area and would be calling to discuss a possible cabin cruiser. On the appointed day, the visiting party turned up at the yard. Drawings were produced and discussed with the technical draughtsman and managers and 'the small, rather gaunt gentleman who introduced himself as Mr MacLean' said he would like to take away some drawings of a particular model to study in more detail.

'Here I was with this motley group,' said Iain Sinclair. 'Not realizing who Mr MacLean was, I in all innocence started to ask a bit more about his background business, his interest in boats and so on; but I was struggling to find any common ground for discussion. There didn't seem to be any warmth in him and he was cagey about giving any inkling of his identity.

'Only when the party left and I looked again at the name – Alistair MacLean – did I refer to the jacket of one of his books and realize it was indeed *the* Alistair MacLean. He must have thought he was dealing with a real innocent . . .'

What Iain Sinclair was discussing was the potential order for a cabin cruiser which would cost £500,000. 'It would have been a real feather in our cap,' he said, with dreams of providing a boat for the man who wrote stories like *HMS Ulysses* and *The Guns of Navarone*.

Complete with plans for the new boat, MacLean, Avdo, Lachlan and Ali prepared to head south to visit his other brother, Ian, and his wife, at Ross-on-Wye in Herefordshire.

They took their farewells of Gillespie, Margaret and family and there came that special moment when Alistair clasped the hand of his dear friend, Tom Fraser. Of all the people he had known down the years, that boyhood bond had ensured there was nobody he knew better, or by whom he himself was known better.

So it was southwards across the border to England and on to that charming corner of Herefordshire, not far from Wales, where Ian and Bunty had finally settled having brought up their two sons, Alistair and Ian, and daughter Margaret in Surrey, then retreated to Scotland; they had later gone back south to be nearer the family.

Now they prepared to play host to Alistair, Lachlan, Ali and Avdo before they all went on to see Margaret in the market town of Wells in Somerset. They had no sooner arrived at the villa in Sussex Avenue, Ross-on-Wye, than Bunty was surprised to see Ali, without a by-your-leave, crossing to the cabinet and pouring himself a drink. This was the preamble to a bigger embarrassment.

Avdo Cimic recounts that there were differences of opinion within the family about the proposed cruiser from the Buckie yard. Avdo felt young Ali was trying to prove his knowledge by advocating a bigger one. With his vast experience of the sea, his uncle Ian argued that the size was right and some bad blood began to be generated.

The upshot was that Ali suddenly announced he had had enough of this family tour; he was bored and was going home to Switzerland. His father was mortified by the discourtesy to Ian and Bunty and didn't quite know what to do. But the lad had made up his mind and soon he was off, leaving his father, Avdo and Lachlan to mend the atmosphere.

After a few days, the remainder of the party headed for Wells, where Ian and Bunty would be pleased to see Margaret and family in the context of a wider gathering of the MacLeans. They checked in at a local hotel, where Alistair played host at a farewell dinner. Avdo was the only one there who was not strictly family, though he was by now very much one of the circle.

It was a pleasant evening of good fellowship, in which much of the hurt and embarrassment of Ali's departure had been forgotten. The significance of that farewell gathering would not come clear for several months. They were simply enjoying themselves.

Sticking to that rural tradition of Scotland, the MacLean boys of Daviot were still early risers, a habit which persisted with Alistair through all his bouts of drunkenness. On the following morning, he and Ian were out and about at the crack of dawn, walking through the town of Wells, recalling the days of their youth. Suddenly they found themselves faced with the twelfth-century cathedral, so they stepped inside and stood in silence, each with his own thoughts but knowing that the other, too, would be remembering Father, up there in his Highland kirk at Daviot, more than fifty years ago, his golden tones echoing from stark walls with his message of hope and compassion and understanding.

They left the cathedral and later that day they left each other, Alistair off back to Dubrovnik and Ian and Bunty home to their villa in Ross-on-Wye. That would be the last time they would ever speak to each other face to face.

Events were moving quickly.

35

Though Alistair MacLean's family structure had long since broken up and Gisela had refused to remarry him, they remained on sufficiently good terms that he was free to go back and stay at Villa Murat whenever he wanted. He would spend four months of the year there and was always present for the festive season, joining his first wife and three boys at the place which should have been their united family home.

It was there that I met her on two occasions, a dignified lady in her early sixties, living alone with her memories in the big house which became the basis of her divorce settlement in 1972. A huge dog lopes out to give warning of a stranger. Gisela hovers by the back door to verify the identity of her visitor, a faded beauty but recognizably the German girl who won the heart of Alistair MacLean more than forty years earlier.

Once settled in the lounge of Villa Murat, she looks out wistfully over Lake Geneva and tries to make sense of those latter days in Alistair's life. After he broke with Marcelle, he would pay visits during which he wrote from a room upstairs and felt comfortably at home. Then he would be off again, back to his seclusion in Dubrovnik.

'I still had great compassion for him but, when he asked me to marry him for the second time, I knew I couldn't take it all again,' said Gisela. 'Once bitten, twice shy. But we would sit here and talk; after all, we had been married for a long time and had a lot in common. I used to tell him about my "eighteen years of slavery", as I called it.'

At festive time, they usually spent Christmas at Villa Murat before all going off for the New Year, to attractive places like Garmisch-Partenkirchen.

'Alistair and I would walk and talk and, at the various hotels where we stayed, he would take great pleasure in asking the pianist to play his favourite music. He liked Scottish tunes but his favourite performer was Hank Williams and he particularly liked his song "The Singing Waterfall".'

Alistair could give a creditable performance on the piano himself and when he was in a happy mood he would break into 'Nellie Dean' or 'I'll Take You Home Again, Kathleen'. He loved drinking songs and took a special liking to Paul McCartney's 'Mull o' Kintyre'.

There was one year when they just stayed at Celigny for the whole festive period and had a most delightful time. There are pictures showing him in an apron, washing the dishes. Gisela remembers him as being on his best behaviour that year, and it particularly pleased her that he was being pleasant to the boys.

'He was such a Jekyll and Hyde. I know there is good and bad in everyone but I could never understand how Alistair could hurt people so much.'

In the mid-eighties Alistair was in such poor physical shape when he travelled from Dubrovnik to see his doctor in Cannes that he was warned about his drinking. The message, bluntly, was that if he didn't give up the whisky immediately, his end would not be far off. Alistair appears to have taken the warning and Avdo Cimic confirms that he then confined himself to his favourite wine, which was the Yugoslav red called Merlot; even then he wouldn't touch a drink till eight in the evening.

'Sometimes he would stop drinking completely, not touching it for a month,' said Avdo. 'So much so that we used to call it his Ramadan.'

But his Ramadan didn't survive. He was still in abstemious mood over the festive season of 1986 and went off to the Black Forest with Gisela, Lachlan and Ali for the customary New Year holiday. As always, he made his 'first foot' telephone calls to his brothers in Britain on New Year's Day 1987, and sounded in good form.

It was into January when disaster struck, triggered off when he met an Irishman who was working as a porter in their hotel at

Hintergarten, making some money to pursue his course as a doctor of theology back home.

It was a classic case of MacLean finding someone who could do with a helping hand, so he invited him to his room to discuss his future. There is evidence that he handed over a cheque for £15,000 to this total stranger in his life; if the generosity had ended there, the dénouement might have been vastly different. Instead, they embarked on a drinking spree which had catastrophic consequences.

'During our holiday,' Gisela told me, 'Alistair had not been touching drink at all, not even on Hogmanay Night. Then he met this Irishman. Well, you know how men can sometimes compete with each other to see who can drink the most. They started on the mini-bar in Alistair's room and drank a great deal. That sparked him off on a bout.'

He wanted to buy Gisela some jewellery so they decided to spend a few days in Munich, booking in at the plush Bayerischer Hof Hotel. Alistair was adept at concealing his condition and Gisela didn't detect the full horror of what was happening.

From London, Sabrina Carver would speak to MacLean by telephone two or three times a week, no matter where he was, and it was during her call to the German hotel that she became worried. He sounded merry enough but there was something halting in his speech.

Leaving the family to their privacy, Avdo had gone off skiing in Austria with his wife and daughter, but after receiving a call from Alistair in Munich he too felt there was something wrong. He and Sabrina discussed it over the phone and it was agreed that he should make his way to Munich without delay to see what was happening. After all, they were two of the very few people who had enough influence on Alistair to stop him drinking.

Avdo caught a train from Nasfeld and arrived in Munich to find his boss in a bad condition. He opened the mini-bar in his hotel room. It was empty. Gisela went to bed that night, leaving the two of them watching television, Alistair equipped (as often) with a bottle of mint syrup, a non-alcoholic drink which needed diluting and to which he was particularly partial.

Gisela rose next morning and went to check in his room. This time she knew that something was very far wrong. 'He was in bed, just looking at me with big eyes. The bottle of mint syrup had been left by his bedside and he had reached out for it, perhaps thinking it was alcohol which would help relieve his pain from a previous fall.'

Before he lost contact altogether, Gisela – she who had spent all those years trying to stop him drinking – ran for some wine and water, held his head and tried to put the glass to his syrup-encrusted lips.

With huge irony, the very last conscious act in the life of Alistair MacLean was to turn away a drink. 'No,' he said gently to Gisela, pushing away the glass. Then he lapsed into unconsciousness, and there was never another sign of communication.

He was rushed to a local clinic and then to the University Hospital of Munich as the various members of the family were summoned, including Lachlan and Ali, who had already left after some kind of falling-out.

Ian and Bunty arrived from England. With her nursing background, Bunty quickly summed up the situation when they were taken to see Alistair in the intensive care unit.

To all intents and purposes, he was a corpse, and they were keeping him alive on a support machine. Ian enquired and was told that he had had several strokes and they had carried out three brain scans. If he survived, would he be a cabbage?

'Yes,' said the doctor.

'Then why are you keeping him alive?' asked Ian.

'Because I am a doctor, not God,' came the clinical reply.

Ian knew when to say no more. In addition, it seemed that Gisela may have wanted to give him every last chance.

Alistair lingered through the rest of January and died quietly in that Munich hospital on Monday 2 February 1987.

'I think he knew, sub-consciously, that something was going to happen,' said Gisela. 'And there was Alistair, who had always been so strong a character, so masterful . . . but in the end we all have to give up our own will. In the end, like all people, he had to take death. To see him lying there in the hotel that morning, so meek, so helpless, I just felt so sorry that things had been the way they were.'

As the world received news of the death of Alistair MacLean, the obituary writers poured out their endless columns on the man described by the *Daily Express* as 'the foremost adventure writer of his day'.

Over a three-column headline, *The Times* called him 'Yarn-spinner for the millions'. They said his output was prolific if repetitious. He wrote to a formula which appealed to a popular readership. 'I know the day I start to satisfy readers of *The Times* I'm finished,' he had said. His name would forever be synonymous with *The Guns of Navarone* and *Where Eagles Dare*, bestsellers which had been made into equally successful films. But his vast wealth lay uncomfortably on his conscience and he lived, if not frugally, then simply.

The *Daily Telegraph* described his early novels as 'models of terse action writing, always well researched and pared down to the essentials':

MacLean was a quiet man, speaking softly with a broad Scots accent that no period abroad could lessen. He had no desire to attend literary occasions and, when he did, he remained a spare figure of middle height standing in a corner, more often than not in a haze of cigarette smoke.

No one grasped the sense of MacLean better than one of his fellow countrymen, Allan Massie, then on his way to becoming a distinguished and award-winning novelist himself. Among his observations in the *Scotsman* obituary, he said:

HMS Ulysses was written at a time when the British cinema seemed to turn out a story of wartime heroism every second month. It owed something to Nicholas Monsarrat's *The Cruel Sea* and, though it was not as fine a novel, it was a very good and gripping one. It contained hints that MacLean might develop into a realistic novelist, whose stories of action also dealt seriously with emotions of men under stress.

Instead, he went in another direction. To say he 'sold out' would not only be impertinent or foolish but it would also be wrong: he merely followed his talent and wrote the books he wanted to write, which were probably those he was best equipped to write. He became 'an entertainer and, I think, a good one', as he put it himself.

The virtues of a MacLean novel are very clear. The action is fast, the incident frequent. It strains at the bounds of credibility but, unlike Fleming, hardly ever breaks them. If there is none of the style that Fleming imparted to the Bond novels, there is very little of the nastiness and snobbery that hang about them either. MacLean valued professionalism, both in his own work and in that of his heroes. There was a definite formula: he offered, as one critic put it, 'a hero, a band of men, hostile climate, a ruthless enemy and, as often as not, a Judas figure who almost upsets the mission'.

Because he lacked the ability of a Buchan or an Ambler to make particular moods his own, to put an unmistakable stamp on certain areas of experience, it is unlikely that his books will last. I can't imagine that this would have worried him. He wrote books to make air journeys tolerable and to take people out of themselves for a few hours; he did it very well. 'I am good at my job. No, I'm very good at my job. I'm a thorough professional,' he said. And so he was.

MacLean's demise was acknowledged in the Swiss newspapers, but sparsely so, for they are about as discreet as they are anonymous as a people. It is one of the reasons celebrities choose to stay there; nobody bothers them.

His former secretary, Jacky Leiper, now a valued assistant to the vice-president of Union Carbide in Geneva, read the notice with pangs of sadness. From leaving the MacLeans back in the seventies, she had never been in touch again.

'My overall feeling,' she said, 'was one of sorrow to have seen someone like Alistair who could have been an awful lot happier. It would have been better if he had been able to remarry Gisela – and better if he had stayed in the United Kingdom. He had some friends in Switzerland but this was not a natural life. This was his hiding place.'

Jacky's mother read the news at her home in Carmunnock, on the south side of Glasgow. A few miles away, one of Alistair's former pupils, Gordon Whitehill, realized that the house he bought in 1979 (343 King's Park Avenue) was where his old teacher had written *HMS Ulysses* – yes, through in the wee back bedroom.

The announcement of Alistair's death brought a special pang of

regret to Willie McIntosh, that other former pupil who, just a few
weeks earlier, had come upon the old class photograph from his
Gallowflat days. He could put a name to most of them: David Yule,
by then a high-ranking officer in Strathclyde Police; Leslie Piggot,
who became a distinguished Scottish athlete; and standing at the
end of the row, the man he remembered best of all – Mr MacLean,
good-looking, solemn-faced schoolmaster, viewing the camera with
caution, right hand clasped on left wrist, the tartan tie fitting well
with the tweed suit, which had long been his uniform.

Willie had always intended to write to Mr MacLean so he would
put it off no longer. He recalled old times and enclosed the photograph, hoping it would find him with an address which said: 'Mr
Alistair MacLean, Geneva, Switzerland'. A few weeks later it was
returned, marked 'Unknown'. And days after that, Willie read of his
death. He told the story in his local newspaper, the *Rutherglen
Reformer*, which finds its way to exiles around the world, and there
was an immediate response from classmates, even a suggestion for
a class reunion. Wouldn't Alistair have been touched to come again
among his 2B class of middle-aged men and to hear the gratitude
which they now articulated in his memory? He had wandered into
another world, far removed from the rugged contours of Rutherglen.
But Gallowflat had not forgotten.

So they came from their various directions to prepare for the private
funeral at Celigny. Avdo had dashed back to Austria, taken his
family home to Dubrovnik and returned to Geneva. Ian and Bunty
arrived from England, Gillespie and Margaret flew in from Scotland,
accompanied by none other than Tom Fraser, Alistair's best friend,
who may have been dying of cancer but had managed to outlive the
old pal who clasped his hand at Daviot that day, knowing they would
never meet again. (Tom survived for two more years.)

The Chapmans, Sabrina Carver, David Bishop and one or two
others flew from London and, together with Gisela and the boys,
they joined in an agreeable dinner at Hôtel Richmond in Geneva,
a warmly reflective evening which was a kind of quiet celebration of
the life of a man who, with his own special mixture of talent, feelings
and frailties, had touched every one of them.

Most of the mourners were staying at Hôtel L'Angleterre nearby,
one of Alistair's favourite haunts. The irony of the dinner location

was that Hôtel Richmond had been the destination of Marcelle on that crisis day, many years before, when she had to be hastily removed from Villa Murat before Gisela arrived back from Germany.

Now that was all in the past and they were remembering the good times. And, in the morning, they drove out to Celigny for the funeral service in the little chapel by the village square.

Apart from family and close friends, they had invited Alistair's favourite waiter, Nikki Tracchia, and his Spanish domestic lady, Gabrielle, who had cooked and cleaned for him in the apartment at Florissant and looked after Lachlan, who was living in the neighbouring apartment.

It was a deeply moving service, conducted by a minister who had previously been in Oxford, and when the hymns had been sung, the lessons read and the prayers offered, the small group of mourners followed the hearse on foot, round the village from the church to the quaint little cemetery by the trees and the waterfall.

Folk from Alistair's homeland, accustomed to the black frock of sober ceremony, observed the solid oak casket and the undertaker's array of uniformed attendants and thought it an expensive funeral.

Contrary to their etiquette, Michael and his wife were seen to walk ahead of Gisela, but only the Scots in the cortège would know a thing like that.

They followed the coffin round the winding path to the plain little corner of the churchyard, not as trim an enclosure as Daviot but a decent enough place just the same. There, Gisela was joined by Lachlan, Michael and Alistair as the minister raised his voice in benediction. On that cold, clear February day by Lake Geneva, they lowered the coffin to its last resting place and lingered for a final thought before shuffling out to the waiting cars and down the road for a lunch at Hôtel du Lac in Coppet.

Deep and private sorrow was overlaid with the chatter of warm recollection at that luncheon table. There was so much to remember.

Now the turbulent life of Alistair MacLean – 1922 to 1987 – had finally quietened to the silence of a grave in that little village by the lake. He deserved his peace. But it was not to be.

Even as they left him to his eternity, a Scottish newspaper was warming to the sensation which would guarantee an enlargement of sales in the weeks to come.

36

A few days after the funeral, there appeared in a Scottish tabloid newspaper the kind of headline which might have caused Alistair to turn in his grave. There wasn't even the decency of a week from his death before the *Sunday Mail* announced its inside sensation with the trailer: 'MY HELL WITH ALISTAIR MACLEAN — A DRUNK AND A WIFE-BEATER: Former wife tells all.'

In characteristic fashion, the paper was revealing 'the remarkable secret life of top-selling thriller writer Alistair MacLean for the first time'. The former Rutherglen schoolteacher was a monster in drink, according to his second wife, Mary Marcelle. He broke her jaw and teeth, punched her in the stomach, hurled her downstairs and pushed her into the canal in Amsterdam.

Marcelle had, of course, threatened him with all this in an attempt to improve her divorce settlement a decade earlier, a blackmailing device which MacLean had answered with the promise to see her in court. Her allegations, however true or false, might have been difficult to substantiate and she could have found herself at the wrong end of a libel action. Little more had been heard of her threatening manuscript but clearly she had not forgotten.

The macabre irony of the story now told was that the accusations were being made from one grave to another, providing a new twist to the role of ghost-writer, which had been taken up by the journalist Robin McGibbon. Marcelle, who predeceased Alistair by two years, had evidently spoken to Mr McGibbon shortly before she died.

The world copyright on the story belonged to the Tauber Press Agency and, according to the *Sunday Mail*, it was due to be published as a book. For their own serialized purposes, they had acquired those parts of the story which told how the lady who had everything money could buy – diamonds, expensive cars and houses around the world – also had violence on a monumental scale.

One minute MacLean was a raging alcoholic madman, intent on destroying Marcelle, the paper's readers were told; the next he was a mild-mannered man, showering her with roses and begging forgiveness.

Whatever one may think of such outbursts, the reason for now giving exposure to Marcelle's accusations is that, for all her tendency to exaggerate, there was very likely a strong foundation of truth in what she said.

To that extent, she helps to flesh out the Jekyll and Hyde character which MacLean undoubtedly became, the only reservation being the extent to which the dead can be monstrously libelled. But, if Marcelle had been warned off in her attempts to publish the damning manuscript in MacLean's lifetime, she hadn't abandoned the idea altogether.

While living in Beverly Hills after the break-up of the marriage, she envisaged the story as a blockbusting television series, along the lines of a *Dynasty*, and told friends like Doreen Kern that she had made approaches to the appropriate companies.

How far she could have fictionalized the story without further legal trouble is a matter for speculation. Clearly, she saw some high dramatic possibilities in the tale of the Scottish minister's son, struggling as an unhappy schoolteacher, suddenly finding fame and fortune as a bestselling novelist and moving on to a life-style of mansions, limousines and diamonds, leading to drink, drugs and violence, two broken marriages and assorted triumphs and tragedies. The scriptwriters could have had no complaint about the ingredients.

Doreen Kern, who was friendly with both parties, remembers visiting Marcelle in the London Clinic when she was recovering from an assault in which she alleged Alistair had so damaged her leg that the kneecap had to be removed.

There was little doubt that she suffered physical assault but, as with almost everything else she tried to instigate, nothing at all came of her attempts to put it on screen. As her previous husband said, Marcelle was a good starter but a bad finisher.

Now, however, it was all spilling out in a Scottish newspaper, causing shock-waves among friends who knew little or nothing of his tendency to violence. In the course of the three weekly instalments, the *Sunday Mail* published a further news story in which MacLean's brothers, Ian and Gillespie, hit back at the way his name was being maligned, defending the man who could no longer speak for himself.

Seeking to tell the other side of the story, they said Marcelle had left him penniless and that he had had to borrow money to make alimony payments after their divorce. They claimed that her account was full of inaccuracies and lies and that the primary reason for the divorce was her extravagance; she was hopelessly improvident with money.

They pointed out that, much against Alistair's wishes, Marcelle had tried to take over the filming of his books but that, despite spending more than a million pounds of his money on trying to launch productions, nothing at all came of it.

It was known, they claimed, that Marcelle took drugs and that during the two or three years prior to the divorce she had deviated into relationships with other men and, in particular, there was evidence of her being beaten up by one of them. It was on those occasions, they said, that she blamed Alistair for her injuries.

Alistair's lawyer wrote a stiff letter to Noel Young, then editor of the *Sunday Mail*, expressing indignation at the way he had chosen to publish the material, alleging inaccuracies in Marcelle's story and pointing out that, if publication had taken place in MacLean's lifetime, they would have sought an injunction to prevent publication of libellous material.

He deplored the 'bad taste' of publishing so soon after the author's death, suggested he should reconsider printing any more of it and called at least for an explanation to the readers that much of the material was disputed.

Well, Noel Young did that, in printing the story of the brothers' reaction, but went ahead as planned to give the full three-week serialization of Marcelle's own story, wherever her spirit might have been by that time. It never did materialize as a book. But wasn't it typical of Marcelle that she could not be silenced, even from the grave?

It was a nine-day wonder which left its own sour taste but Bishop had more practical matters to attend to. He had met Alistair in Geneva on 26 September 1986, when the author completed a new will and settlement of his copyright position. Uppermost in his mind was a determination that Gisela should be handsomely treated in the event of his death, notwithstanding that this could give rise to substantial Swiss taxation. (For one thing, she was no longer a relative.)

He had also taken a curious decision that Michael, the adopted son, should be excluded from the will, saying he had been well treated in connection with the shop he opened in Geneva. When Michael met and married the beautiful Marie Madeleine Mees from Paris, Alistair was suspicious of her motives and bluntly challenged her on why she was showing an interest in his son. Wasn't she just after the money because of who the young man's father was?

But he met his match in Marie, who was able to draw on her own considerable background, pull herself to the full height of her dignity and freeze out his insulting suggestion. Perhaps MacLean was over-sensitive on the question of attractive Frenchwomen, having already had his fingers burned with another, who had at one stage reduced him to the point of bankruptcy.

David Bishop told him the exclusion of Michael would be most unfair and that he should be treated equally with the other two boys. He had merely been given a helping hand, the same as Lachlan and Alistair.

So the will was finalized, and now it was time to reveal its contents. For a highly successful international writer, who had earned somewhere around £20 million in his thirty years at the top, there was surprisingly little left at the end. Properly invested and nurtured, his money should have multiplied over the period. Instead, outwith the value of continuing copyrights, Alistair MacLean left a gross estate of only £1.68 million. It was all to go to Gisela and the three boys. Having given the Geneva house to Gisela at the time of their divorce – Villa Murat came to be worth £1 million in itself – he had no property to leave. Since the first marriage ended fifteen years earlier, he had led that nomadic life in rented property, from Geneva to Cannes, Beverly Hills to Dubrovnik. The sons had been costing him a lot of money and, at the time of his death, there was a substantial overdraft to be cleared.

As a result of those debts on the estate, repayment of loans and

Swiss inheritance tax, the final amount to be distributed between
Gisela, Lachlan, Michael and Alistair was £870,000.

In those last two years, MacLean knew he was a poor survival
risk and became more and more concerned about the position of
Gisela, whose income had been geared to his lifetime. As it was,
the arrangement from the time of his death meant that she could
count on an annual income of around £60,000, with the three boys
receiving just under £34,000 each.

There has been some agitation within the family as to why they
don't get more from the copyright settlement which has produced
an average annual gross income of £425,000 since MacLean's death.
Michael MacLean defends Bishop's position as literary executor.
'He is very cautious with the money and that's a good thing. He
doesn't want to put it all out and see it blown in a short time. As it
is, we have guaranteed payments from the trust for the next twenty
years. I don't know about the others but I'm quite satisfied with
what I get. Of course, perhaps I don't need as much as the others.'

In leaving everything to his first wife and children, Alistair felt he
had done well enough by the rest of his family and friends down
the years, as indeed he had. He had no interest in leaving legacies
to anyone else, but Bishop did suggest one exception: that he should
leave his boat, *Insan*, to Avdo Cimic. That was done.

Avdo's commitment to looking after Alistair, for which he had
received an advance of twenty years' salary, had come to an end
after just eight years, by which time he had used the money to
establish himself in that handsome art gallery in the centre of
Dubrovnik. Studio 57 is popular with tourists and locals alike and
Avdo now devotes himself to the role of gallery owner, hovering to
assist potential customers with that easy manner which charms old
ladies.

Since Alistair died, Avdo has encountered other foreigners with
money to spend, like the gent who wandered in from a cruise ship
in the harbour and turned out to be Mr Heinz, the American soup
man. His purchase of pictures from Avdo's gallery presented one
problem – how to ship them directly to the United States. Never
stuck for an answer, Avdo volunteered personally to convey the
paintings to California, for which Mr Heinz paid a first-class air
fare!

Having suspended his pension payments when he left Hotel

Argentina for the service of Alistair MacLean, Avdo did make an approach to David Bishop about a possible contribution in that direction.

'The family said "no" and I didn't feel too badly about it,' he shrugged.

Indeed, one could be forgiven for thinking Avdo had done quite well out of his association with MacLean. He had certainly remained faithful to their verbal agreement and was due what he had received. But, considering he had also been left the boat in Dubrovnik Harbour, there could be no tears over the family's refusal of further payment.

Avdo subsequently sold the boat for £18,000, still enough to square up his pension deficiencies and there, surely, the books were well and truly balanced.

All that remained was the collecting of Alistair's personal effects from Villa Sandra, which had been his main base those last eight years. There wasn't a great deal to collect since he had lived such a simple life. His wardrobe contained a few pairs of trousers and some nice suits which he never wore. There was the tuxedo, which he kept for the Christmas rendezvous with Gisela and the boys. There were some books and manuscripts to take away in the car, which Lachlan came to collect in Dubrovnik.

The master himself was gone, but Avdo has left the apartment as it was, so far not letting it out to visitors. Alistair's table and typewriter are still there, as if poised for his next fictitious adventure; his *Times* atlas and magnifying glass lie at the ready. His portrait looks wryly down on the scene of his creations and the leather swivel-chair awaits his arrival.

Outby, the ships sail down the Adriatic in a setting which begins to remind you of another place.

37

From penniless Scottish schoolmaster to one of the biggest-selling authors the world had seen, Alistair MacLean enacted a personal drama which was little known to his vast following of readers. They knew the public persona but practically nothing about the human being behind it, that mass of contradictions which lay within a deeply divided personality.

The statistics show that he wrote a book for almost every one of the thirty years in which he was a fulltime professional, all but one of them as fiction, the exception being his biography of Captain Cook. His book on cancer was never published and an intended story of the American Civil War got no further than thirty pages.

He had dreamed of writing great literature, which he hoped would take the form of his 'Rembrandt Quartet', as he called it. In the end, he settled for what he did best and that brought a huge commercial success.

Having struck that winning formula with *Navarone*, he gave each book an original story-line and maintained it with an exquisite craftsmanship, entertaining a mass market which recognized him as a master story-teller.

It was an art he expressed without the explicit sex, sadism or snobbery which he deplored in others, a legacy to the reading public which they still accept with gratitude.

The question of his appeal to the young brings forth an interesting response from Alastair MacNeill, the young man who carries on the tradition by turning those MacLean outlines into full-scale novels.

Born as recently as 1960, MacNeill represents a third generation of Alistair MacLean readers. His grandmother, now in her late eighties, discovered the books, his parents read them, and he himself has been enthralled by them since he was a teenager.

'As far as I am concerned, that is the secret of his immense success,' said Alastair MacNeill, 'that ability to produce a novel which could be enjoyed by any generation. He never used swear words, sex or gratuitous violence, which meant parents could let their children read his books satisfied that there was nothing to corrupt them.'

If MacNeill has a criticism, it concerns the tendency to push his female characters into the background. Plainly, he was ill at ease with women in his books but the readership had no complaints.

Similarly, in an age when contemporary authors are intent upon 'realism', the style of Alistair MacLean could be seen as an anachronism; but once again, the answer lies in the popularity of his books, as reflected in the continuing level of sales. Theories tend to melt away in the face of pleasure – and that was what he gave to millions of people.

It was all the more of a sadness, therefore, that the deeper satisfactions of life eluded him. On the private and personal side, he struggled with a disarray of marriage and money matters; with that sense of guilt about high earnings, which not even his immense kindness and generosity could assuage; with an addiction to alcohol which blurred the margins between his fact and his fiction and, worse still, affected his health to the point of premature death.

If escape was a prime characteristic of Alistair MacLean's fiction, it was no less a feature of his own life. He was searching for greater meaning and fulfilment while running away from the chances of finding it.

His bachelor flat, etched into that rockface of the Dalmatian coast, was a picturesque setting, of course, with its view of sea and ships and sense of Hebridean melancholy, especially on those stormy days when little islands would peer helplessly out of the mists, just as they would do in Colonsay or Iona.

In the solitude of Dubrovnik, almost certainly he found his greatest peace. Yet there must have been times when he questioned his presence there. With human contact limited to those lunchtime drives to Zaton Bay or evening meals with some locals, he was a foreigner without a common language.

Perhaps he was a fugitive from himself, searching always, finding seldom, just hiding and quietly harking back to those happier times when life was simple and rounded and innocent, and happiness needed no analysis; when Janet ruled in the kitchen and Father was closeted in his study and Tom Fraser was stopping by and Lachlan was there and life was sweet.

He never got over his brother Lachlan's premature death, coming at such a delicate stage in his own young life, and mourned him privately as surely as Catherine Mackintosh still nurses the memory today.

'If you had seen Lachlan, you would never have looked at me,' he kept telling Gisela.

With his father's death in the prime of a distinguished career, the double tragedy somehow dimmed the rest of his days. He was deep and private, and Gisela knew only that he believed in God, though he did not discuss his religious beliefs, even with her.

Having been subjected to a great deal of religion in his early days, he did write:

I have come to the reluctant opinion that, despite their hardly gained reputation as dedicated church-goers, men of God and even religious fanatics, the Scots are primarily interested in the trappings of religion and not in religion itself.

Even from the days of John Knox, who should never have been allowed near an Edinburgh pulpit, and the Calvinists, who carved up everybody in sight for the greater glory of God, down to the latter-day meaningless confrontations of Catholic Celtic supporters and Protestant Rangers supporters, precious few of whom ever darken the door of chapel or church, the true spirit of Christianity had burned with a low and guttering flame indeed ... I fear that with religion, as with nostalgia, the element of hypocrisy is never far from the surface.

As his own man, he roamed far and wide, as surely as the tinkers his father would meet on a Highland highway – a gypsy in his caravan who should have felt at home in Vaccares.

When Graham Lord of the *Sunday Express* asked him where he regarded as home, there was a long silence before Alistair replied,

'I haven't got a home basically. I suppose home is where my love lies.'

And where was that? In the Scottish Highlands, with its memories of childhood and the tugging ache of Father and Lachlan? Somewhere in the isolation of the sea with its warships and dramas and camaraderie? In Dubrovnik or Cannes or Beverly Hills – or most of all with Gisela in Geneva?

From questions like these, Dubrovnik was as good a hiding place as any, anonymous, respectful, uncaring, even largely unaware of his presence. Switzerland, so picturesque yet so bland, had served that purpose too.

He and Gisela had recovered a basis of good understanding and friendship. There would always be the Jekyll and Hyde in his nature but the enigma had come much closer to being unravelled.

Having firmly rejected all his overtures on the subject of remarrying her, Gisela had ensured her emotional independence. It was unthinkable to her that Alistair could ever control her life again.

With that matter established, Avdo Cimic was in no doubt about where Alistair's thoughts were turning more and more. As the man living upstairs and devoting years of his life to looking after him, he gave a revealing clue to this Scot who had been so critical of his native land. 'Alistair spoke all the time of Scotland, of his father and brother Lachlan. He had a tape-recording of his mother's beautiful singing voice and I used to hear him playing it over and over again when he was alone. He knew his Robert Burns and spoke of his intention to go home one year for a Burns Supper.

'I am in no doubt that his heart lay in Scotland, perhaps most of all at Daviot.' (Was the man who poked such fun at the mentality of the exiled Scot now himself a victim of the nostalgic pull?)

So to Daviot they came that late spring day of 1987, for a memorial service which should have satisfactorily completed the circle which started there, sixty-five years earlier. But, in the ridiculous confusion of whether or not it was a public service, the respectful folk of Scotland erred on the safe side and stayed away, denied their only chance to bid farewell to a distinguished son.

For the limited congregation of family and friends – the only absentee was son Michael, who has never set foot in Scotland – there was all the more of a close-knit poignancy about the occasion.

Here, before his father's pulpit, from which that golden voice had raised the rafters of the little kirk, Alison Rapson now echoed that other voice, as she sang that Gaelic song, 'I Love the Shepherd', which Alistair's mother had performed on the day she won the gold medal at the Mod.

The lessons were read by his brother Ian and his best friend, Tom Fraser, still fighting his last illness. And the eulogy came from the man who brought Alistair MacLean to prominence in the first place.

Ian Chapman said: 'It was in this church, Sunday after Sunday, that he would listen to the eloquence of his father's preaching. Let me quote from one of those sermons.

'"But His words were like a sunrise. One sees such a sunrise in a beautiful island of the Hebrides. I have lived in such an isle of dreams and my spirit has been held, as in a secret spell, by the miracle of God's dawn. Oh youth, oh youth, oh the beauty of it – oh the wonder! The crooning sea breaking on a hidden shore; the scented winds blowing from across the far spaces; the island wrapped in dreamless sleep, waiting for the dawn. And the dawn comes. The saffron changes to grey, the grey to misty white, the white to blue and suddenly a beam of silver shoots up the sky. And it is morning. And the isles are jewels, flashing to the sun and to the sea."

'Can you imagine the effect on the young Alistair of listening, week after week, to the beautiful literary cadences which fell from his father's lips? This must have been a time when his own latent descriptive gifts were being nurtured. There is no doubt in my mind that those early years greatly influenced his character, his psyche and much of his later outlook on life.'

He described Alistair as 'a good, if sometimes difficult, friend for more than thirty years'. Like many very shy and private people, he could be brusque, even surly, reserving his warmth and charm for a small number of close friends. But he had always remained 'a wonderfully warm-hearted, complex, fascinating, intelligent man who bore no grudges, and lived his life his way'.

Among the few outside folk who turned up at the service was Charlie Dunbar, the cinema projectionist from *HMS Royalist*, who had returned to his job at the Playhouse in Keith after the war and then became manager of cinemas in Glasgow. There he came to know a Mr MacLean, who was assistant manager of the Grant Arms Grill in Argyle Street, an acquaintance which was furthered when they met up again at the Roy Bridge Hotel on Loch Laggan, where the same Mr MacLean had become mine host.

The subject of the war had never been raised and it was not until he appeared at the memorial service that Charlie Dunbar realized that his Mr MacLean was none other than Gillespie, brother of his friend on board the *Royalist* during the war! Similarly, Charlie had moved on to a job as a mobile librarian in rural Banffshire before he realized that this writer called Alistair MacLean was again his former shipmate.

So they wandered out to a fine, clear day and cast their eyes around the childhood territory of Alistair MacLean – his father's beloved kirk and the manse across the brae, now a boarding house for tourists; Tom Fraser's derelict home and the Mackintoshes' handsome house on the hill.

The birds sang in the trees and picked up the echoes of distant voices, long gone from this parish but lingering still for those with the memory or the soul to hear.

Alistair's name was already engraved on the granite slab and folk lingered by the stones which commemorated his father and mother and Lachlan.

So they tore themselves away from Daviot that day and, much later in Switzerland, I walked with Gisela to that other churchyard at Celigny, not far from Villa Murat, to that unpretentious corner by the leafy shade. Only a few graves cluster there, the first on your left so plain that it might mark the resting-place of a local labourer; except that it catches your eye with the name of Richard Burton, the neighbour from down the road who would pass Gisela from time to time as they walked their dogs.

Across the narrow pathway, at fifty degrees to port, you come upon the stone of Alistair MacLean, a simple little setting bereft of all the wealth and trappings of those two remarkable figures: the man who wrote *Where Eagles Dare* and the actor who starred in it, now resting within a few yards of each other. No more fisticuffs.

We stood by the grave and heard, from over the dyke, the singing waterfall which tumbles down the ravine like a sparkling Highland burn.

For all the hurt and the heartache, there is no doubt that Gisela loves him still.

From that glade in Celigny she walks away with her thoughts, a woman who knows that, in this bewildering world, we live and love but seldom learn.

The life and times of Alistair MacLean, warm, wayward, fallible human being, were finally over. His considerable talent had flared and flourished and sometimes flickered and left him with a simple epitaph: that he brought entertainment to the lives of millions.

For all the lack of deeper satisfaction in his own life, I suspect he would have settled for that.

The Cruise of the
Golden Girl

IT STILL LACKED TWO HOURS to sunrise on a morning late in June when the hoarsely asthmatic starting splutter of our ancient Kelvin engine desecrated the Sabbath stillness of that far north-westerly Scottish fjord. In those high latitudes in midsummer, it was still the middle of the night. But quite apart from the inhumanly early hour and the corresponding depth of our spirits, it must be admitted that we were in pretty bad shape before we set out.

Our weariness was excusable. We had arrived on board on the same night, and for the previous seventeen hours the four of us had been travelling north non-stop in a dilapidated and almost springless vehicle of incredible vintage. Comfort there was none: even before we had clambered aboard the car, its interior had been more than comfortably loaded with provisions, bedding, luggage and equipment. Nor were matters helped by the condition of the roads during the last four or five hours: it was such as the city or suburban motorist encounters only in nightmares.

But we were well content. The worst, we happily believed, lay behind. We were now the proud and still somewhat unbelieving owners of a 34-foot Loch Fyne skiff, of unknown age but sound construction; and all that we had to do was to sail her back to the Clyde. We had the charts and the tide-tables; we had two excellent compasses; and were weighed down with the advice and admonitions of two fully qualified master mariners; some of us had even been to sea before, but not for long. Our preparations were complete. We had reckoned on everything – well, almost everything. 'Almost' is used advisedly, for there proved to be a flaw in our calculations. In our ignorance, we had failed to take into account just one factor – the Atlantic.

We had not long to wait for an intimation of its presence. Its first manifestation took the form of a slight but unmistakable wallowing which, as we rounded the southern headland of the fjord, changed swiftly to a lively pitching – this to the accompaniment of a furrowing of inexperienced brows, a cocking of ears to the imagined rising note of the wind, and a nervous inspection of the open sea ahead.

With dismaying suddenness the open sea was no longer ahead, but all round us. The *Golden Girl* was butting straight into the long, grey swell of a heaving Atlantic, the aftermath of a storm. With a graceful buoyancy, her bows soared high and easily over each rounded crest, and the resulting sheets of spray, cascading over decks and down the unprotected five- by twelve-foot hatch of the amidships fish-hold, brought out the oilskins for the first time. After that we lived in them.

It was dawn. The clock said so, but all we could see was gloom and murk, the driving cloud-wrack, and the menacing heave of the sea. If any crack-brained producer ever wishes to present *King Lear* in a nautical setting, I know the very place for him.

An inspection of the studiously unconcerned faces might have failed to elicit the fact, but we were not happy. Dougie, the engineer – a lifelong admirer of Para Handy, and whose great misfortune it is to bear the name of the mate instead of that of the engineer of the *Vital Spark* – looked at me, and I looked at him. Doctors C. and M. regarded each other with professional detachment. We all looked at each other. Nonchalance was the order of the day. Then we smiled tentatively. We smiled more broadly. We even laughed, the north-west wind lending to the sound of our mirth a peculiarly hollow note. We pressed on. The time had not yet come – although it was not very far distant – when the first man to suggest turning back in bad weather received the heartfelt thanks, the admiring praise, and the unstinted approval of his fellow voyagers. So keen, indeed, did each become to forestall the other in this practice, that eventually we had great difficulty in leaving harbour at all, even on a very fine day.

Keeping up this air of cheerful nonchalance now called for great skill and effort. With no cargo and practically no ballast, the five feet of water which a Loch Fyne skiff draws aft is considerably more than offset by her ten-foot beam, and she tends to sit high in the water. At least, the *Golden Girl* did, and she rolled southward in a highly spectacular fashion. But I daresay that things looked worse than they really were; and by the time we had run into the lee of Raasay we were able to prise locked fingers free from stanchions, remove splinters of wood from our fingernails, and resume the practising of our rolling gait. With the advent of calmer waters, breakfast, and the first gleam of sunshine, all was well again in our watery world.

Of the matchless scenery of Skye and the west coast of Inverness-shire, and of the gratifying speed with which we shot through Kyle Rhea with a six-knot spring tide behind us, it is not my purpose to write fully. But I would like to pay tribute to the good manners of the people of Kyle who watched us come alongside the pier there. A vintage Kelvin has neither clutch nor reverse, which means shutting off the engine far enough away to bring the boat to a stop where required. But an eight-ton Loch-Fyner doing seven knots has a surprising amount of way on her, and we were deeply grateful to these Highlanders for that native courtesy which prompted them to fall into an absorbed conversation and to point out to each other distant objects of interest as we overshot the pier by a hundred and fifty yards.

Four hours after leaving Kyle, Dougie and I, blissfully asleep in the fore cabin, were startled into wakefulness by a violent jolt, a loud crash, and water rushing into the cabin above our heads. We knew at once that we were doomed. This was it. Sinking fast, and helplessly trapped below decks. Take to the boats! Only we had no boat.

The scene on deck ten seconds later – the delay in arriving there being due to a cabin door never designed to allow two people to get through at once – did little to reassure us. On the beam, dimly visible through the mist and driving rain, loomed the sullen mass of Rhum. On the starboard bow the island of Eigg could be seen at fleeting intervals. And right aft, with four hands on the five-foot tiller, stood Doctors C. and M., no longer looking nonchalant, peering worriedly ahead into the gloom of the gathering storm.

The engine was throttled back to dead slow. Although it was only afternoon, sky and sea alike were visibly darkening. With every wicked, seething comber, the bows reared high into the air until the forefoot was entirely clear of the water, then plunged down into the following trough with a sickening, shuddering smash which must have thrown an immense strain on every beam and plank in her aged frame. At the same time would come the harsh and menacing metallic vibration of the propeller shaft in its casing as the screw rose clear of the water. We blew up our lifebelts.

The need for urgent action became all too plain. We knew that several planks had already sprung from the stem-post and that their hold was gravely weakened. If they lifted clear of the apron, it was going to be a black day for various insurance companies in the city of Glasgow. Realizing this, one of our gallant medical men, ignorant of the conditions in the fore cabin and so still preserving a vestige of unshattered nerves, disappeared below to get the Summer Isles–Ardnamurchan chart from the chart locker. He returned at great speed.

We did not even pause to congratulate him. A quick bearing on the islands, now fast vanishing in the mist, an estimate of the wind and the set of the sea, and a swift glance at the chart, convinced us that Mallaig was our best hope. And even then it appeared at the time to be none too good a bet; for an interminable five minutes of vicious, hammer-blow pitching elapsed before we could seize the opportunity to jerk the throttle wide open and, our hearts in our mouths, swing the *Golden Girl* round in a tight half-circle in an exceptionally long trough. And so we ran up the Sound of Sleat for some miles, with the heavy seas eagerly pursuing, until opposite the mouth of Loch Nevis, where another, and rather less dangerous, hundred and eighty degree turn let us beat our way south into Mallaig Harbour.

'Relieved' is a trifling word to describe our feelings. We would have declined any inducement to take to sea again within the hour. But nothing would have made us confess our true feelings to the weatherbeaten and genuine sailors who thronged the Mallaig waterfront. Talking on the pier to these fishermen afterwards, we leaned professionally against stacked herring-boxes and, with an air of fearful nonchalance, agreed that it was blowing up outside and might very likely become quite choppy towards evening. I do not think we cared what we said. We were safe, safe, safe – safe in Mallaig Harbour.

We almost lost our lives in Mallaig Harbour. Leaving the pier at nine p.m., we sought to anchor in the inner harbour, but it was hopelessly crowded with vessels of every description which had run there for shelter. So we anchored the *Golden Girl* just outside, letting her ride on about ten fathoms of chain, and retired to the tiny fore cabin. Here we built up a roaring fire in the stove, for the night had turned cold, shut the door, clamped down the skylight, and prepared for a night's peaceful slumber in much warmth and on little oxygen.

But we did not sleep. A strong south-west wind had been sweeping down over the town even as we anchored. We were lying just outside the protection of the houses and hill, and our apprehension steadily mounted with the rising howl of the wind. There was much thoughtful rubbing of unshaven chins, incessant cigarette-smoking, and continuous, brooding regard of the dark patch of skylight over our heads.

The first sharp grating from the bows had us up on deck in record time, shivering in the sudden cold and blindly peering through the rain and blackness. Gradually objects took shape, and suspicion became demoralizing certainty. Our anchor was dragging and we were drifting swiftly out of harbour.

Ten minutes later, the engine cut back to just above stalling speed, we nosed our way with infinite caution between two yachts – barely distinguishable shapes of inky blackness in the almost imperceptibly lesser darkness around us – and let go anchor. This time we paid out every possible foot of chain.

We remained on deck watching. At the full extent of our chain we were about sixty feet outside the inner harbour. The wind became still stronger, and the *Golden Girl*, riding so exceptionally high in the water, got the full benefit of every ounce of the wind pressure. Within twenty minutes we were dragging anchor again.

Three times in the next hour we repeated this cycle of movement – returning to the inner harbour, anchoring, then drifting out again. Finally, at about one o'clock in the morning, tired beyond words, soaked with lashing rain, and chilled to the bone by the icy fingers of the gale, we determined to go alongside the pier. With no clutch, no reverse, and no idea of where the pier lay in that darkness, this decision was indeed the counsel of despair.

After several false starts, the engine spluttered into life and we got slowly under way, Doctors C. and M. hauling frantically on the chain as we came up over the anchor. It was barely clear of the bottom when the engine suddenly coughed, just once, and as suddenly died.

Dougie's energetic efforts to locate the cause of engine failure – spurred on by the frantic comments of shipmates who watched with fascination the rapid approach of jagged rocks and foaming white breakers – were of no avail. The engine would not start.

The rocks drew perilously near. Beyond the outer harbour mouth now, we were exposed to the full force of the sea, and we knew that the *Golden Girl* could not last long if once she struck.

At this dramatically perfect moment – there were only seconds to go – the *Golden Girl* brought up with a violent jerk and suddenly ceased to drift. We had no idea of what had happened – only that it was a miracle. And we were in no mood to question a miracle, but accepted it with proper gratitude. And there, for the next half-hour, the *Golden Girl* tossed and rolled, riding jerkily at the full length of her iron-taut anchor cable, her stern swinging wildly twenty yards from the waiting rocks, in the rain, the wind and the blackness, while we numbly wondered when the chain or bitt would go, or the anchor work free.

Because of the weather and our preoccupation with the rocks, we did not see the lights of the big, powerful fishing-boat until less than half a minute before it came alongside out of the darkness and made fast to us. We were too worn-out, exhausted and frozen for rejoicing or even wonderment at this fresh miracle. But in retrospect, we can safely say that while the general public may still choose Beethoven's Ninth Symphony the beautiful purr of those diesels was the loveliest music we had ever heard.

It took seven men to get our anchor clear of the bottom, but after it was raised we were safely alongside the pier within ten minutes. From start to finish that rescue operation was a magnificent object-lesson in seamanship in the worst conditions. The fishing-boat skipper made never a mistake. We made one by mentioning salvage money to him; but I think he generously attributed our breach of good manners to ignorance. He brushed aside our thanks, and vanished as quickly and with as little ceremony as he had appeared. We slept well that night.

We learned later that a young lady, kept awake by the storm in the middle of the night, had seen our torches flashing off the rocks as we moved about the decks. She had phoned to the police, and then to her father, who had immediately collected a crew and taken out the fishing boat.

We owe much to the people of that port. Gavin Maxwell (author of *Harpoon at a Venture*) says that their unspoken motto is 'I'll not see you stuck.' For as long as we and *Golden Girl* continue our happy partnership, we shall not forget that we do so solely by courtesy of Skipper Sutherland of Mallaig and his volunteer crew.

The next morning we looked over the side at our anchor, still hanging just awash. It weighs about fifty pounds and was hooked round the anchor flukes of another, weighing at least three hundred, which must have lain untouched at the mouth of Mallaig Harbour for many years. We can, fortunately, produce numerous and reliable witnesses to this incredible stroke of fortune. Were this fiction, I could never dare claim any coincidence so fantastic.

We did not sail the next day. The wind had dropped to the merest whisper, and a sea of limpid blue stretched away beckoningly to the haze-blurred southern horizon; but we remained steadfastly blind to the invitation. Had any one of us suggested leaving, we would doubtless have gone. But nobody made the suggestion. The unanimity of silence was wonderful.

We sailed early on the Tuesday, out into a morning of grey swell and grey mist. Resolutely ignoring the first lift of the Atlantic, we chugged confidently out of harbour, again falling into attitudes suggestive of easy and careless nonchalance. We even felt nonchalant, a feeling that rapidly became one of chagrin and intense mortification as the engine broke down beneath the expressionless gazes of the watchers on the pier. For the next two and a half hours our engineer and his assistants toiled in a sulphurous silence at the task, doubled in difficulty by the continual wallowing of the craft, of stripping and cleaning the carburettor. We found later that these stoppages were due to the lack of a filter in the paraffin tank.

By the time repairs were completed, the tide had literally carried us over the sea to Skye. It is a delectable island, but it was not included in our itinerary; and we were not sorry when the engine coughed into life and we left Skye rapidly astern. We rounded the notorious Ardnamurchan in almost a flat calm, left Loch Sunart on the port hand, and brought up in that wonderful bay which, with Portpatrick in Wigtownshire, was to become one of our favourite harbours on the West Coast – Tobermory.

We spent a restful night there, Messrs McBrayne allowing us to tie up alongside one of their steamers, and sailed again before dawn to catch the flood-tide racing south-east through the Sound of Mull. Rounding Calf Island in slight drizzle and a cold half-light, we found that the weather had repented of its smiling mood of yesterday afternoon. A strong wind blew from the west, and heavy, sullen seas were sweeping silently along between the shores of the Sound.

Once fairly out in the open, our light craft was caught up and carried away with dismaying speed. Deep furrows again settled upon our brows, and a dark pessimism upon our souls; but we pressed resolutely on, largely, or, to be honest, solely because we had no alternative. A Loch-Fyner full out in a heavy stern sea is a sea-boat without rival; but we found that the first tentative reduction of engine speed resulted in so wild and alarming a yawing from side to side that we abandoned all idea of keeping anything but the most elementary control over what would next happen.

Abeam of the Grey Rocks, we passed the *Lochinvar, en route* from Oban to Tobermory, a hundred times our size and yet making heavy weather of it. Several hardy gentlemen, braving the elements on deck, were observed to doff their headgear in our general direction. Forty-eight hours previously we would have attributed this courtesy to a deep admiration for our seamanship and gallantry. But in our apprehensive gloom just then, the only possible interpretation to see in it was a premature token of respect to those already visibly rising above mere mortality. The Sound of Mull, at that moment, bore close resemblance to our nightmare imaginings of the River Styx.

Lismore and its lighthouse now loomed inhospitably ahead, effectively barring further flight – flight, mark you, being an ignominiously accurate term and compelling us to abandon the channel on the Morvern side and to quarter to the south-east to round Duart Point. The heavy seas, no longer directly aft, pounded enthusiastically on the starboard quarter, soaking the unfortunate steersman; and the crossing, although at length managed successfully, considerably shook both the *Golden Girl* and her long-suffering crew. We speculated on what would have been the effects had we tried to make headway diagonally against such a sea instead of with it. Later, we found out.

As we rounded Duart Point, the Firth of Lorne, stretching away to the south, gradually revealed itself. We would have infinitely

preferred that it hadn't. Seas of seething white-caps, so ably depicted
by Conrad, sound infinitely picturesque; but the appreciation dimin-
ishes markedly when they are seen from the elevation of the deck
of a Loch-Fyner. One look at the Firth, and the Sound of Mull
changed retrospectively in our minds from an unpleasant experience
to a fond and nostalgic memory. Our hearts could not sink lower,
for they were in our boots already. But, as ever, we pressed on.

The sea, sweeping in from the Atlantic round the Sound of Mull,
was setting east-north-east towards the mainland; so for several
miles we clung to the east coast of Mull, partly for protection but
chiefly to have the sea as nearly as possible astern when we set out
over the Firth. Finally, at about eight a.m., we altered course ninety
degrees to port and struck out for Pladda Lighthouse.

Half an hour later, fully out in the open, the *Golden Girl* was
yawing in a fashion calculated to daunt the most fearless, shipping
copious quantities of water, and taking a wicked hammering. (We
were later told by a Meteorological Office friend in Prestwick that
we had picked the worst possible four days of the season to take our
boat south. Continuous gale warnings were being broadcast – but
we had no radio. Neither, apparently, had anyone else on the West
Coast.)

When the helmsman altered course thirty degrees to port and
brought the *Golden Girl*'s stern into the sea, we made not a murmur
of dissent. I must again pay tribute to the behaviour of a Loch Fyne
boat in the heaviest of stern seas; it is really magnificent. The *Golden
Girl* became unbelievably steady and gave the comforting impression
of being practically unsinkable.

Ten miles away to the east lay Easdale, a wonderful little natural
harbour protected by a large island, with a narrow entrance to the
north-west and a still narrower one to the south. Borne swiftly along
by the heavy seas astern, we covered the distance in an hour, making
for the southern entrance – the other being obviously unapproach-
able that day. At low water this southern entrance is narrower,
tortuous, and extremely dangerous, strewn with rocks and only a
few feet deep. Also, the leading buoy to the channel, as shown in
the 'Clyde Cruising Club Pilot', was missing. But there was no
alternative, or time to seek one: and there could be no second
chance. Doctors C. and M. stood in the bows, one on either side,
sounding desperately for depth and bawling back instructions with

a wholly unprofessional lack of restraint. Behind was a four-knot sea – and we required at least another two knots for steerage way. Our speed was remarkable, our trepidation was considerable, our skill was negligible, and our luck was incredible. We made it. We tied up at the pier and went ashore, seeking fuel for the boat and breakfast for ouselves.

In the three days since Sunday we had become changed men. In our possibly lowered state of morale, we had come to detect an unpleasantly personal element in the unswerving malignity of the Atlantic, and the *Golden Girl* had lost many of her magnetic qualities for us. We were in no hurry to return to sea, and would have lingered long in Easdale had we not struck up an acquaintance with a couple of retired fishermen, as kindly and helpful as all whom we met there. When the tide turned, they said we would have an easy crossing to Pladda. They told us that the sea was falling away already – and, indeed, the sky was now a cloudless blue and the merest breath of a wind stirred the harbour surface. Having lived there all their lives, they obviously knew what they were talking about; so we had no excuse to tarry longer. We sailed at two p.m. on the top of the tide, with our elderly advisers, standing on what was left of the pier, wishing us good luck and assuring us of a safe journey and a pleasant passage.

We bear them no ill-will. They meant us no harm. But their weather forecast was a blunder of the first order, and brought us within a hair's-breadth of next morning's headlines.

The rest of the voyage south from Ross-shire has now drifted into the realm of kindly memory and rose-tinted nostalgia. But not Easdale Sound. Not that forty-minute stretch from Easdale Harbour to Pladda Lighthouse. That remains permanently etched in our minds, sharp and clear. We have sailed through full gales in the Antarctic, typhoons in the Bay of Bengal, and would gladly do so again, a dozen times, rather than recross that Easdale Sound. Within five minutes of leaving harbour the *Golden Girl* was pitching and rolling heavily as she sliced diagonally south-south-west against the heavy swell. At last we found how she behaved cutting into instead of away from a cross sea. Abominably. Still relying, however, on the advice of the fishermen, and expecting to find an increasing moderation, we pushed on. Within another five minutes came the cold realization that a ghastly mistake had been made. And by then it was too late.

We had never encountered anything like it before. Gone were the serried ranks of waves, gone were the decorative white-caps – here we had only huge, sullen, moving walls of water, broken masses of grey, heaving and agonized, hastening to the east, like the confused and despairing ranks of a defeated army, in a dreadful silence; then smashing themselves, in a foaming frenzy of self-immolation, on the bitter shores of Lorne.

We had to go on. Turning back to make for Easdale would almost certainly have meant broaching to and foundering in one of these gigantic, precipitously walled troughs. Nor could we turn and run as we had done twice before. This time we were on a lee shore.

One thing above all weighed heavily on our spirits – the ironically incongruous element of the macabre. It was now a perfect summer's day. The wind had died completely. A cathedral stillness invested the air, and a glorious sun shone down smilingly out of a hot June sky. We would have welcomed the faintest cat's-paw of wind, the lightest sprinkling of rain, anything. But nothing changed. There was only the sunlight and the silence – a silence broken by the regular harsh rattling of our airborne screw and the explosive smash as the bows and side of the *Golden Girl* fell smoothly, noiselessly, down the steep side of a wave and then crashed solidly, shockingly, into the rising shoulder of the next wave. She was now corkscrewing in a completely uncontrollable fashion, and on two heart-stopping occasions was flung back from a wave-top into the trough she had just left, and lay there on her beam ends, the port gunwale dipping under, while the massive wall of water, which had thus contemptuously flung her back, bore down remorselessly from above and sought, in a lethal silence and with a kind of animistic savagery, to thrust her under.

Those who have never clung desperately to the deck of a boat heeled over to forty-five degrees mentally registering passing aeons of time and wondering, in a strangely detached numbness, whether she will ever right herself again, can have no conception of the feeling that all eternity can be compressed into the space of a few seconds.

Yet both times the *Golden Girl* came back. Slowly, imperceptibly slowly at first, then with a swift lurch and roll, she righted herself and steadied; and after the second time our fears slowly began to clear. Barring engine failure or sheer disintegration which, in all seriousness, remained a danger to be reckoned with, the *Golden Girl*, we knew now, would take us anywhere. There followed another twenty minutes of vicious yawing through an angle of sixty degrees, of cascading sheets of water, of wild staggering over wave-tops, and of the stunning, jarring, pistol-shot impacts that followed. Then, magically, all became quiet and peaceful, calm and still. We had reached the lee of Pladda, and counted as nothing the cost of cuts, bruises, smashed crockery and two more planks new-sprung from the stem-post.

The remainder of that day was a beautiful anti-climax. Down the length of the inner Sound we sailed, from Pladda to Scarba, in a kind of blissful dream, over a calm sea of that translucent blue usually associated only with the Aegean and the isles of Greece. We held over to the west to cross the mouth of the dreaded Coire-bhreacan – how tamely innocuous after the Easdale Sound! – then swung east, jogged our jerky way across the overfalls and races of the Dorus Mor, and so over the Sound of Jura to arrive at Crinan in the early evening.

There we learned that we were the only boat to arrive from the north that day. We still had wit enough to appreciate that this information was offered not so that we might congratulate ourselves, but to make abundantly clear to us the superior sense of more experienced mariners.

Three hours later we had laboriously traversed the length of the canal and were in Ardrishaig. There we spent the night, and had the uncommonly good fortune to meet the man who had helped his father build the *Golden Girl* half a century before. We watched with flinching gaze and shuddering fascination as he plunged the blade of a huge clasp-knife into frames and planks all over the boat, and manfully gouged large chunks out of the heavy overhead cross-beams. He then pronounced her to be in as sound a condition as when built, and gave us a verbal guarantee extending over the next fifty years.

We awoke to a hushed and breathless dawn, and by breakfast-time were far down the sapphired mirror of Loch Fyne. The weather was ideal, and the eight-hour trip home, by way of the Kyles, was completely uneventful. We were in no way bored by this unaccustomed peace.

Our anchor rattled down in the Gareloch at three o'clock in the afternoon. The *Golden Girl* was home, and, dirty, weary, unshaven, and bloodshot about the eyes, we stepped ashore at Shandon. We knew exactly how Eric the Red felt when he first set foot in the New World, and how Drake felt as he sailed up the Plymouth Sound after his voyage round the world.

We were conscious of many things – relief, satisfaction, happiness, a certain regret that it was all over and, especially, a most gratifying sense of accomplishment. But when one or the other of us is asked, as frequently he is, what he actually did during the voyage, all else fades except the imperishable memory of Easdale Sound, and he echoes feelingly the answer of that eminent Frenchman, who, when asked what he did during the Revolution, replied simply, 'I survived.'

INDEX

All Chapmans books are available at your local bookshop or newsagent, or can be ordered direct from the publisher. Indicate the number of copies required and fill in the form below.

Send to: **Chapmans Publishers Ltd**
              141/143 Drury Lane
              Covent Garden. WC2B 5TB.

or phone: **071 379 9799 quoting title, author and**
              Credit Card number.

Please enclose a remittance* to the value of the cover price plus: 60p for the first book plus 30p per copy for each additional book ordered to a maximum charge of £2.40 to cover postage and packing.

*Payment may be made in sterling by UK personal cheque, postal order, sterling draft or international money order, made payable to Chapmans Publishers Ltd.

Alternatively by Barclaycard/Access:

Card No. ☐☐☐☐ ☐☐☐☐ ☐☐☐☐ ☐☐☐☐

Expiry date: _____

Signature: _____

Applicable only in the UK and Republic of Ireland.

While every effort is made to keep prices low, it is sometimes necessary to increase prices at short notice. Chapmans Publishers reserve the right to show on covers and charge new retail prices which may differ from those advertised in the text or elsewhere.

NAME AND ADDRESS IN BLOCK LETTERS PLEASE
....

Name _____

Address _____

_____

_____

Post code _____ Tel. no. _____